Strengthening the Shepherds

Strengthening the Shepherds

Andrew Kane

All proceeds from the sale of this book go to

The Andrew Kane Partnership Trust

Registered UK Charity No: 1124971

www.partnershipinfo.org.uk

Strengthening the Shepherds

Some years ago, I published a little book that, in the economy of God, has had strong legs. It is currently being published in Poland. Through testimony, teaching, and narrative theology, it told the story of God's life renewing a small, struggling, traditional congregation. A few years after this glorious adventure, my own association with that congregation came to a screeching halt.

The shock and bereavement of the parting plunged me into despair. It also drove me to better understand the pressures, trials, and temptations facing pastors. But above all, it led to a desperate grabbing hold of God for a stronger experience and for knowledge of his character, ways, and grace. It was a crisis of some proportion for this servant of God.

Most denominations recognise the need for pastoral support for their ministers but operate with limited resources. In practice, it is often senior ministers who distil the wisdom of the years and pass on a kind of tribal oral tradition. Such conversations are invaluable and can prove life giving. By definition, however, they tend to be anecdotal and spasmodic, not geared to regular support or systematic exposition. What I have tried to do here is bring together, in a cohesive way, insights from pastoral ministry and from the purpose that God might have through them for the good, and for the strengthening, of his servants.

This little volume is my contribution to such conversations and is an offering of love to those brave and courageous people called pastors.

It occurs to me that two other groups may benefit from this writing.

Because I am a pastor, I have written for those with that particular vocation. However, other leadership vocations in the wider work of the Kingdom of God face similar challenges. If the reader is missionary, evangelist, administrator, worship leader, or follower of any other calling, then it will be easy enough to substitute title and work milieu and hopefully to your encouragement.

Finally, there will be those who, though not pastors themselves, are likely to have a pastor. My hope is that by reading this you may gain greater insight into the pressures that pastor's feel so that you may better support them with your prayers. Paul's apostolic pattern was to be quite candid about his circumstances so that he might appeal to his readers for their prayers. Understanding breeds compassion, which leads in turn to intercession. May that be so, for there is not one true servant of God who is not dependent on the faithful prayers of God's people for the effective working of his ministry. God deliberately makes us interdependent in this way.

Underpinning

Included at the end of each chapter is a section for those who appreciate help with application. The format, conjured from my time as a chartered quantity surveyor and my work in the building industry, draws on the practice of underpinning. Underpinning is not done when a building has failed; it is a response to cracks. These are usually due to bad ground, inadequate construction, or increased pressures. It does not replace a foundation; rather it undergirds it, thereby strengthening it. The procedure is a careful one, effected section by section, and comprised in three stages:

- Exploration to test the existing foundation

- Excavation where necessary to create room under the foundation

- Underpinning, which is the pouring in of new concrete to the underside of the foundation; this is a strengthening of the existing to better support the superstructure.

Underpinning is therefore a helpful metaphor for this practical purpose serving pastor, church leader, and church member alike.

My Thanks

Having completed my first draft manuscript, I asked a number of colleagues for their critique. I am grateful for their encouragement and the honesty of their comments. My thanks therefore to the Rev. Dr. Chris Voke, vice-principal of Surgeon's College; the Rev. Dr. Ian Stackhouse, pastor of Guildford Baptist Church; Philip W. Greenslade, head of the Department of Theology and Biblical Studies at CWR; the Rev. Giles Williams, formerly vicar of St. John's Church, Woking, and of the Burundi Bible Society. Some members of my Baptist Cluster Group also read the manuscript and made helpful comments: the Rev. Dr. Graham Holliday and Revs John Bridger, John Berry, Peter Jackson, and Tony Taylor. I am grateful to the Rev. Christine Parker for reading the manuscript and for her wise comments, especially on the subject of gender inclusiveness. None of the above saw beyond the first draft and of course hold no responsibility for the views expressed in the book, which remain mine alone. My thanks to Judy Powles, librarian at Spurgeon's College, for use of the college library. Also to Gordon Taylor, archivist at the Salvation Army International Heritage Centre, William Booth College, for his enthusiasm and time generously given to my research on the visions of William Booth. Thanks to two book editors who, without reading the full manuscript, helped point me in the right direction: Martin Manser in the United Kingdom and Larry Stone in the United States. My thanks to Natasha and the talented team at Lulu for their design and production; their courtesy and efficiency has made this partnership a pleasure. Finally, grateful thanks to Kate King for help in presenting the manuscript and for her sterling work for the Trust.

For Marilyn,

whose love and loyalty

has made this journey of
life and ministry possible.

Contents

1. The God We Serve 1

2. The Work We Do 19

3. The Discipline We Face 37

4. The Season We Dread 59

5. The Cross We Hold 79

6. The Identity We Own 99

7. The Training We Engage 121

8. The Company We Enjoy 141

9. The Spirit We Receive 161

10. The Accountability We Owe....................................181

11. The Dependency We Confess 197

Chapter 1

The God We Serve

My God whom I serve
2 Timothy 1: 3
These qualities of gentle kindness and ruthless severity that exist side
by side in God
Romans 11: 22, The Message

God's call to pastoral ministry is a high calling and a huge privilege. It also becomes a rollercoaster of adventure for those who respond. Pastoral ministry will pull you and stretch you emotionally and spiritually more than any physical callisthenics can do to the body. It takes you to the peaks of joy and throws you into the pit of despair. You observe at first hand the noblest qualities imaginable in human beings and stand alongside those who still carry the sulphurous whiff of hell. Occasionally there comes an oasis of calm, soon to be dispelled by the rush of activity – the very unpredictability of pace a strain for some of our temperaments. At times, the job seems to call for talents and gifts way beyond our grace. We feel ourselves at best a jack of all trades but needing the wisdom of a Solomon, the energy of a Paul, and the patience of a Job. In the midst of pressured seasons, we can know ourselves drained and exhausted, ending up feeling spent on others with little left for ourselves. We can be pulled in so many different directions at once: the demands of the flock, the needs of the family, and the lure of the enemy with temptations of 'the girls, the gold, and the glory'. And in and behind it all is the God who called us to this work in the first place.

    This book was written by a pastor for pastors. It is not, however, about pastoring. The focus throughout has more to do with 'being' than 'doing'; with the 'who we are in God' than what we might do for him or what he might want us to do. I want to explore the workings of

God in the lives of his servants to the end that we might be called men and women of God, Godly pastors. My simple conviction is that this is the work of God. It is his loving purpose to form us and mould us inwardly. As we are about the job of spiritual formation in the lives of our congregation, so God is about the job of spiritual formation in us. This on-the-job training is a lifelong task. For those of us involved, it is also a rugged school of learning and growth.

In the Beginning, God

So it is with this God that we must begin. The first sermon I preached in my new church following ordination and induction was titled 'In the beginning, God' – from Genesis 1: 1 of course. I was raw and green and very wet behind the ears, but I did at least know that everything had to start with God. So it is with pastoral ministry. The beginning has to be not that of the volunteer (wonderful as they are in much of the work) but for those press-ganged by heaven. The continuance of it has to be not in the accumulation of experience (valuable as that is) but in the daily dependence on God. The ending of it has to be not in the grit and determination of human character (though that is involved) but in the grace of he who is Alpha and Omega – the one who by that name is committed to complete what he initiates. For only then will he, and he alone, get the glory: 'For from him and through him and to him are all things. To him be the glory for ever! Amen.'[1]

What of this God who is integral to every phase and aspect of this calling, the calling within which he shapes us? Where do we begin with him whose names, nature, character, and ways are rich beyond all knowing?

Let's begin with the text at the head of this chapter, where Paul urges that we need 'to stay alert to the qualities of gentle kindness and ruthless severity that exist side by side in God'. In context, the apostle is bringing the majestic sweep of his argument through Romans chapters 1–11 to a climax. Having spelled out a salvation by grace through faith, culminating in the glorious security and unity of both Gentile and Jewish believers in the love of God, he deals with the question of God's purpose for Israel. During this, he counters any

---

[1] Romans 11: 36

tendency to arrogance or complacency in Gentile believers by reminding them of Israel's loss through unbelief. Many in Israel failed to make it to the end because their dependence on God shifted from God himself to other bases – trust in national identity, a presumption of righteousness derived from works, or confidence drawn from their illustrious forefathers. God had to prune the deadwood of unbelief in Israel, an act of some severity. Such an act is set alongside the overwhelming kindness of God in persistently reaching out to those facing this danger.

Now if God acts in that way to 'his people'[2], says Paul, all Gentile believers need to heed the warning. This is the God with whom we have to deal. As C.K. Barrett comments, 'The whole process is a revelation of the nature of God.'[3] It is to this nature of God that we need to stay alert.

In the forward to the second volume of his autobiography, Frederick Buechner makes a helpful observation about recognising God at his work. He is answering the natural diffidence he feels about writing it. Why would anyone be interested? Is he just being a little geriatric, an old codger putting his affairs in order as the end approaches? But he comes to the conclusion that, by looking back over one's life, he sees 'certain themes and patterns and signals that are so easy to miss when you're caught up in the process of living them. If God speaks to us at all other than through such official channels as the Bible and the church, then I think that he speaks to us largely through what happens to us, so what I have done in this book (Buechner writes) is to listen back over what has happened to me – as I hope my readers may be moved to listen back over what has happened to them – for the sound, above all else, of his voice.'[4]

Buechner's search was among the apparently random happenings of his life. He believed that what he came to discern were not in fact haphazard, unrelated events. Rather, he recognised the dictates of a sovereign, loving God. And the discernment of that voice is what made sense of not just his life but, he submits, all our lives.

---

[2] Romans 11: 1

[3] C.K. Barrett, *The Epistle to the Romans,* 2nd edn (London: A & C Black, 1971) p. 218

[4] Frederick Buechner, *Now & Then, a Memoir of Vocation,* (San Francisco: Harper Collins 1991) p. 3

Reflecting on pastoral life, mine and that of colleagues and friends over many years, those 'themes and patterns and signals' begin to appear. Straining to hear the sound of 'his voice' and discern the evidence of his hand, it's as if something of God's style slowly emerges. He has a way of doing things. His character becomes recognisable: the fingerprint of God detected. And one of the key means I have come to see that he employs is his 'gentle kindness and ruthless severity'. All this, I believe, is then directed towards our spiritual formation.

God's Appointed Setting

If the aim of God is to form in his children the image and likeness of Christ, then the context of our lives is his chosen setting for that process to occur. It is among our people that we pastors are exposed to this kindness and severity of God. It is in the daily business of routine and drama that God forms our spirit, cultivates our soul, and develops our character. Eugene Peterson puts it like this: 'The congregation provides the rhythms, the associations, the tasks, the limitations, the temptations – the conditions – for this growing up "in every way into him who is the head, into Christ" (Eph. 4: 15). These conditions are, perhaps, neither more nor less favourable to the life of faith in Jesus than those of the farmer, the teacher, the engineer, the artist, the clerk – but they are *ours.*'[5]

Many think 'if only I were full-time for the Lord my walk with him would be easier' – this is simply not the case. God is no respecter of persons. I am convinced that for every true follower of Christ, God takes whatever is the context of our lives and works it toward our growth in Christ. There is no workplace more or less congenial or preferential for that task.

For pastors, however, the setting is the congregation. It is here that we are to discern God at work, not just through us but in us, for our personal good. This God who calls, this God of 'gentle kindness and ruthless severity', intentionally places us in this chosen setting – the congregation, with all its rich and raw experiences of life. It is here that he prunes at our deadwood. It is here that he nourishes our

---

[5] Eugene H. Peterson, *Under the Unpredictable Plant*, (Grand Rapids: Eerdmans 1992), p. 22

smallest shoots of green. It is here that he invites us to hear his voice, not just in the traditional modes but the very warp and weft of life. And all this in order that we may acquire what Peterson neatly terms 'an interior adequate to the exterior'[6] - the development of a spirituality and character appropriate to our calling as pastors.

Cracked Pots

I was about fourteen when, walking down a corridor in my school, I saw the headmaster coming toward me. As he drew near, he paused, looked at me, and in his characteristic stuttering way spoke. The conversation went something like this:

'Er, Kane, isn't it?'

'Yes, sir.'

'Er, Kane, 4B, isn't it?'

'Yes, sir.'

'Kane, you're what we call a slow learner. Er, you've got it all there somewhere, Kane. But, er, you're a slow learner. Keep at it; keep at it. You'll get there.'

And with that he walked on. I was left somewhat bemused, and at fourteen, I didn't know what on earth to make of his comments. But I've obviously not forgotten them!

He was right of course. I am a slow learner. I suspect that when it comes to matters of the soul we might all be, for some lessons are best learned slowly. This is especially true when God teaches us our true dependence on him. Our cultural moulding prizes self-confidence, self–reliance, and self determination. These are not healthy qualities in believers at any stage of maturity, let alone in pastors. They are also notoriously hard to undermine and penetrate, and any quick dismantling of those attitudes could lead to an identity crisis. What the Lord seems to do is work us over slowly until we come to understand the need for the removal of all those 'selfs'! He then leads us to a new confidence, reliance, and determination found in him, not us. His chosen method invariably is that of pressure and suffering. This process is uncomfortable, disorientating, even discouraging. Under his hand, however, it brings us to the point of honest recognition that we

---

[6] Peterson p. 3

are no more than 'earthen vessels' or, as Brennan Manning picturesquely puts it: 'cracked pots'[7].

The dawning awareness of our earthiness is simultaneously the birthing of hope's true focus, God himself. Christian ministry, like the Christian life, is not the purview of the spiritual superman. We may conceivably start out thinking that and try to act accordingly, but it won't be long before we buckle and another perspective begins to form. God's dismantling of any self misconception in a pastor is only a prelude to a life and ministry more fully into and more fully dependent on Christ.

Not long ago, my wife was in a cycle of chemotherapy treatment. Halfway through the six treatments, we began to recognise the pattern. Following the procedure, she was very rough for a week to ten days: very down, very low. But we learned that those days would pass; her renewal was on the way. So it is with the rhythms of a pastor's life in concert with the Holy Spirit. Through cycles of pressure and suffering, the Lord causes us to become increasingly aware of our own limitations and the extent of our dependence on him. Like chemo, the dosage will vary with each individual. Some cycle of pain, humbling, and renewal however will occur to all.

Pressure Points

In the next three chapters, we look at some ways in which the Lord works on us in what might be termed his 'ruthless severity mode'. Even this, of course, is an expression of his kindness, and long before we get to the good bits, evidence of his graces become evident.

In chapter two, we explore some of the issues that we pastors face day to day. It is through these challenges and pressures that God tests our mettle, identifies our weaknesses, and shapes our character. As we look at Paul in the setting of his Corinthian congregation, we will get the first clue as to what God is after for our souls. We will be forcibly brought back to the primacy of God himself. Scott J. Hafemann, in the introduction to his commentary, writes, 'Second Corinthians is a letter stained with Paul's blood, sweat, and tears. To know this letter is to be moved by Paul's life. What is most striking however is not what this letter reveals about Paul, but what it says

---

[7] Brennan Manning, *Ruthless Trust*, (London: SPCK, 2000) p. 133

about God… For him (Paul), all things derive from and relate back to the sovereign and good hand of God. This "God ward" orientation remains true whether he is speaking about his intense suffering or his change in travel plans, the coming of the new creation of the new covenant or the repentance and rebellion of the Corinthians, the collection of money for Jerusalem or the future of his own ministry. Thus, in the end, the most personal of all letters, in which his struggles and triumphs ooze out of every paragraph, becomes a letter about God. In writing this commentary, I found my own "practical atheism" constantly challenged.'[8]

Congregations, God's chosen setting, and our daily work among them have the capacity to pull us every which way: blood, sweat, and tears. The design behind it all is to pull us ever Godward.

Chapters three and four explore further ways in which God heats the metal to remove the dross – to change the metaphor. Discipline and exile are probed as expressions of his love: pressure points strong enough to harness the most wilful, independent of spirits. In these chapters, we consider the nature of God as a true father and the fear which is his due. Even in the process of chastening, graces and serendipities break out like showers on a wasted desert.

Discipline and exile are experiences common to all believers. What is perhaps important to note is that pastors, missionaries, and the like are not exempt. God will introduce these seasons, and the conscientious worker will struggle all the more because of them. If the work itself was not enough, they might say, now there is this to contend with.

But what then if the pastor fails? What if he buckles under the pressure? What if he gives into temptations and betrays his trust? Is that then the end? Or can that be, in itself, part of the process at the end of which there can still be hope?

One of my biggest struggles when I began to feel the promptings of God to put some of these thoughts down on paper was the realisation that at some point I would have to share somewhat of my own story. Not a wholly edifying story as it turns out. I was one who, under the pressures, buckled. My diffidence, however, was not just that of embarrassment.

[8] Scott J. Hafemann, *The NIV Application Commentary*, (Grand Rapids: Zondervan Publishing House, 2000) p. 15

There have been many failures in Christian leadership in recent years, some of whom would be considered high profile names. Without trying in any way to absolve such, or deny the simplicity of saying 'no' to temptation, I suspect there is a need for those more qualified than I to do some research into this. There is a vulnerability that pastors face when a number of spiritual dynamics converge. Put together heightened spiritual fervour, a revival atmosphere, an outpouring of brotherly and sisterly love; mix it with neglected marriages; add in the potential for abuse of authority and the fact that we are all damaged people in process and you have a potent and dangerous cocktail. Counsellors and clinicians could bring helpful insights with their skills – skills and expertise that I do not have.

I was however encouraged by something written by Herman Wouk in the dedication to his book *This Is My God, an Introduction to Judaism*. He wrote, 'Nobody can be more aware of the deep lacks in *This Is My God* than I am. The theme needs a prophet. The subject needs monumental scholarship. I offer the book relying on the maxim of Rabbi Tarfon in *The Ethics of the Fathers:* "The work is not yours to finish; but neither are you free to take no part in it."'[9]

If there is much that needs to be contributed by specialists, there is value in a pastor's perspective. If I too am not free to opt out, what I can offer is an answer to my earlier questions: 'Is that then the end? Or can that be for the fallen in itself part of a process at the end of which there is hope?'

The workings of God we look at in the next three chapters will occur in every pastor's life. Most, thankfully, will not buckle in the process. Most, hopefully, will respond wholesomely to God – his seasons of pressured work, discipline, and exile – and grow through it. But when that is not so, when failure has occurred, I am happy to testify that there is no failure so final that God's grace cannot restore. For me at least, even the failure was not outside of God's careful handling. 'Ruthless severity' it may have felt at times but all in the greater purpose of his loving kindness. If that is of some help to a minority of our community, then no embarrassment should stand in the way.

Richard Baxter, in his classic *The Reformed Pastor,* speaks in a forthright manner about the sins of the ministry. Despite the style of his language in seventeenth century English, his words are a clear call

---

[9] Herman Wouk, *This is My God*, (London: Collins, 1973), The Dedication

to transparency and confession. In his introduction he says, 'The world already knows that we (pastors) are sinners. And is it not highly necessary that they also see that we are penitent sinners?... Our penitent confession and speedy reformation are the means that must silence the reproaching adversaries.... The leaders of the flock must be examples to the rest in this as well as in other duties.'[10]

The one thing this process must accomplish is to strip us of any illusions concerning ourselves. God is under no such illusions; he knows every bit of us there is to know. Our frailties are no hindrance to his call to ministry, and our limitations are no hindrance to his using us greatly. The one thing that gets in the way is any sense of our thinking of ourselves more highly than we ought to think. His ruthless severity is designed to take the pride and self-misconceptions from us, to strip out all illusions. Is the process painful? Yes. Is it necessary? Without a doubt.

Reconstruction

What the stripping, humbling process I have just outlined does is to lead us to look afresh at the cross. If everything from start to finish is about God, then this, his most awesome gift, must be revisited. Where do we go when we come to an end of ourselves? The cross. What hope is there for those whose integrity has been compromised? The cross. Where can we find relief and healing? The cross. Where is our inspiration when the call and task seems overwhelming? The cross.

Chapter five becomes a pivotal chapter; for any exploration of the cross clarifies it as a place of exchange: from death to life; from sin, self, and shame to conviction, forgiveness, and the birth of compassion. Poets and preachers, princes and paupers, all manner of men and martyrs have gloried in the cross. The first and last verses of Isaac Watts's classic hymn express it perfectly:

When I survey the wondrous cross

Where the young Prince of glory died,

My richest gain I count but loss,

And pour contempt on all my pride.

Were the whole realm of nature mine,

---

[10] Richard Baxter, *The Reformed Pastor*, (Lafayette IN: Sovereign Grace Publishers, 2000) p. x.

That were a present far too small,

Love so amazing, so divine,

Demands my soul, my life, my all.

Rededication becomes the only appropriate response. Even as we do so, we discover that further graces come to us – all designed to better shape this 'interior adequate to the exterior', graces that need incorporating more securely into our lives as people and as pastors.

Chapters six to the end of the book explore some of these. We shall look at our identity, the call to training, the need for a harmonised life in fellowship with others, the resources of the Spirit, and the value of ultimate accountability.

At the end of the day, however, amid all the talk of spiritualities, only one thing should dominate and that is the reality of Jesus in our lives. Spirituality is a buzzword today; it comes in all shapes and sizes and appeals to followers of many faiths and none. What this journey has established for me is the magnificence and sufficiency of the person of Jesus.

Ministry is all about Jesus. Ministers, therefore, have to be all about Jesus. Whatever notions we may entertain to the contrary, all we are and all we have to offer is Jesus. The disciples in the upper room certainly understood this with panicked certainty. The news that Jesus was going away but that he wanted them to continue the mission stirred their emotions like dark churning waters. They understood perfectly well that they were very small fry in this enterprise. It was all about him; it always had been; it was inconceivable without him. The reassurances Jesus brought to them, through those upper room discourses, were based primarily on the promises of his return, the presence of the Father, and the gift of the Holy Spirit. God was going to invade their being in ways even greater than they had known during Jesus' earthly ministry – God no longer beside them but soon to be within them. God in them – that was going to be the secret, that was the treasure in the cracked pots. It was that which would carry them to the ends of the earth, inspire them to work like Trojans and die as willing martyrs.

The same is offered to us, and this indwelling is what life and ministry is all about.

Crucial to this is the understanding that his indwelling does not override our own personalities, characters, or idiosyncrasies. It does not eliminate or absorb the earthiness that we have been referring to. Samuel Chadwick expresses it like this, 'The indwelling is that of a real, personal, spiritual Presence. It is not a gift that can be located somewhere in the brain or heart of a man, but a personal Spirit that indwells another personality; a personality within a personality by which the Spirit becomes the life of my life, the soul of my soul; an indwelling that secures identity without confusion, and possession without absorption.'[11]

The Paradoxical Pastor

For a while I toyed with entitling this book *The Paradoxical Pastor*. It proved inadequate overall, but if we stay with it a moment, we can see its value at this point.

I have said enough already to indicate that my journey reflects that of a slow learner, a cracked pot, and a testimony to the great truth that 'the heart is deceitful above all things'[12]. Through rugged schooling, through fresh insights at the cross and a desperate grasping for all the resource of his grace, I was comforted to know that Jesus still lived in me, as he had since I prayed the sinner's prayer as a teenager. But what I learned as never before is how utterly dependent I was on him. And he has done all this while in pastoral ministry just as he does it for those working in schools, in hospitals, on farms, in offices, or anywhere else on his earth.

But there is a paradox here. Men and women of God, pastors, missionaries, are supposed to look good and have it all together aren't they? There will always be members of our congregations who want us to be all they know themselves not to be, to put us on a pedestal and encourage us to share their illusions. Some television channels seem to stereotype an image of the successful pastor. But is it really about the perfect haircut, tailored suits, word perfect oratory, and large churches? Is this a helpful image of leadership? It has its appeal, but surely we buy into it at our peril. For all the years of God's rugged schooling, grace, and indwelling, I for one am still very conscious of my vulnerabilities.

And yet... when we look at a more biblical model, perhaps we are not so far off track. Murray J. Harris comments on Paul's apostolic

---

[11] Quoted by Philip Greenslade, *The Legacy of Jesus*, (Farnham: CWR, 2002) p. 77
[12] Jeremiah 17: 9

ministry in these terms: 'Christian existence is often marked by *paradox*: divine comfort in the midst of human affliction, divine strength in the midst of human weakness, life in the midst of death, spiritual rejuvenation in the midst of physical debilitation, joy in the midst of sorrow and generosity in the midst of poverty.'[13]

Walter Luthi, the Swiss scholar-preacher, in his commentary on 2 Corinthians recalls a picture from an old calendar that used to hang in his home when he was a child: it was a picture of a messenger – limping with a wooden leg. The title? 'The Limping Messenger.' And Luthi goes on: 'The natural man prefers to picture a messenger in the way that the ancient Greeks picture their god, Hermes, with wings on both feet. It is the winged messenger, not the man with the wooden leg, who corresponds to our wishful thinking. But the messenger of Jesus is no winged Hermes. The apostle Paul is more like that limping messenger.'[14]

The paradoxical pastor does have a pleasantly subversive ring to it! It certainly undermines that sharp-suited CEO image of a pastor. It reminds us of our humanity, still very much a work in process, yet at the same time our high and holy calling as shepherds of the flock. We stand before the people to declare God's truth, aware that it has challenged us long before it will the congregation. We offer the sacrament in bread and wine, knowing that it is the celebrant who is unworthy to come before this table. We counsel those whose lives are falling apart, knowing how close at times ours feels to be doing the same. Ministering within this paradox undermines any tendency to pomposity or pretence, while still raising valid expectations that God himself might use us in his service. In the wilderness seasons of ministry, it reminds us that it is all ultimately his responsibility. In the fruitful times, it emphasises the need to give him all the glory. It teaches us that no presenting circumstance of itself is ultimately decisive, whether within us or external to us, for all the riches of God in Christ are available to us. Paradoxical indeed.

Nigel Watson puts it well like this, commenting on the phrase 'the power of the gospel'. 'If the bearer of such a word of power is,

---

[13] Murray J. Harris, *The New International Greek Commentary, The Second Epistle to the Corinthians,* (Grand Rapids: William B. Eerdmans Publishing Company, Milton Keynes: Paternoster, 1995) p. 123

[14] This story is quoted by Nigel Watson, *Epworth Commentaries, The Second Epistle to the Corinthians,* (London: Epworth 1993) p. xl in Introduction

in his own person, transparently powerless, without presence or eloquence, no superman but rather one who is all too human, then that simply proves that the source of the *transcendent power* does not lie in himself but in God alone. The glaring disparity between the power of the message and the powerlessness of the messenger serves only to protect the truth that 'salvation is of the Lord' (Jonah 2: 9 A.V.).'[15]

Wise pastors have always known that this is so. C.H. Spurgeon in his *Lectures to My Students* includes a chapter entitled 'The Minister's Fainting Fits'. (As with many of the divines of the past, we need to decode their metaphors to bring their thoughts in fresh language to our day!) The title refers to depression and other seasons when the minister is overcome to the point of being barely able to struggle on. Spurgeon himself, the greatest preacher and pastor of his generation, was prone to depression as he acknowledged at the beginning of the chapter: 'Knowing by most painful experience what deep depression of spirit means, being visited there-with at seasons by no means few or far between.' And in a broader observation, he writes of fellow pastors, 'The strong are not always vigorous, the wise not always ready, the brave not always courageous, and the joyous not always happy'.[16]

Perhaps none have brought the frailties of the pastor's humanity and the potential of the pastor's service together as tellingly as Henri Nouwen. Nouwen's name has become synonymous with the phrase 'the wounded healer' – not just the title of one of his most famous books, but a statement which embodies his philosophy of ministry. Amid his giftedness and genius, he honestly acknowledged his own frailties: his breakdowns, psychological flaws, battles with loneliness, and grapplings with sexuality. Michael Ford, in his biography of Nouwen, explains this philosophy of ministry, including Nouwen's warning to ministers: 'A deep understanding of their own pains, however, makes it possible for them to offer their own experience as a source of healing to those "who are often lost in the darkness of their own misunderstood sufferings". But in doing so, he writes, ministers have to walk the tightrope: they should neither conceal their own

---

[15] Watson p. 43

[16] C.H. Spurgeon, *Lectures to My Students,* (London: Marshall, Morgan and Scott, 1965) p. 154

experiences from those they want to help, nor be tempted by any form of spiritual exhibitionism – "open wounds stink and do not heal".[17]

I have come to believe that this is what a Christian is supposed to look like, what a pastor is supposed to look like. This kind of paradoxical living is not something we mature out of or rise above. It is not comfortable, but neither can we escape it. To the end of our days, we will know ourselves to be cracked pots filled with treasure. It is this balance and creative tension that the severity and kindness of God is committed to produce in us.

God Meant It for Good

In the mist of that work of God, however, it is easy to lose perspective. And in losing perspective, one temptation is to walk away from our commitments. Pressures can seem unbearable such that relief is sought away from a difficult church, difficult spouse, or difficult people. Unfortunately, there is not a little 'Christian' literature circulating today that subtly validates such abandonments.[18] Ajith Fernando comments on such departures from previous loyalties in these words, 'It is almost as if liberation from pain and stress is regarded as a sign of God's will in this decision'.[19]

Joseph seems to be one who lost sight of neither the big picture nor his place in it. After a long season of trial, his brothers came to beg forgiveness for the aggravation and pain they had inflicted on him. He replied with clarity, 'You meant evil against me, but God meant it for good....'[20]

Yes, he did know 'experience without explanation, adversity without purpose, hostility without protection'[21] – a telling phrase Alec Motyer uses to describe how life can appear at times for the earthly people of God. Joseph knew abandonment by family, false accusation by Potiphar's wife, and failed hopes while in prison. Life bordered on the unendurable, and all this was initiated by his brothers. Never, however, did he cut and run.

---

[17] Michael Ford, *Wounded Prophet*, (London: D.L.T. 1995) p. 58

[18] I am thinking here of books such as Jake Colsen, *So You Don't Want to go to Church Anymore,* and some of the Emerging Church literature.

[19] Ajith Fernando, *An Authentic Servant,* (OMF Publication) p. 14

[20] Genesis 50: 20 ESV

[21] Alec Motyer, *The Message of Exodus*, BST series, (Nottingham: IVP, 2005) p. 28

But if he knew 'the severity of God', he also knew something that transcended all the pain – an unshakeable confidence in the sovereignty of God. The cry of the Psalmist would later echo the conviction of Joseph, 'You are good, and what you do is good'[22]. God was at work here. He was shaping Joseph for high office, and he was using Joseph as one small part of a greater plan.

That understanding is crucial to our exploration here. Nothing that we go through is outside God's good and loving purpose. In our lives, God always means it for good. With that confidence, we can turn to the first area of the pastor's challenge: that of his daily work.

---

[22] Psalm 119: 68

Underpinning

Exploration – *based on the following hymn of William Cowper:*
God moves in a mysterious way,

His wonders to perform;

He plants his footsteps in the sea

And rides upon the storm.

Deep in unfathomable mines

Of never-failing skill

He treasures up his bright designs

And works his sovereign will.

His purposes will ripen fast

Unfolding every hour;

The bud may have a bitter taste,

But sweet will be the flower.

Blind unbelief is sure to err

And scan his work in vain;

God is his own interpreter,

And he will make it plain.

- Which of God's ways of working are recognised in the hymn?
- To what end does Cowper suggest these workings of God are designed?
- How might they represent something going on in your life at present as discussed in this chapter?

Excavation – *recommended for digging deeper*

- *Wounded Prophet* – *A Portrait of Henri J.M. Nouwen*, by Michael Ford, published by D.L.T.

Exchange – *new foundation for old*
A response of worship in the words of Matt and Beth Redman:

Blessed be your name in the land that is plentiful,
Where the streams of abundance flow,
Blessed be your name.
And blessed be your name when I'm found in the desert place,
Though I walk through the wilderness,
Blessed be your name.
Blessed be your name when the sun's shining down on me,
When the world's 'all as it should be,'
Blessed be your name.
And blessed be your name on the road marked with suffering,
Though there's pain in the offering,
Blessed be your name.

Every blessing you pour out I'll turn back to praise,
And when the darkness closes in, Lord,
Still I will say,

Blessed be the name of the Lord,
Blessed be your name.
Blessed be the name of the Lord,
Blessed be your glorious name.

You give and take away,
You give and take away,
My heart will choose to say,
'Lord, blessed be your name.'[23]

Chapter 2

The Work We Do

I have laboured and toiled and often gone without sleep....
And who is equal to such a task?
2 Corinthians 11: 27 & 2: 16

A friend of mine, a Baptist pastor in his mid forties, left his church in the West Country to serve in a Christian evangelistic organisation. This move was precipitated by pressure and stress he and his family walked through as they handled the pastoral implications of a key church leader being imprisoned for sexual offences against young people in the church. In the highly charged atmosphere of such pain, the conflicting demands of ministry to victims, families, and the perpetrator itself generated criticism from a wider circle. Some deemed it almost his responsibility that this happened in the first place, some said it was distracting him from their needs, others said it was affecting his preaching. Balancing the need for confidentiality, the directions of police and legal teams, the interest of the media, and the demand for explanation and information from the membership produced an intolerable strain on my friend and his wife.

Another friend, an Anglican vicar in the midlands, has yet again had to have time off work due to stress. He was called to his parish on an agenda of change. This was the message from the interview committee and reinforced in his selection process. He began to preach the gospel and expound the word of God in the somewhat traditional, sleepy community. Life began to spring up, a few new families joined the church, some young people showed interest in the midweek club, and before too long, there was a small group of new believers enjoying new life in the Spirit. This began to be reflected in the worship – and in wear and tear on the building. Change no longer appeared so attractive to the original members. Demands began to be made for honouring the prayer book and reverencing the building. Private meetings were called to raise petitions, complaints were made to the bishop, hate mail was received, and open resistance demonstrated to my friend's ministry. Should he stay, keep faith with the new converts, battle it out, or shake off the dust and seek new pastures? And what was the cost either way?

Still another friend pastoring a Baptist community church in the southeast of England has a wonderful gifting to minister to needy people on the fringes of society. He finds and attracts those with multiple marriages and children, troubled with substance abuse, dabbling in the occult, work-shy but brilliantly adept at working the social services system to great advantage. Many respond to the demonstration of loving acceptance and the grace of the gospel, but the complexity of social problems is such that he and his team are stretched to the limit of expertise and strength. Called to the ministry of the word and prayer, he finds himself wearing so many other caps he needs a larger rack to store them: social worker, financial adviser, marriage counsellor, deliverance exorcist, lifestyle guru. All the while, he pastors the church, which, surprise surprise, suffers from low income.

Those three cameos reflect the crisis in pastoral ministry in the west. Care for the Family suggests that as many as 80 per cent of pastors experience depression and burnout. The attrition rate is high; sustainability over a lifetime is increasingly rare.[1] Of the group that left Spurgeon's College with me, less than half continued doing the job for which we all set out with such high hopes. No wonder Bill Hybels has said that pastoring a church is the toughest job in the world.

Before settling into further gloom and depression, however, we must ask has it ever been any different. Certainly many of the social issues we face have real complexities, but mankind in sin is the raw material that pastors are called to deal with in every generation. The fact that sin and Satan are remarkably ingenious at devising ever-more-twisted ways of operating is but a call to seek wisdom from above, which has to be more than adequate to the challenge. Most of the pressures pastors face come, in fact, from 'friends' within, rather

---

[1] Further statistics and analysis are available from the Evangelical Alliance web site: www.eauk.org/careforpastors.cfm

than foes without, and any reading of the epistles shows that it has ever been thus.

A Reality Check

In a moment of pastoral angst, the apostle Paul cried out, 'Who is equal to such a task?', 'Who is sufficient for these things?' (RV). As Peterson translates it, 'This is a terrific responsibility. Is anyone competent to take it on? No.'[2] Although this book is more about *who* we are as pastors than *what* we do as pastors, we need to establish some scope of the work in order to feel the weight of it and be able to assess the internal cost to us. This question of Paul's in second Corinthians is a good place to start. In this most personally vulnerable of letters, we can get the feel of what caused his angst, recognising it is likely to be similar for ministers of the gospel in every generation.

Servants of God (6: 3). Paul begins this letter in his usual manner by introducing himself in terms of his call, an apostle of Jesus Christ by the will of God. He concludes it with one of the clearest statements of the Trinity in the New Testament and throughout has God central and dominant in every argument. Paul is a man consumed by his relationship with the Father, through the Son, in the person of the Holy Spirit. It is a theocentric life, so he views his ministry quite naturally as a servant of God.

This for all of us is both elegantly simple and wonderfully mysterious. To know the grace of the Lord Jesus, the love of God, and the fellowship of the Holy Spirit is a relationship available to any childlike spirit. It is also a lifetime of high calling to adventure and discovery, which will take us into all eternity. It encompasses immanence and intimacy, transcendence and awe.

Our calling to be servants of such a God means in the first instance to be preoccupied with him, learn his character and ways, discern his voice, pursue his truth, worship his majesty, and seek him in prayer. As the apostle expresses it elsewhere, 'I want to know Christ and the power of the resurrection and the fellowship of sharing in his sufferings, becoming like him in his death, and so, somehow, to attain to the resurrection from the dead.'[3]

---

[2] 2 Corinthians 2: 16 The Message
[3] Philippians 3: 10

Exodus 30 provides a helpful insight. Here the priests are instructed in the blending of the anointing oil, a fragrant mixture of spices and oils that was to be burned on the altar. This ministry in the inner court of the temple was their primary calling. They were firstly to bring offerings to the Lord. During this, their clothing would become impregnated with the fragrance of that holy place. Later, as they moved to minister among the crowds in the outer courtyard, the people would smell the fragrance that represented the presence of God coming from the servants of God. With this picture obviously in mind, Paul speaks of being the aroma of Christ, a fragrance of life to those being saved or the smell of death to those who are perishing.[4]

It was said of Duncan Campbell of Hebredian Revival fame that he only had to utter the word God in his Scottish accent, drawing out the vowel to great effect, to cause people to fall on their knees. As a preacher, I have often thought a Celtic accent would be a great help, but what was at work here with Campbell was the fragrance, the awe, the breath of God – the anointing of a man who came from the courts of heaven to the congregations of men with telling effect.

This is the God we are called to serve, initially by devoting time and seasons in his presence. It is a call to worship, meditation, prayer and reading – and among all the other demands, who is equal to such a task?

We have this treasure in jars of clay (4: 7). Nowhere is the humanity of Paul so clearly seen as in this extraordinary letter. We feel with him in his hardships in Asia, under great pressure, beyond ability to endure, in despair of life itself feeling the sentence of death. We identify with him as the verbs of his experience cry out: hard pressed, perplexed, persecuted, struck down, given over to death. We hear him as the servant of God straining for integrity: in great endurance; in troubles, hardships, and distresses; in beatings, imprisonments, and riots; in hard work, sleepless nights, and hunger; in purity, understanding, patience, kindness; in the Holy Spirit and in sincere love; in truthful speech; and in the power of God, with the weapons of righteousness in the right hand and in the left. We hear him through glory and dishonour, bad report and good report, genuine yet regarded as impostors, known yet regarded as unknown, dying and yet living

---

[4] 2 Corinthians 2: 14ff

on, beaten and yet not killed, sorrowful yet always rejoicing, poor yet making many rich, having nothing and yet possessing everything. We look with awe at his struggles with false apostles and physical sufferings in chapter eleven and can only watch from afar at the holy ground of his agony as he battles with his thorn in the flesh, a messenger of Satan, in chapter twelve and begs God, without the answer hoped for, to take it all away.

I suspect that anything said after that litany of troubles will seem trite, but the fact is that all the Lord's servants face battles that expose and challenge their humanity, even if not of the same range and intensity as that of Paul. Reality calls for the simple acknowledgment that in handling these mysteries we are limited and flawed, we have patterns of life as sinners that change slowly at best, and we as often as not would rather flee than fight.

My first introduction to the writing of Brennan Manning was his little book *The Ragamuffin Gospel*. Since then, through his writings, he has become a firm friend and trusted director, for I love his raw honesty and transparent spirit. His writings reveal a man fractured and vulnerable, yet ablaze with a passion for God. He also happens to be a Godsend for any preacher for his storytelling is supreme – a rich source of illustrations, perception and compassion, humour and poignancy. For example from the above book: 'After reading the entire Gospel of Luke for the first time, a girl said, "Wow! Like Jesus has this totally intense thing for ragamuffins." The young lady is onto something.... In short, Jesus hangs out with ragamuffins.... Just as a smart man knows he is stupid, so the awake Christian knows he/she is a ragamuffin.' [5]

At those times when we are overwhelmed by our humanity, we do well to remember that God is probably not shocked nor wringing his hands in anxiety over our state. The solution may not be to rebuke the devil nor the deacons nor the technology of Bill Gates – being the generation I am, not a few of my frustrations are technological! What we are more likely to be in need of is learning how our humanity fits into the call, something which I have already indicated is a large part of this book. For now, however, given our humanity, our jars of clay, the question is valid: who is equal to such a task?

---

[5] Brennan Manning, *The Ragamuffin Gospel,* (Harpenden: SP Trust Ltd, 1997), p. 47

Ministers of a new covenant (3: 6). In this section, Paul is explaining the greater glory of the new covenant by contrasting it to the old as administered by Moses. This is now a ministry of the heart, by the Spirit, bringing righteousness, never to fade, and wonderfully glorious. Such ministers no longer have to wear veils like Moses for we enjoy a freedom in Christ. Glory is referred to over and again in the passage. Glory indeed. Heady stuff for those called to continue this work. Later, Paul describes the role as Christ's ambassadors (5: 20). This too is a high calling.

In acknowledging 'heady stuff' and 'high calling', however, the serpent lays waiting. The ambassadors of Christ are not those who live in Victorian embassies echoing the grandeur of empire. The world is full of pictures that portray the splendour of high office whether crimson gowns in the Lords, the crowns of kings, the tunics of generals, or the ancient uniform of high chancellor. The role model for the minister of the new covenant is rather that of the master of the universe carrying bowl and towel. Even those called to preach and proclaim the Word do well to remember the injunction of St. Francis of Assisi, 'Go into the world, witness to the good news of the Kingdom, if necessary use words.' Who we are will always be more important than what we say or do.

One of the consequences of this job at a practical level is that pastors spend much of their lives dealing with ultimate issues: life and death, heaven and hell, incarnation and eschatology, weddings and funerals. This is an abnormal way to live. Most believers have these as their background; pastors have them as their foreground. As such, it is easy to have false expectations of our congregations, laying on them our own work milieu. Equally, perhaps more dangerously, we can develop a distorted view of normality, becoming harsh and severe with those who do not match up to our own perspectives and commitments. It is said that pastors, along with doctors and lawyers who also daily deal with big life issues, are prone to depression, for who can live with ultimate issues all the time? The danger is that to live with the abnormal is to become abnormal. If our objective in ministry is to make everybody's background like our foreground, we are doomed to failure. Our job is to shape people to Christ, the mediator of this glorious new covenant, not to us – and I suspect he is a lot more holistic and merciful than we tend to be. Approximately eighteen years at the carpenter's bench would have significantly shaped his understanding of a normal worldview. Perhaps a bit of tent making from time to time would help us.

One of the most enjoyable aspects of pastoral work is to visit people in their workplaces. I mainly sit and listen, try to understand the issues they face, watch the colleagues they work with, and attempt to ask moderately intelligent questions. Whatever benefit they may accrue from such a visit pales in insignificance to the benefit to me. This is one of the key arenas where the glory of the new covenant has to work, where followers of Christ are being salt, light, and leaven. If it doesn't work in the workplace, then it's no more than religious jargon and irrelevant. We need to be kept in touch with the sharp end, which is not the study but the builder's yard, the solicitor's office, the nurses' work station, the teacher's classroom.

Ministers of a new covenant of glory, Christ's ambassadors, what a job! Who is equal to such a task?

So we make it our goal to please him (5: 9). One of the running sores that is reflected through the Corinthian correspondence is the challenge Paul faced to the competence of his ministry from both regular members of the congregation and the 'super-apostles' whom he addresses in chapter eleven. Earlier Paul had said, 'I care very little if I am judged by you or by any human court; indeed I do not even judge myself.'[6] Barrett comments on this verse, 'If Paul had attended to all the criticism of himself and of his work made within his own churches (to go not further) he would have given up his apostolate. He was not thick-skinned, but simply recognised the truth that man is not qualified to act as his brother's judge. It is a reasonable inference that the criticism of the apostle, which in 2 Corinthians will appear as a full-scale attack, had already begun.'[7]

So the 'full-scale attack' is underway. Paul reacts passionately and launches into 'foolishness and boasting'. Philip Hughes urges throughout his commentary on chapter eleven that it is not self-esteem that causes Paul to speak about himself as he does. 'To suggest that this humblest of God's servants was moved by injured pride to write as he now does is to show a complete misconception of the situation. It is

[6] 1 Corinthians 4: 3
[7] C. K. Barrett, *The First Epistle to the Corinthians, Black's New Testament Commentaries*, 2nd edn (London: A&C Black, 1971), p. 101

concern, loving anxious concern, for the spiritual welfare of those who are his children in Christ which moves him so strongly.' [8]

I am sure we do well to hold to Hughes' observations of Paul's overarching concern, but to suggest that his writing is wholly altruistic seems both untrue to the natural reading of the chapter and an unnecessary denial of human reactions. His interpretation also puts Paul into such a different league to most of us that he would be hard to relate to. A more helpful view perhaps might be to recognise Paul's sense of rejection and the pain that causes; after all, the pain of rejection was clearly evident in Jesus' grief over Jerusalem, both for their loss and his. Yet Paul was not so consumed by it that he did not rise to the challenge it presented, which was their higher good – even if he had his 'mad moment' in the doing of it.

A pastor's job is not easily assessed or evaluated. Business tycoons study balance sheets, craftsmen and artists display their works, even police officers produce arrest figures. The temptation for the pastor is to reduce the criteria for job satisfaction to statistics – bums on benches or pounds in plates, being the most obvious. While both form important aspects of stewardship, neither is a true measure of faithfulness and neither is solely attributable to the pastor anyway. Fruitfulness is both seasonal and collegiate: one sows, another reaps, but even then it is the Lord who alone gives the increase – and gets the glory.

A nagging question for the conscientious pastor is am I doing a good job? How can I tell? Two people come out of church and shake hands with the pastor on the door. One says, 'Wonderful sermon pastor, thank you. What a blessing you are to this church.' The other cannot meet your eye, mumbles inanities, and hastens away. This is a critical moment. The pastor is depleted and vulnerable. In his humanity, he craves affirmation and encouragement. This is perfectly valid, but it is not the same thing as an evaluation of a job well done; these functions are different and must not be confused. What is going on in the hearts of the two people coming out of church? Unless they say something, you may never know – that's the problem. The first is a gift with their affirmation and encouragement, the second not so. But

---

[8] P. E. Hughes, *Paul's Second Epistle to the Corinthians*, *The New London Commentary*, (London: Marshall, Morgan & Scott, 1962) p. 372

who is to say whether the service and the sermon were not doing a more powerful work in that life, thus shaping his reaction on the door?

The danger of confusing words of appreciation and encouragement with a job well done is obvious. It will lead eventually, if fed on, to the shaping of words designed to elicit such response. The Word of God is thereby both prostituted and neutered. If compromises of this sort are practiced at the heart of the ministry, who can tell where such compromises will run to? The bottom line is that people are no guide to faithful pastoral ministry. They may be an encouragement or a discouragement, but only the Lord is able to determine its true worth.

Much of Jesus' ministry was in the context of religious politicking – his radical message and lifestyle provoking animosity from conservatives more concerned with position and tradition than truth. There will always be this subversive aspect to the gospel, undermining confidence in anything other than God's magnificent Son. Preaching therefore must have its prophetic element, 'to uproot, tear down, destroy and overthrow'. This is never popular as the blood of the prophets testifies. For a pastor to pursue this subversive ministry is exhausting, not least because it absorbs so much time and energy. At a political level it cost Jesus his life; many pastors feel it will do for them as well.

The Puritans put great stress on what they called living before the Audience of One. Os Guinness quotes John Cotton's exposition of the phrase in Ephesians, 'not with eye-service as man-pleasers': 'We live by faith in our vocations, in that faith, in serving God, serves men, and in serving men, serves God and he doth it all comfortably though he meet with little encouragement from man, whereas an unbelieving heart would be discontent that he can find no acceptance, but all he doth is taken in worse part.' Guinness develops this by adding, 'Similarly we who live before the Audience of One can say to the world: "I have only one audience. Before you I have nothing to prove, nothing to gain, nothing to lose".' [9] And also we might add say it to our churches as well.

We live in a different age to the Puritans. Ours is governed by opinion polls and consensus politics, conformity and blandness,

---

[9] Os Guinness, *The Call*, (Carlisle: Paternoster, 2001) p. 74

consumer surveys and trend-following, which, if reflected in the church, can all too easily shift focus from the Audience of One to the audience of many.

So we too (in our better moments) 'make it our aim to please him', and who is equal to such a task?

A messenger of Satan (12: 7) A biblical worldview demands that we recognise the presence and activity of Satan. Paul clearly does here, as did Jesus – as the gospels graphically portray. John Calvin wrote, 'It is an artifice of Satan to seek some misconduct on the part of ministers which may tend to the dishonour of the gospel; for when he has been successful in bringing the ministry into contempt all hope of progress is destroyed: therefore the man who wishes to serve Christ with usefulness must apply himself with all possible diligence to preserve the honour of his ministry.' [10]

It is not my purpose here to add to the speculations as to what the nature of Paul's thorn in the flesh was other than to observe he considered it satanically originated. It is worth noting, however, that his response to such was not to rebuke the enemy but to pursue the matter with God, as had Job before him. This is not to deny the place for deliverance ministry, only to say that the primary recourse for servants of God is always to be God himself.

Some years ago I was talking to a man who worked on the production side of the film and theatre industry. He said that it was a tough sphere of work and in his view all the men who worked in it were either into women, gambling, or drink. I suspected he had a rather jaundiced view of his industry, but if that be rewritten as sex, addictions, and money, I doubt many, in any industry, would be excluded from those spheres of temptation.

In addition to all that, of course, the pastor has his own unique occupational hazards. A vicar confessed with remarkable candour to a group of us one day, 'I was counselling a young lady recently and suddenly had this great insight: I knew just what she needed – me!' It is, however, the more subtle temptations, those that lie at the core of our being, not yet fully yielded, not yet fully understood, that provide the greater danger areas: the platform for our egos, the descent into the professionalism of man management, the messiah complex that urges

---

[10] Hughes p. 221.

us to control and manipulate (all in the name of service), the competitiveness between colleagues, the attendance to things external at the expense of the internal, the avoidance of prayer, the pandering to the consumer mentality of the day, the treatment of people as commodities. Eugene Peterson puts it like this, 'The religious leader is the most untrustworthy of leaders: in no other station do we have so many opportunities for pride, for covetousness, for lust, or so many excellent disguises at hand to keep such ignobility from being found out and called to account.' [11]

In the margin of my Bible against Luke 22: 31 is the date 16.3.85. That morning in my time of prayer and meditation, I had a strong sense that the Lord was speaking these words to me. The verse says, 'Simon, Simon, Satan has asked to sift you as wheat. But I have prayed for you that your faith may not fail. And when you are turned back, strengthen your brothers.' I had no idea what it meant, how I would be sifted, what the trial of my faith would involve, and especially how long would be the turning process – probably just as well.

Within a matter of months, I was involved in a personal failure. The point I wish to draw out here is that at no point in those months did I ever sense or feel Satan near. I had no dark clouds, no brooding presence, no evil dreams. The battles were of the flesh, but I do not doubt that Satan was involved – not only because the Lord had so clearly spoken that to me, but because as the quote from Calvin reminds us, he is always lurking around seeking to undermine ministry. The fact that there is no lingering sense of evil, of burning sulphur or demonic manifestations, only makes the battle more subtle and insidious.

What the whole episode eventually did was to set me on a course to understand how such a failure could have occurred (i.e., to better understand myself). David Benner, in his excellent book *The Gift of Being Yourself,* quotes three theological heavyweights: 'John Calvin's opening words in *The Institutes of Christian Religion:* "There is no deep knowing of God without a deep knowing of self and no deep knowing of self without a deep knowing of God" ... Thomas à Kempis argued that "a humble self-knowledge is a surer way to God than a

---

[11] Eugene H. Peterson, *Under the Unpredictable Plant,* (Grand Rapids: Eerdmans, 1992) p. 15.

search after deep learning" ... Augustine's prayer was, "Grant, Lord, that I may know myself that I may know thee".' [12]

I may have known quite a bit about aspects of church, Bible, and theology, but I was woefully blind to my own inner world. Mine had been a pretty average upbringing, but flaws and damage there were aplenty, which made me vulnerable in some settings. It was my inner world that needed understanding then repairing. What I needed was that 'interior adequate to the exterior'. [13] I have been amazed at the extraordinary lengths to which God goes and the great patience he shows to save and to win back. He does this not only for our own sake, for he then uses our stories and discoveries to the aid of others. So what I seek to articulate here are principles and practices, the ways of God, a vocational holiness, which I should have known before and was found wanting of but am now learning again. Ultimately, of course, they are lessons of grace and mercy, which are of universal application, not just to those called to this job.

What Satan meant for destruction, God had meant for good so that now, these many years later, I can seek to fulfil the prophecy and 'strengthen my brothers'. And of course, this dynamic is at work in all of us. The interaction between a God who foreknows, a Satan who sifts, and servants who are so lacking should fill us with a sense of awe, a reverent humility, the touching of a profound mystery – it certainly does me. And who is equal to such a task?

Meanwhile we groan, longing to be clothed with our heavenly dwelling (5: 2) This second Corinthian letter was written by Paul probably no later than AD 54, some ten to fifteen years before he was to be martyred. Churches have been planted in Galatia, Pamphylia, and Cilicia, over into Greece, and he is probably currently in Ephesus, where he was to stay for nearly three years, the longest sojourn in his travelling life. The work was to grow profoundly and affect the hinterland of the province of Asia with a string of daughter churches formed from the great trading centre. Yet even here, at the height of his powers and effectiveness, he reveals a clear focus on the end of his life. The troubles he has been through have forged in him a firm grasp on his own mortality and eternity, so his eyes are fixed on the unseen.

---

[12] David Benner, *The Gift of Being Yourself,* (Guildford: Eagle, 2004), p. 20.
[13] Peterson p. 3

His hope is set on the heavenly dwelling, and the criteria which shapes his lifestyle and actions is his accountability before the judgement seat of Christ. He is determined to finish well, whether that moment comes tomorrow or in decades' time.

When we were pastoring in Worthing, we had the privilege of ministering to many senior saints, not a few of them retired pastors. Some of these did better than others in handling retirement. It seemed to me, those who fared best were those able to distinguish between their calling and their employment, their vocation and their occupation. Popular wisdom would have us believe that 'there's no retirement in the Kingdom of God'. That, I think, is only partially true. Numbers 8: 23–26 legislated for the retirement of the Levites at the age of fifty but helpfully provided them a support role in a useful arena of service without all the responsibilities they previously carried. This is a careful and compassionate distinction. It honours the aging process, recognises the decline in natural powers, acknowledges that there will come a time when a person should no longer be employed full time, but affirms that the calling of that individual remains and, in the appropriate context, has much to offer.

Who could doubt the achievements and influence of men and women over sixty-five, let alone fifty? The Bible and church history is redolent with stories of their fame: Moses and Caleb at eighty, John on Patmos at ninety, John Wesley at ninety and Billy Graham and Mother Theresa in their late eighties just to cream the headlines. However, what they and all who successfully negotiate what is being called 'the third age' have done is to find the right niche. The key is surely a servant heart to outwork the gift of God.

I love the phrase used in the NIV, 'full of years', as in the sentence, 'He died an old man and full of years'. It is used of only five people in scripture: Abraham (Genesis 25: 8), Isaac (Genesis 35: 29), David (1 Chronicles 29: 28), Jehoiada the priest (2 Chronicles 24: 15), and Job (Job 42: 17). In meriting this accolade 'full of years', these men have demonstrated a capacity to enjoy life to the full at every stage, to have learned contentment not least with the unresolved and unresolvable, and to have found reconciliation with death. Alexander MacLaren comments on the phrase: 'these men were satisfied with life; having exhausted its possibilities, having drunk a full draught, having nothing more left to wish for. The words point to a calm close, with all desires gratified, with hot wishes stilled, with no desperate clinging to life, but a willingness to let it go, because all which it could give had been attained.'

One of the most famous pieces of Christian literature is the passing of Mr. Valiant-for-Truth in Bunyan's *Pilgrim's Progress.* 'Sensing his time had come, he called his friends around him and said, I am going to my Father's, and tho' with great difficulty I am got hither, yet now I do not repent me of all the trouble I have been at to arrive where I am. My Sword I give to him that shall succeed me in my Pilgrimage, and my Courage and Skill to him that can get it. My marks and scars I carry with me, to be witness for me, that I have fought his battles, who will now be my rewarder. When the day that he must go hence was come, many accompany'd him to the river-side, into which as he went, he said, *Death where is thy sting?* And as he went down deeper, he said, *Grave where is thy victory?* So he passed over, and all the trumpets sounded for him on the other side.'

Finishing well – and who is equal to such a task?

Frailty, Fallibility, and Failure

I am not concerned at this point with genuine failure, by which I mean loss of integrity. That this happens among pastors and priests is indisputable as I have already indicated.

What I want to tease out here is a more difficult, subtle area. It is the lingering sense of it all being too much, induced by the combination of the issues outlined above. Given the God we serve, who we are, the job we are called to do, the context of that job, the enemy present, and the need to see it through to the end, it is not surprising that pastors, at times, feel woefully inadequate. Such feelings can cripple and make us more vulnerable to temptation. Men and women who undertake this job are mostly sincere, dedicated folk who pursue the call with a genuine desire to serve the Lord, his people, and his kingdom. They do not, by and large, undertake the job for financial gain, social status, or considerations of an easy life. Such conscientiousness, however, in the light of the question 'who is equal to such a task' is likely to lead to the conclusion of 'not me!'

This, however, is the very force of Paul's own conclusion. In and of himself, even he was not up to it, and God had ordained it so; this is the first place that God's rugged schooling brought him and will also bring us. Paul had to come to this place of acknowledged frailty, for it is only at such a place that we throw ourselves on God for his help. The only true failure is the failure to acknowledge our impotence and his sufficiency.

The danger is that instead of surrendering we bolster up our effort with false comfort. Pastors have a couple of ways of doing this.

The first has to do with the numbers game. Within the first few minutes of newly meeting another pastor, I can guarantee that the question will arise as to how big my church is. These days I try to answer along the lines 'big enough'. I have been there and done that enough in the past, however, to understand that underlying such enquiry is the insecurity that seeks to know if I am doing a better job than he or she. Pride or dejection quickly follows. Such comparison is, of course, asinine as any rational, objective thought would quickly tell, but the heart has its moments of betrayal too!

The subtlety is that numbers are not unimportant. The gospel is expansionist. Our commission is to go into all the world and make disciples. Our history has been shaped by the numbers in Acts and the stories of revival. And you will never know who the lost sheep are if you don't have some system for counting them.

The 'who is equal' question, however, can never be answered by counting or, more importantly, by comparing numbers. Used in the wrong way, they can only induce a dangerous lure to pride or a probably wholly unwarranted sense of failure.

The second factor arises from the first and is the temptation to view colleagues and companions as competitors. There have been moments in pastoral *extremis*, when almost the last thing I could bear was the story of another great triumph, of growth, of revival and blessing on my brothers – usually in South America, Asia, or Africa. The unsanctified cry barely gets strangled in the throat: why not in Europe, why not the UK, and especially why not here? R. T. Kendall confessed that on hearing news of the 'Toronto blessing' reviving the South London Vineyard and Holy Trinity Brompton, he did not first enquire what it was about but felt grieved that any visitation of the Spirit had not come first to Westminster Chapel; they had, after all, sound doctrine and a track record of praying for revival.

The moment colleagues become competitors, the very collegiate, relational nature of the Kingdom of God is undermined, resources are lost, complementary ministries become alienated, and the unity that commands the blessing is lost.

Grace

Ministry today is challenging, demanding, complex, and tiring! The simple conclusion of this quick dip into 2 Corinthians is that it has never been any different. It is some inverted sense of pride to suggest that it is more difficult today than for first century Paul; in the days of the Reformation; during the Great Awakenings; or in China, India, or any place else in any age. If there is any difference, it has probably less to do with the nature of the job than the superficiality that dogs our generation to imagine that these things can be done without recourse to the disciplines and depths that our forefathers knew to be essential.

The great danger then is that we accuse God of not being able to fulfil his part, that having called he is not able to sustain. Not that this would be articulated, we know the stories of Korah too well for that, but if it festers inwardly, it will poison the spirit and disable the servant.

The trick is taking the time and patience to make them work for us first. Most frequent air travellers pay scant attention to the valiant efforts of the flight attendants as they explain the emergency procedures. The one that always registers with me, however, is the instruction if the oxygen masks drop down put your own on first before you attempt to help anyone else. Compassion and loving concern might suggest that this is wrong tactics; surely, what could be more helpful, indeed sacrificial, than attending to others first? The airlines' advice is sound, however, for it is a long-term solution: if you don't breathe, your ability to help others is short-lived. The same is true of pastoral ministry.

Paul later answered his own question 'who is equal to such a task?' with the confident statement of faith, 'our competence comes from God'. The fact is God's grace is sufficient, his promises are dependable, his resources adequate. To suggest anything less is blasphemous.

It has been necessary, however, to feel the weight of the task, the substantiality of the load we carry day-to-day. This is often one of the first severities that God uses in our spiritual formation – part of what is, for many of us, the dawning realisation that more is needed than one seems to be able to come up with.

Underpinning

Exploration – *based on 2 Corinthians 1: 3–12*

- v. 3 Are you able to sing just now, or like the exiles in Psalm 137, has the song grown faint on your lips? Is your current spiritual / emotional tank full, half, or empty?

- v. 4 In the troubles of life, how is Father comforting you, or is the heart heavy with God apparently distant? Do you know which spiritual exercise helps refresh you in God's love?

- v. 5 & 6 Is there any sense of purpose in your present distresses, or do they seem to end with yourself? Is there one thing you could change to help?

- v. 8 Have you been able to inform someone else about your hardships suffered, or are you bearing them alone?

- v. 12 How is your confidence level just now? Where do you experience gaps between reality and expectations in your role?

Excavation – *recommended for digging deeper*

- Eugene H. Peterson, *Under the Unpredictable Plant,* Eerdmans

Exchange – *new foundation for old*

- The prayer of St. Theresa of Avila

Lord God remind me always
Let nothing disturb thee
Nothing affright thee
All things are passing
God never changeth
Patient endurance
Attaineth to all things
Who God possesseth
In nothing is wanting
Alone God sufficeth

Chapter 3

The Discipline We Face

For what son is not disciplined by his father?
Hebrews 12: 7

We are asking questions about a pastor's spirituality. What kind of interior do we need to sustain the exterior pressures of the job? As we are about the task of spiritual formation in the lives of our congregation, how does God go about that task in us? So far we have seen that he uses 'trials of many kinds' [1] including the nature of the job itself. These pressures and challenges, however, should never be understood as other than loving acts of healthy Fathering. We need to know to the core of our being the Fatherhood of God and the security that results. That very Fatherhood, however, needs to be mingled with another biblical truth, the fear of the Lord: a healthy respect and awe of the God whom we serve. These truths, as working realities, are essential ingredients of spiritual health.

How, then, does God go about bringing us into the substance of these truths, and what might the results be in terms of further maturity – 'so that you may be mature and complete, not lacking anything' [2]? We begin with a look at what has been assumed so far, the call of God to pastoral ministry in the first place.

The Call of God

The call of God to Moses, recorded in Exodus chapters three and four, is a classic example of God's call in scripture. Commonly understood, there are four features present in those encounters when

---

[1] James 1: 2
[2] James 1: 4

God apprehends his man or woman. All these key elements are explicit in the Moses story, whereas in some other calls they may be only implicit.

In chronological order, the first feature is the apprehension of an individual. 'When the Lord saw that he had gone over to look, God called to him from within the bush, "Moses! Moses!"' (3: 4). A similarly clear example in the New Testament is the conversation between Saul of Tarsus and the Lord Jesus on the road to Damascus. 'He fell to the ground and heard a voice say to him, "Saul, Saul, why do you persecute me?"' (Acts 9: 4) There is no mistake in either case over who was being called.

The second feature is the revelation of the God who is calling. 'I am the God of your father, the God of Abraham, the God of Isaac, and the God of Jacob' (3: 6). Later in the conversation, this is developed, 'I AM WHO I AM. This is what you are to say to the Israelites: I AM has sent you' (3: 14). And again in the New Testament, 'Who are you, Lord?' Saul asked. 'I am Jesus, whom you are persecuting,' he replied. 'Now get up and go into the city, and you will be told what you must do' (Acts 9: 5). Again, there is no question as to who was doing the apprehending.

Next is the communication of a message to be delivered or the assignment of a job to be done. God draws Moses into his concern for Israel's plight as they suffer at the hands of the Egyptians, then God entrusts the job to him of bringing 'my people the Israelites out of Egypt' (3: 10). Again looking at the New Testament example, 'This man is a chosen instrument to carry my name' (Acts 9: 15). For Moses, the job specification was to head the exodus, for Saul to witness and proclaim the name of Jesus Christ.

Finally, there is the location, the people who are to benefit from the message given or the job undertaken. So Moses was to go to Pharaoh in Egypt to secure deliverance for the people of Israel (3: 10). Saul was given the brief to exercise this call 'before Gentiles and their kings and before the people of Israel' (Acts 9: 15).

I hope the above is not too tediously obvious, overly simplistic, or individualistic. In practice, these elements come in various ways and order and with degrees of clarity and understanding. Laying out the simple biblical model, however, helps draw a couple of important deductions.

Assurance of the Call

We have already stated that with the call from God there comes the resourcing and equipping to do the job. That 'sufficiency' however can only be for those genuinely called. God has no mandate to supply those whom he did not call. Therefore, it is incumbent on everyone undertaking pastoral ministry to have the assurance that they are genuinely called by God, for then they can have the confidence of his grace. There are spheres of work in the Kingdom where volunteers are welcomed but not the pastoral ministry: that is for those press-ganged by heaven. Appointments to pastoral ministry are the work of the ascended Christ; it was when he ascended that he gave gifts to men: 'It was he who gave some to be apostles, some to be evangelists, and some to be pastors and teachers.'[3]

Happily studying quantity surveying, the last thought in my mind was that I would ever stand and preach before people. Over a three-week period in the summer of 1963, however, God hijacked my plans and reoriented me completely. On successive Sunday mornings in different churches, God contrived to send me three different preachers with the same message of calling young men to pastoral ministry and at the same time drop the name of Spurgeon's College into two of the sermons. The thought terrified me on many levels. I was not an upfront person; I had never spoken in public. What would Marilyn, my fiancée, think? What about those who were helping orientate me toward a professional partnership and lifelong security in a satisfying career, not least my father, also a quantity surveyor? Having nearly qualified, did I now have to begin studies all over again? 'Reluctant' hardly describes the emotions.

However, God's intrusion was not to be ignored. Thankfully, most denominations have procedures for testing such calls. Mine went through various Baptist denominational and college committees who added their confirmations along the way. God had broken in: it was clearly me he had in mind. (After three weeks tracking me round the country, I didn't want him mobilising anyone else in the cause!). The job was defined, at least as far as I understood it. And when I was inducted at the Durrington Free Church Worthing in September 1970, the final piece was in place as a people were prepared to believe God

---

[3] Ephesians 4: 11

was in it too. Ordained – part of that mystical company who through the generations have had hands laid on, the Holy Spirit imparted, and the commission to pasturing delivered.

I cannot tell how grateful I am for the clarity of the call or how essential it has been. Without it I would certainly not have survived in the job. Notwithstanding the best effort of Spurgeon's College, for which I am profoundly grateful, I did not understand much of what pastoring was about. Even now, after all these years, the mysteries of both divinity and humanity perplex me constantly. If anything, I suspect I thought of the job in terms of decisive, charismatic leadership, clarifying the vision, and rallying the troops to the cause; I knew little of listening, suffering, and self-denial. Neither did I understand much about the dark stuff of my own heart. I have often wondered if the Lord did not call me to ministry as a means of keeping me close to him, for I did at least know it was his work. I am more than convinced that any benefit to others through the ministry is a bonus – the grace is that I am being saved through it.

What I did know and have never doubted since is that I was called and the assurance of it has grown with confirmations and understandings along the way.

Each call of course will be unique, individually shaped. Not everyone gets a burning bush or a Damascus Road ambush. What is needed for each of us sensing God's call is to pursue it and understand it until it becomes part of the fabric of our lives. Dave Hanson puts it like this, 'Call is its own kind of knowledge. A call demands that it be known. It is a kind of information that contains within it the imperative that it be searched for and comprehended as if it were a matter of life and death.... Knowing the call takes time. It begins with an inkling about a road we sense we are being asked to take and ends with a deep knowing of one's self.' [4]

Diffidence Tinged with Fear

If it is imperative to know a clear call, I note from the biblical encounters that such is invariably met with reactions similar to my own, what I would define as diffidence tinged with fear.

---

[4] Dave Hansen, *The Art Of Pastoring*, (Downers Grove, Il: IVP, 1994) p. 30

God's call is accompanied by a sense of diffidence at best, rank fear or disobedience at worst (Jonah). In Exodus 3 there is a profoundly moving sequence in which Almighty God expresses his emotions and intentions: 'I have indeed seen the misery of my people.... I am concerned about their suffering.... I have come down to rescue them... so now, go, I am sending you.' Who would not quail before such passion, purpose, and energy?

Moses' excuses in the face of the divine call are almost humorous, as if the Almighty might need reminding of human frailties. Surely he was disqualified by his previous track record, including manslaughter, and if murder wasn't enough, what about his speech impediment: vocally challenged and a preacher? If all that was not enough, surely his age was against him? If Moses might have considered himself too old, Jeremiah thought himself too young. Gideon knew he was from the wrong side of the tracks, Isaiah was pole-axed by conviction of sin, Amos was in the wrong career, Hosea was in a dubious marriage, and Peter, James, and John were unlearned and ordinary men.

So the list goes on until you realise that this is the way it's supposed to be. Diffidence tinged with fear is the appropriate response. The problem is not the presence of those reactions in face of the call but any subsequent loss of them once we become familiar with the territory of ministry. I wonder if Uzzah's death during David's ill-fated attempt to return the ark to Jerusalem was not in some measure due to his familiarity with the ark, it having been part of the household furniture in his father's home for some twenty years; familiarity bred contempt.

Diffidence is the appropriate response because it reflects an accurate assessment of our humanity, which is why so many of those ancient characters echoed Moses' cry, 'Who am I that I should?' Their excuses may be laughable, but that is only because we know the end of their stories and celebrate their triumphs of faith. The best of these biblical characters, however, would have felt diffident all the way through. It was not as though they reached a magical plateau where suddenly they felt up to the job. As an elderly preacher said to me on one occasion, 'These butterflies have almost become friends.'

Living with such awareness is difficult, but it lies to the heart of the calling, indeed more than our calling, our very being. As pastors, we are to model weakness in order to demonstrate his strength and power, a model so completely different from every leadership role offered by the world. Even 'model' sounds too intentional, too contrived; this weakness, this diffidence is more innate than that; it is part of the very warp and weft of our fallen nature. Philip Yancey in "Grace and Gravity", his final chapter in *What's so Amazing about Grace,* puts it like this: 'We creatures, we jolly beggars, give glory to God by our dependence. Our wounds and defects are the very fissures through which grace might pass. It is our human destiny on earth to be imperfect, incomplete, weak, and mortal, and only by accepting that destiny can we escape the force of gravity and receive grace. Only then can we draw close to God.' [5]

If diffidence has to do with ourselves, then being tinged with fear has to do with the God who calls.

Father and Fear

The final word in theology is of course 'God is Love', but I suspect we have tended to lay a cultural filter over the word love, which has eliminated some of the stronger pigments. What is left is true but somewhat wan and incomplete, lacking the vibrant colours that command attention: Van Gogh's sunflowers without gold, Rembrandt's self portraits without black, or the pre-Raphaelites without their crimsons: God's love without God's awe.

The restoration of the fear of the Lord in particular seems to me a necessary ingredient to spiritual health. We humans tend to be lopsided in our approach to God, veering instinctively toward his nice side. Given our orphan spirit, this is perfectly understandable: lost child runs to father's embrace for comfort and reassurance. To know him in one part, however, is to be drawn into all the knowledge of God. This is the high adventure that will absorb us for all eternity. 'That I might know him' [6] was the heart cry of the great apostle, and not just the easy bits either but the tough ones too: identification with suffering and death as well as resurrection.

---

[5] Philip Yancey, *What's so Amazing about Grace*, (Grand Rapids: Zondervan, 1997) p. 273
[6] Philippians 3: 10

Could it be that Jesus' explanation to the Sadducees is equally applicable to us today, 'you are in error because you do not know the Scriptures nor the power of God'[7]? Any cursory glance at the word of God is enough to convince us of the necessary place of the fear of God in our lives.

Isaiah thunders, 'The Lord Almighty is the one you are to regard as holy, he is the one you are to fear, he is the one you are to dread'[8]. The indictment against fools, those who reject the wisdom of God, is that 'they hated knowledge and did not choose to fear the Lord'[9] – which also shows the need to be intentional in this matter. Part of leadership responsibility is to instruct other in this attitude: 'So I continued, "What you are doing is not right. Shouldn't you walk in the fear of our God to avoid the reproach of our Gentile enemies?"'[10] Or as David put it, 'Come, my children, listen to me; I will teach you the fear of the Lord.'[11]

And of course this is not just an Old Testament reaction to God as if with the coming of Jesus everything was changed – far from it. The record of the early church's life in Acts identifies the fear of God as an integral part of their community: 'everyone was filled with awe,' 'Great fear seized the whole church and all who heard about these events,' 'Then the church throughout Judea, Galilee and Samaria enjoyed a time of peace. It was strengthened; and encouraged by the Holy Spirit, it grew in numbers, living in the fear of the Lord'[12].

Paul's indictment of the ungodly was that 'there is no fear of God before their eyes'[13]. So he sees fear as a virtue, as an incentive in the pursuit of the Christian life: 'perfecting holiness in the fear of the Lord'[14], 'work out your salvation with fear and trembling'[15]. As A.W. Tozer put it, 'No one can know the true grace of God who has not first known the fear of God'[16]

---

[7] Matthew 22: 29
[8] Isaiah 8: 13
[9] Proverbs 1: 29
[10] Nehemiah 5: 9
[11] Psalm 34: 11
[12] Acts 2: 43, 5: 11, 9 :31
[13] Romans 3: 18
[14] 2 Corinthians 7: 1 AV, RSV, NASB, NKJ
[15] Philippians 2: 12
[16] Quoted by John Blanchard, *Gathered Gold,* (Welwyn: Evangelical Press 1984) p.105

Walter Eichrodt has a vivid phrase to describe this fear of the Lord – 'the inward agitation produced by the *mysterium tremendum*'[17]. The phrase accurately describes a man's initial encounter or exposure to the glory of God. For a working attitude, however, we may need to downgrade its intensity, much as weather forecasters downgrade a hurricane from grade five to two as it approaches land: still dangerous, respect needed, but normal life can continue. What usually assists this is God's quick response over and again, 'Do not be afraid'. 'And there were shepherds living out in the fields... and the glory of the Lord shone around them, and they were terrified. But the angel said to them, "Do not be afraid. I bring good news...."'[18].

I was raised to go to church and have been in and around churches all my life; I love the people of God, worship, and prayer. If anything other than simply a Christian, I am a Baptist. I have visited Anglican, Orthodox, Catholic, and house churches in over thirty countries in four continents. But consistently, the one biblical experience of God missing from the vast majority is this fear of the Lord, this awe, this respect, this holy awareness of his otherness.

In that conversation with the Sadducees, Jesus was explaining that their error arose from a failure to grasp the scriptures and the power of God. I wonder if our shortcomings in this area do not have more to do with the latter than the former. It is at this point that I want to add another strand to the discussion, that of discipline.

Father and Corrective Discipline

One of the seminal stories the early church wove into its definitive narrative was the moment of divine discipline meted out on Ananias and Sapphira.[19] This was not a glorious moment for the church; sin was found in its midst, revealing 'it was not all romance and righteousness'.[20] It must have occurred to them to quietly drop the story, much as a media agency might drop a news item if its political implications conflict with editorial ideology. Far from this occurring

---

[17] Walter Eichrodt, *Theology of the Old Testament Vol 2,* (London: SCM, 1964) p. 269

[18] Luke 2: 8–10, 15

[19] Acts 5:1–11

[20] John R. W. Stott, *The Message of Acts,* BST series (Downers Grove, Il: IVP, 1990) p. 109

however, the story is front page news: couple lie to Holy Spirit, cheating discovered among Jesus' followers, two dead. As John Stott comments, 'It illustrates the honesty of Luke as historian; he did not suppress this sordid episode'.[21] The story was obviously told and retold in the manner of oral tradition until it found its place in the founding stories of the church. Why? Because it was further evidence that God was present and active among his people.

There was much evidence of the continuing work of Jesus[22] to record: the poor heard good news, the sick were healed, the dead were raised, prisoners were dramatically released by angels, and God spoke in visions and dreams. All this was only attributable to a supernatural presence among very ordinary, mainly uneducated, people – the acts of the Holy Spirit. Among these acts to be honoured and recorded on a par with the happier workings was this one of discipline, judgement, and purification. Twice in the short bulletin it is recorded that the primary consequence of this event was that great fear came upon them. F. F. Bruce comments, 'The fear which fell upon the whole community suggests that many a member of it had reason to tremble and say to himself, "There but for the grace of God, go I"'.[23] Surely so, and in every generation, given the lifelong span of the sanctification process. The legacy for the church was the realisation that a holy God was in their midst and prepared to act when necessary to preserve purity and integrity among his people. Such a God could simply not be ignored if he was likely to intervene in such a manner.

If we ask if that is a good or a bad thing, most would affirm it a good thing. Indeed, it is the sort of thing a loving father would seek to impress upon his children in order to keep them safe and sound. This is the fear of the Lord. 'The fear of the Lord is pure, enduring for ever. The ordinances of the Lord are sure and altogether righteous.... By them is your servant warned; in keeping them there is great reward.'[24]

---

[21] Stott p. 108–9

[22] C.f. Acts 1: 1 'I wrote about all that Jesus began to do and teach until the day he was taken up into heaven', the implications being 'I now write of all he continued to do subsequently'.

[23] F. F. Bruce, *Book of Acts (New London Commentary)*, (London: Marshall, Morgan & Scott, 1968), p. 115

[24] Psalm 19: 9, 11

I mentioned earlier a personal failure of some twenty-five years ago. This was not adultery in the technical sense but was an inappropriate relationship with a church member and a clear violation of pastoral trust. As a result, I was brought before a meeting of all church members and required to make public confession, which I did. As may have been anticipated, the turnout was extremely large! The occasion was without doubt the worst of my life as I was humiliated and shamed before so many. The outcome was the loss of the church that had absorbed my life for seventeen years, the ending of a wider role of support to churches along the south coast, and the need to move from the district. Everything was stripped away, leaving me bloodied and raw. A few friends stood by us, but most faded away, increasing the sense of isolation and dejection. The biblical model that I now understood as never before was that of exile, compounded by the knowledge that it was all my fault. It was in this season that I began to learn the fear of the Lord.

For me it had to do with the realisation that dire consequences are contingent on his judicial acts. When the certain knowledge of judgement was near, it was the fear of loss that griped me: loss of honour, esteem, position, work. What else may he not take? I deserved it after all.

God is determined to secure our salvation. He has gone to unimaginable lengths to make it possible – he who did not spare his own beloved Son but freely gave him up for us all. He is not, therefore, going to be held back by our finer feelings and sensibilities but seems quite resolved to drive a coach and horses through such worldly niceties in order to get at us. Surely God would not do this, take that, humiliate, destroy, or pain, would he? You better believe it; so committed is he to removing anything that stands in the way of his fierce, jealous embrace. If he turned a deaf ear to Gethsemane, he is certainly not going to listen to our whimpering and whining. He knows better than to allow us to hold onto our dummies when we could be at the breast. Grace is our only hope, but we fool ourselves if we imagine grace to be always congenial. The fear of the Lord is the hammer that beats steel into our souls against the anvil of his love, an attribute as unyielding as his fear.

A couple of years after those events, the elders of the church wrote me a most gracious letter. In it, they kindly affirmed the role I had played in laying the foundation on which the church was continuing to build. They expressed their sorrow for the pain caused through the actions they felt led to take and apologised for any unnecessary hurt to myself or the family, and where this had happened 'we would sincerely seek your forgiveness'.

In my reply, I thanked them for their generosity and assured them there was no unforgiveness, resentment, or bitterness on our part. I reproduce my last paragraph as it is relevant here: 'Through those difficult days, the Lord made it perfectly clear to me that it was He that I had to deal with. He was still my sovereign Lord and nothing could touch me or my family but with His express permission. My dealings were with God, and He used who and what He would to work His mercy and grace into my life. You were just one of his instruments. Thankfully, we never confused the tools with the Craftsman.'

Commenting on the corrective discipline given to King David, John MacArthur summarises well: 'Yet David was a better man because of God's discipline. God had a purpose in the discipline – to draw his servant closer to himself, to convince him not to sin again, and to help him grow and mature.'[25] Or as the Psalmist puts it, 'Before I was afflicted I went astray, but now I obey your word…. It was good for me to be afflicted so that I might learn your decrees.'[26] There is a raw cleanness to the fear of God; it banishes any sentimental notions of his love, compels a realistic recognition of his agency, and yields a deeper respect of his Fatherhood. When set within the context of a call, this fear eclipses lesser fears and forges a cry for integrity. It brings us back to him with whom we have to deal and helps us grow up fast.

Hopefully only a very small number of pastors will experience this corrective discipline themselves. I pray that the reminder of it, however, will gird the loins and determination of all to avoid anything likely to bring it about.

Father and Preventative Discipline

The story of Ananias and Sapphira is a dramatic, attention-grabbing incident. The same principle of God at work through

---

[25] John MacArthur, *Hebrews (The McArthur NT Commentary),* (Chicago: Moody Press, 1983) p. 386
[26] Psalm 119: 67, 71

discipline but set in the more prosaic ways of life is addressed by the writer to the Hebrews in chapter twelve. Quoting Proverbs, he argues the case for discipline at the hand of a loving father for the good of his children. The Greek word that translates 'chastening' or 'discipline' means enforced learning. It does not have to do with punishment but God making sure that we are learning and staying educated. If we have known this from our earthly fathers, how much more should we expect it of our Heavenly Father? God is Abba Father; therefore, he treats us as his children with hard training. Any failure to discipline would raise the question of paternity: perhaps this is not just a careless father but, in fact, not the father at all, perhaps the children are illegitimate? Not so, our Heavenly Father does in fact discipline. At the time it is painful, but later it produces a harvest of righteousness and holiness and is reassuring evidence of parentage and family relationship. To be so disciplined demonstrates our sonship and his Fatherhood.

Again it needs be said, what the writer is talking about here is not corrective discipline, where there has been judicial punishment for sin, but what might be called preventative discipline, enforced learning. Just as good parents will put boundaries down for children for their good, so God sends fences and limitations to us for our protection and restraint. These circumstances may be painful, frustrating, or any other manner of difficulty, but behind them lays the working of our Heavenly Father to slow us down, make us think, and turn us more to prayer. Being preoccupied with these matters often keeps us out of mischief and retunes our ear to his voice.

These disciplines should create in us as much a sense of awe and reverent fear as the lightning strike from heaven. To be in the hands of such a Father brings forth the widest range of emotions imaginable, not least lives tinged with fear. 'Therefore since we are receiving a kingdom that cannot be shaken, let us be thankful, and so worship God acceptably with reverence and awe, "for our God is a consuming fire".'[27] This is the privilege of our filial relationship, and it is one goal of his ruthless perfecting.

We live in an age when the effect of children without fathers is all too evident not least in the despair and disillusionment of the young toward adults, who are perceived to have failed them. An indulged life

---

[27] Hebrews 12: 28, 29

without boundaries and discipline leads not to happiness but anger. Tom Wright writes, 'We are horribly aware, not least in the big cities of the Western world, how dangerous, to themselves and to others, are children who have never learned limits, have never discovered the meaning of 'No', backed up with appropriate restraints. Spoiled children on the one hand, and ignored children on the other, are a menace and a nuisance to everyone else, and are unlikely to grow up as happy, well-rounded characters, able to sustain a normal adult life. Clearly some kind of discipline, as one aspect of genuine love and care, is vital.'[28]

Tragic as that is the greater tragedy would be for the church to be no different from the world.

Abba Father and His Pastors

If these things are true for all God's children, how much more is it important for those of us called to pastoral ministry not just to understand them academically but be shaped by them. Discipline, either in the trials of life or the more incisive acts of judgement, is one of the ways in which our heavenly Father works. This must surely include the various pressures and trials of our calling; they must be seen as an integral part of Father's grace at work in our lives. Much as we might want to quit or fold under the pressure, these stresses are part of the shaping of us as men and women of God. We do well, therefore, to have a healthy respect for his dealings and so pursue our calling with diffidence tinged with fear. Such a posture before our Father positions us to grow, for the prime requirement in learning is attitude of heart: 'the fear of the Lord is the beginning of wisdom'.[29]

Let me briefly comment on three areas of growth related to and emanating from such a posture; three virtues intrinsic to our lifestyle, central to our calling and all derived from knowing the fear of the Lord:

Wisdom

Would to God that I knew as much as members of my church sometimes thought I did. Other times of course they knew full well that I

---

[28] Tom Wright, *Hebrews for Everyone,* 2nd Edn (London: SPCK, 2004) p. 152
[29] Proverbs 9: 10

was bluffing my way through. Feeling my woeful lack of knowledge some years ago, I was somewhat comforted with the thought that what I don't know will always vastly exceed what I do. Knowledge, however, is not the same as wisdom, far from it; some of the cleverest people live like fools – and fools are the antithesis of the wise, the constant counterpoint drawn in Proverbs.

Biblically, of course, one's mind gravitates at this point to the wisdom literature of the Old Testament. Wisdom, however, is honoured throughout the scriptures and characters of wisdom portrayed as heroes and role models: Solomon and Ester in the Old Testament, Anna and Simeon at the birth of Christ, Priscilla and Aquila among the early church. Gerhardt von Rad portrays the person of Joseph, who 'through discipline, modesty, knowledge, self-mastery and the fear of God had given a noble form to his whole being.... Before Pharaoh he proves himself a shrewd counsellor, and before his brothers the man who can be silent... and finally the one who "covers up all sins with love"'.[30]

A friend recounted how he had been asked to arbitrate in a neighbouring Baptist church where the relationship between pastor and people had reached breaking point. Initially, his sympathies had been with the pastor, but it was not long before he realised that much of the trouble the pastor complained of was self inflicted – the fellow had been so lacking in common courtesies and good manners that finally the congregation replied in kind. The man was simply a fool!

When I was a chartered surveyor working in a professional practice in London, I was surrounded by fellow professionals. There were times we might disagree and debate practices or procedures, but this was usually done with appropriate manners. There was also a clear structure of authority, which meant that men with greater experience were deferred to. The place hung together and worked. It makes for an interesting comparison with pastoring a church where not a few can perceive themselves to be the expert and knows the best way of doing things. Taking a positive slant on this, it at least shows that people are passionate about church. The flip side is that pastors tend to work in an environment where their judgements, and

---

[30] Quoted by Derek Kidner, *Proverbs, Tyndale OT Commentaries*, (London:Tyndale Press, 1964) p. 16

sometimes their integrity, are constantly under scrutiny. Mind you it could be worse; at least we are not politicians with the media snapping at our heels! Thankfully, I have pastored very happy churches, but my heart goes out to men where not a little abuse comes their way. In such situations, the call to wisdom has never been more needed. 'A man's wisdom gives him patience; it is his glory to overlook an offence.'[31]

James offers good counsel, 'If any of you lacks wisdom, he should ask of God, who gives generously to all without finding fault, and it will be given to him.'[32]

Holiness

I freely acknowledge that I find the word 'holiness' difficult. It's not that I don't understand its technical meanings: the Hebrew *qadosh,* the Greek *hagios,* denoting to separate, used of persons or things from profane to divine use, then developing into the ethical character and purity of the god to whom devoted. I've read the standard works on holiness and some of the lives of the saints and holy people, and I'm fully persuaded that it's a good thing. The problem is imagining it as nice; it sounds so sombre and earnest. Holiness, I think, has a poor image, sadly, often further marred by some who advocate it strenuously!

If the word is to be redeemed, it can probably only be achieved by the Redeemer. Gabriel's words to Mary included the phrase, 'the holy one to be born'.[33] Jesus is the perfect representation of holiness; our greatest goal is to be conformed to his likeness. In asking what God is like, we do well to remember Blaise Pascal's shrewd observation, 'God made man in his own image and man has returned the compliment'. Even so, every study of the life of Christ can only enhance our sense of wonder at the sheer magnificent vitality of this man wholly separated to God.

'The first thing we must learn about him is that we should have been absolutely entranced by his company. Jesus was irresistibly attractive as a man... young, vital, full of life and the joy of it, the

---

[31] Proverbs 19: 11
[32] James 1: 5
[33] Luke 1: 35

Lord of life itself, and even more the Lord of laughter, someone so utterly attractive that people followed him for the sheer fun of it.'[34]

'In particular, Jesus' characteristic behaviour spoke as many volumes as his characteristic teaching. Wherever he went, there was a party. After all, if God is becoming King at last, who wouldn't want to celebrate? But he celebrated *with all the wrong people*. He went into low dives and back alleys. He knocked back the wine with the shady and disrespectable. He allowed women of the street to come and fawn over him.... What had happened to all the old taboos, to Israel's standards of holiness? They seem to have gone by the board. Jesus was saying – in his actions as much as his words – that you didn't have to observe every last bit of the Torah before you could count as a real member of Israel..., you could be healed, restored and forgiven right here, where Jesus was, at this party, just by being there with him and welcoming his way of bringing in the Kingdom.'[35]

Working out a holy life in the midst of such company has a noble ring to it when describing Jesus. Living among such a bunch of ragamuffins does not always offer the same appeal to most pastors, especially after the initial buzz. Yet such is Father's assigned context for our holy calling, a ruthless appointment for 'the congregation is the pastor's place for developing vocational holiness.'[36]

What holiness does have to be is somehow consonant with the very earthiness of the setting of our lives. The essence of this holiness is perhaps that, despite everything, it is a life that carries with it the blessing of this God we serve. And in all the mix of life, both fears within and struggles without, that blessing remains. In a moving recollection, Frederick Buechner, in his autobiography *Now & Then,* graphically expounds such a holiness: 'I saw, I think for the first time, that holiness is not something hazy and elusive that we know apart from the earth but something we can know only as it wells up out of the wells of the earth, out of people as clay-footed as Jacob, the trickster and crook, out of places as elemental as the river Jabbok, where he wrestles in darkness with a Stranger who was no stranger,

---

[34] Quoted by Nicky Gumbel, *Questions of Life*, (Eastbourne: Kingsway, 1994) p. 35, from Lord Hailsham, *The Door Wherein I Went*

[35] N. T. Wright, *Who Was Jesus?* (London: SPCK, 1992) p. 99

[36] Eugene H. Peterson, *Under the Unpredictable Plant*, (Grand Rapids: Eerdmans, 1992) p. 21

out of events as seamy as the time he gulled his half-blind father out of Esau's blessing. "See, the smell of my son is as the smell of a field which the Lord has blessed," and there it is all in a moment: Jacob betrays his brother, dupes his father, all but chokes on his own mendacity, yet the smell of him is as the smell of blessing because God no less than Isaac, has chosen to bless him in spite of everything. Jacob reeks of holiness. His life is dark, fertile, and holy as the earth itself. He is himself a bush that burns with everything, both fair and foul, that a man burns with. Yet he is not consumed because God out of his grace will not consume him.'[37]

Holiness, another of those virtues best sought in the fear of the Lord – and a little more of the party spirit!

Fathering

Some years ago when I first read Henri Nouwen's story of homecoming, *The Return of the Prodigal Son,*[38] I remember being brought up sharp by his conclusion. I had happily followed his journey of identification with both younger and older son and felt the warm embrace of the father in words and touch. I felt known, understood, and received unconditionally. It was a cosy and reassuring place to be and deeply relevant personally. Then at the end, Nouwen explores the role of the father. Initially, this reinforces the earlier truths as the fatherhood of God is beautifully portrayed, resulting in appreciation and worship. Then the shock as he asks a number of questions:

'But what of the father? Why pay so much attention to the sons when it is the father who is the centre and when it is the father with whom I am to identify? Why talk about being like sons when the real question is: Are you interested in being like the father? It feels somehow good to be able to say: "These sons are like me." It gives a sense of being understood. But how does it feel to say: "The father is like me"? Do I want to be like the father? Do I want to be not just the one who is forgiven, but also the one who forgives; not just the one who is being welcomed home, but also the one who welcomes home; not just the one who receives compassion. But the one who offers it as well?

---

[37] Frederick Buechner, *Now & Then,* (San Francisco: Harper Collins, 1991), p. 19–20
[38] Based on Jesus' parable in Luke 15: 11–31.

'Isn't there a subtle pressure in both Church and society to remain a dependent child? Hasn't the Church in the past stressed obedience in a fashion that made it hard to claim spiritual fatherhood, and hasn't our consumer society encouraged us to indulge in childish self-gratification? Who has challenged us to liberate ourselves from immature dependencies and to accept the burden of responsible adults?

'Perhaps the most radical statement Jesus ever made is: "Be compassionate as your Father is compassionate."'[39]

Growing up isn't easy, but then remaining a child isn't really an option either. Through it all, then, God means it for our good. He sees us in the hard work of the job. He issues the call in the first place, knowing it to produce diffidence tinged with fear. Like a good father, he maintains awe and respect through his discipline, leading to our pursuit of wisdom, of holiness, and of vision to see the need for fathering in others. So is our Father raising up fathers and how our generation is desperately in need of them.

A Story of Fathers

Through the voice of Reuven Malter, Chaim Potok in his novel *The Chosen* tells the story of his friendship with Danny Saunders. It is an unlikely friendship set in Williamsburg, New York, over the period of the second world war. Danny's background is that of a Russian Hasidic Jew whose father, Reb Saunders, is the rabbinic leader and dynastic ruler of the sect. Reuven has been raised by his own father, David, who is also a rabbinic scholar but more progressive than the ultra-orthodox Hasidim. The shaping influence of the two fathers is key to the story, especially that of Reb Saunders with his brilliant son, Danny. His extreme method of parenting pervades the whole book, and it is only at the end that the old rabbi offers any explanation.

'Reuven, I did not want my Daniel to become like my brother, may he rest in peace. Better I should have had no son at all than to have a brilliant son who had no soul. I looked at my Daniel when he was four years old, and I said to myself, How will I teach this mind what it is to have a soul? How will I teach this mind to understand pain? How will I teach it to *want* to take on another person's

---

[39] Henri J. M. Nouwen, *The Return of the Prodigal Son*, (London: D.L.T., 1994) p.122–3.

suffering? How will I do this and not lose my son, my precious son whom I love as I love the Master of the Universe Himself? How will I do this and not cause my son, God forbid, to abandon the Master of the Universe and His Commandments?

'He closed his eyes and seemed to shrink into himself. His hands trembled. He was silent for a long time. Tears rolled slowly down alongside the bridge of his nose and disappeared into his beard. A shuddering sigh filled the room. Then he opened his eyes and stared down at the closed Talmud on the desk. "Ah, what a price to pay.... The years when he was a child and I loved him and talked with him and held him under my tallis when I prayed.... 'Why do you cry, Father?" he asked me once under the tallis. 'Because people are suffering,' I told him. He could not understand. Ah, what it is to be a mind without a soul, what ugliness it is.... Those were the years he learned to trust me and love me.... And when he was older, the years I drew myself away from him.... 'Why have you stopped answering my questions, Father?' he asked me once. 'You are old enough to look into your own soul for the answers,' I told him. He laughed once and said, 'That man is such an ignoramus, Father,' I was angry. 'Look into his soul,' I said. 'Stand inside his soul and see the world through his eyes. You will know the pain he feels because of his ignorance, and you will not laugh.' He was bewildered and hurt. The nightmares he began to have.... But he learned to find answers for himself. He suffered and learned to listen to the suffering of others. In the silence between us, he began to hear the world crying."

'Then he spoke his son's name.

'There was silence.

'Reb Saunders spoke his son's name again. Danny took his hand away from his eyes and looked at his father.

'"Daniel," Reb Saunders said, speaking almost in a whisper, "when you go away to study, you will shave off your beard and earlocks?"

'Danny stared at his father. His eyes were wet. He nodded his head slowly.

'Reb Saunders looked at him. "You will remain an observer of the Commandments?" he asked softly.

'Danny nodded again.

'Reb Saunders sat back slowly in his chair. And from his lips came a soft, tremulous sigh. He was silent for a moment, his eyes wide, dark, brooding, gazing upon his son. He nodded his head once, as if in final acknowledgment of his tortured victory.

'My father was in the kitchen and there was a strange brooding sadness on his face. I sat down and he looked at me, his eyes sombre behind their steel-rimmed spectacles. And I told him everything.

'When I was done, he was quiet for a very long time. Then he said softly, "A father has a right to raise his son in his own way, Reuven."'[40]

I trust this rather long quote from the end of Potok's book will carry the impact intended. The punchline, of course, is the final sentence: 'a father has a right to raise his son in his own way'. And if that is so among good men, how much more is it true of our Heavenly Father who works all things for our good, even those things which have the first, and perhaps every, appearance of acts of severity. For 'the Lord disciplines those he loves…, and God disciplines us for our good, that we may share his holiness. No discipline seems pleasant at the time, but painful. Later on, however, it produces a harvest of righteousness and peace for those who have been trained by it.'[41]

---

[40] Chaim Potok, *The Chosen,* (New York, Fawcett Press, 1967), p. 269
[41] Hebrews 12: 6, 10, 11

Underpinning

Exploration – *based on Hebrews 12: 4–11*

- Can you identify your present 'struggle against sin' (verse 4) and the nature of your 'hardships' (verse 9)? It might be good to write them down; doing so helps eliminate those that are purely imaginary and not real.

- Are you able to receive these trials not as the agency of men or demons (though they may well be involved) but as 'the Lord's discipline' (verse 5) and for 'our good' (verse 10)?

- If you are close to 'losing heart' (verse 5), what can you do to re-affirm Fathers' profound love for you and have it the more settled in your heart?

- Fathers' purpose is stated as 'sharing his holiness' (verse 10) and 'righteousness and peace' (verse 11). What other virtues can you see coming in your life from this season?

- Can you discern what methods Abba Father has been using to raise you as his son?

Excavation – recommended for digging deeper

- Chaim Potok's novel *The Chosen* – just because it is a great read and contains penetrating insights to fathering.

Exchange – new foundation for old

- From 'Praise to the Lord the Almighty', by Joachim Neander (English translation by Catherine Winkworth)

Praise to the Lord, who o'er all things so wondrously reigneth,

Shelters thee under his wings, yea, so gently sustaineth;

Hast thou not see?

All that is needful hath been

Granted in what he ordaineth.

Praise to the Lord, who doth prosper thy work, and defend thee!

Surely his goodness and mercy here daily attend thee:

Ponder anew

What the Almighty can do,

Who with his love doth befriend thee.

Chapter 4

The Season We Dread

So the people of Israel were taken from their homeland into exile.
2 Kings 17: 23
My God, my God, why have you forsaken me?
Psalm 22: 1, Matthew 27: 46

In these opening chapters, we have been looking at some of the ways in which the Lord orders adverse circumstances, pressures, and disciplines to effect his work in our souls and in our character. As we respond, there is a weaning away from false confidences to a hope in his graces. Healthier inner understandings and attitudes move us to better appreciate his indwelling and power. We come now to one of the more dramatic actions of God in this process, that known as exile. We begin with the experience of Israel.

Six hundred years before Christ, the big name in the news was Nebuchadnezzar, King of Babylon and leader of the world's greatest power, the mighty Babylonian Empire. At the head of his armies, he rampaged his way through the Middle East, defeated the Egyptian forces at Carchemish, and effectively brought Israel into its sphere of influence. After a show of rebellious bravado by King Jehoiakim[1], the Babylonian army finally marched on Jerusalem in 597 BC. It was a fatal error, costing Jehoiakim his life, probably to assassination. In an attempt at a more appeasing line, his eighteen-year-old son, Jehoiachin, was placed on the throne. Nebuchadnezzar was not to be diverted however. The city offered little resistance and within three months surrendered. Implementing his usual foreign policy, Nebuchadnezzar transported the leading citizens of the conquered country to Babylon. As a result, King Jehoiachin, the queen mother,

---

[1] See 2 Kings 24, Jeremiah 35

the chief priests, army generals, and landed citizens were deported. Two further deportations were to follow in 587 and 582 BC, which included a twenty-five-year-old priest called Ezekiel and a fifteen-year-old lad called Daniel. Few of those leaving would see the holy city again, for the cream of the nation's society was exiled in Babylon for seventy years.

For the people, the experience was traumatic. John Bright speaks of 'the hardships and the humiliations that these exiles endured', while acknowledging that 'their lot does not seem to have been unduly severe'.[2] Peter Ackroyd opines, 'The uncongenial nature of the situation should not, however, be understated. The heartfelt cry of Psalm 137 suggests real sensitivity to its oppressiveness; so too, does the distress of Ezekiel (e.g., in 4: 14) and that of his compatriots who feel themselves as "dry bones", crushed under the weight of disaster, and either complaining of the injustice of what has befallen them (Ezek 18) or the impossibility of escape from the consequences of divine judgement (Ezek 37).'[3]

What we have here is a displaced people separated from previous familiarities and securities, people knowing dislocation, loss of freedom, and restriction. This would have induced disorientation and trauma. Through the medium of television today we can catch something of that in the haunted look on the faces of refugees as they move from their homelands as a result of natural disasters or man's inhumanities: shuffling, clutching meagre belongings, and facing an uncertain future.

The Place of Exile

Over 25 per cent of the Old Testament is devoted to this period of Israel's history. I believe that statistic tells us exile is important, not simply as a phase of this people's history but as an experience common to life. Just as God took Israel into exile for a specific purpose, so he uses exile in the experience of his children in all generations.

At one level, exile is a motif for the whole of the Christian life: 'our citizenship is in heaven'[4] so here we are 'aliens and strangers on earth.'[5]

---

[2] John Bright, *A History of Israel*, (London: SCM, 1967) p. 326
[3] Peter R .Ackroyd, *Exile and Restoration*, (London: SCM,1968) p. 32
[4] Philippians 3: 20

Even within that, however, there are seasons in which individuals, churches, and communities more particularly endure an exilic type experience. Through any number of circumstances, life becomes ravaged and dislocated, with displacement, loss of freedom, and restriction, even to momentous proportion. We live in a dangerous world where the saints are caught up in its unpredictability, whether tsunamis, terrorism, rail crashes – so the list could go on. In a moment life can change with frightening implications.

It can happen to individuals, sometimes as result of their own sin and stupidity, sometimes through no apparent fault of their own. Illness, bereavement, imprisonment, redundancy, retirement, old age, an overseas posting can all equate to the sense of exile.

Our leaving Worthing in 1987 felt like such a banishment. Though we were, and remained, grateful for the people who called us to Woking, the overwhelming sense of loss was palpable. The new, while clearly God's appointing, felt full of pain, a deep ache of the in-between. In time, I slowly came to understand that this new exilic setting would be the place of reform. That very understanding, however, took a long time to dawn so great was the sense of loss and the alienation of the present. I felt abandoned and echoed the cries of many of the psalms: we are given no sign, no prophet is left, and none knows how long this will be (Psalm 74: 9). Something of this is captured in a later meditation on Psalm 66: 8 and 12.

A God appointed prison
With burden laden back,
Under people riding roughshod,
A daily fiery hack.

By this he saved my life
And made my foothold firm.
Dross pressured out of silver,
Long years of soul reform.

---

[5] Hebrew 11: 13

61

His goal: to lead out pris'ners
With singing on their lips,
Renewed through fire and water,
More steel, more grace, more his.

Consider then this God of ours,
Redeeming life through pain,
Severity and kindness both,
Plan for eternal gain.

As well as individuals, it can happen to communities. Dietrich Bonhoeffer described the church in Germany in the 1930s as having gone into exile. The same could be said of the church in China following the revolution of 1948 or perhaps today's church in Indonesia or the Sudan with tens of thousands of martyrs in the past few years. Brueggemann suggests that the American church today is moving into exile: 'God may be discerned as moving against the Enlightenment until it is dismantled.... Serious believers are indeed an alien community in American culture.'[6]

The heart of it seems to me to be this: once I was there, now I am here, and here is very different and very difficult.

Clearly as pastors we must have a biblical view and understanding of exile as a paradigm so we can stand alongside our people in their distress and provide perspective for them in their trials. I suspect, however, we may not be so good at recognising when the same is happening to us.

Jim Bakker, the American TV evangelist, was sentenced to forty-five years in prison for fraudulently raising money. He was subsequently vindicated but only after spending five years in prison. They were very rough years of ill treatment, media character assassination, and alienation from much of the Christian world (Billy Graham being one notable exception who visited regularly). Initially, he hated every moment. Bakker now testifies that he is convinced that God put him in prison to get his attention. In that period, he met with

---

[6] Walter Brueggemann, *Hopeful Imagination*, (Philadelphia: Fortress Press, 1986) p. 18 & 133

God in a powerful way and by the end was able to say it was the best thing that could have happened to him. Prior to that he was far too busy maintaining the business of Heritage City USA and the PTL network to wait on the Lord, but all that got very changed in prison – the kind of circumstance C. S. Lewis called 'a severe mercy'.

Exile, of course, is not the only metaphor for this experience; it is otherwise known as 'the Sahara of the heart' (Richard Foster), *Deus Absconditus* (a term used by theologians), or the dark night of the soul (St. John of the Cross). Seasons of suffering and darkness are honestly reflected in scripture, not least the Psalms, which Calvin calls 'songs for all the seasons of life' – winter as well as the brighter ones. Walter Brueggemann divides them into Psalms of orientation and Psalms of disorientation. Writing after the death of his wife, Martin E. Marty speaks of the wintry season of the heart, the frigid cold blasts that come in the wake of pain or death – an absence in the heart. 'Wintry frost comes in the void left when love dies or a lover grows distant.... The absence can also come, however, to a waste space left when the divine is distant, the sacred is remote, when God is silent'.[7]

Silence and darkness are the two images that most conjure such times. Every generation has grappled with attempts to make sense of life and its capricious wiles. Our contemporary society has moved that forward with the principle of 'the right to know'. We demand access to information and see it as an inalienable human right. Such knowledge enables us to organise and control and find a logical explanation. We do not do well, therefore, with secrecy, much less mystery. Yet God operates in both word and silence, light and dark – they are all alike to him, and he operates on a strictly need to know basis!

What is paramount is to recognise that such times are not outside the sphere of God's compassion, indeed may even be at his initiation. 'Jesus full of the Holy Spirit returned from the Jordan and was led by the Spirit into the desert.'[8] From such a recognition we can begin to seek Father's purpose, for there are things that can only happen in our souls through exile.

---

[7] Quoted by Ronald Dunn, *When Heaven Is Silent*, (Milton Keynes: Nelson Word Ltd. 1994) p. 130

[8] Luke 4: 1

One day, the disciples asked Jesus a question concerning a man born blind: 'Rabbi, who sinned, this man or his parents, that he was born blind?' Jesus replied it was neither, 'but that the work of God might be displayed in his life.'[9] Commenting on Jesus' response, Helmut Thielicke writes, 'He tells the people: your question is wrongly put.... Thus by rejecting the question, Jesus helps to liberate us from the constant complaint against God and from the injury we do ourselves thereby.... For he teaches us to put our question in a way that is meaningful. He tells us that we should not ask, "Why?" but "To what end?"'[10]

Ezekiel and Exile

For generations, Israel had a working theology that assured them that Zion was God's earthly address, Israel the focus of divine favour, and his choice of David's line inalienable. Despite warnings from the prophets that God's favour was not unconditional, the people continued to rest in the assurance that God would intervene to protect them from their enemies and eventually roll back all opposition to see the full flowering of Israel's promise in triumph and glory. As Bright picturesquely puts it, 'Nebuchadnezzar's battering rams breached that theology beyond repair.'[11]

For Israel, the very status of their God was thrown into question. All they had so acceptingly believed about him now needed radical review. They found themselves subjugated to a more powerful people, in a more sophisticated society, with a more buoyant economy, living in more developed cities, all of whom worshipped a pagan god, a god they had always been told was no god. It did not begin to look that way now. The result was a theological emergency of the greatest proportions.

For the common people, even the simplest rituals followed for generations were now impossible. Since Solomon's day, three times a year they had journeyed up to Jerusalem for the feasts and worshipped God in his temple. Now they were separated. God was back there in Jerusalem where he had always been, and they were here in Babylon, access denied by 600 miles of inhospitable desert. As the years went

---

[9] John 9: 2
[10] Quoted by Dunn, p. 84.
[11] Bright p. 328

by, God was even more back there and back then, an experience past not present, a memory of easier days and naïve faith. It began to look a little like a gossamer dream, a pleasant memory signifying nothing meaningful or substantial for the present reality.

Scripture is too full of such crises to leave us in any doubt that the desert is a finding time where God himself is the one waiting to deconstruct inadequate theologies and impact his child with a more profound awareness of himself. It would be nice to think that pastors and spiritual leaders had no need of such, that our training and learning has set us up for being God's vehicle of truth. Not so. None of us comes to the job without our background, traditions, and thought forms that will almost certainly be imperfect, not least our sentimental notions of how God acts. For those hungry to know him, some spell in exile is often his ordained way for adjustments to be made.

Jacob by Jabbok, Joseph in an Egyptian jail, Job in a week the worst of all weeks, Jonah in a fish, and so it goes on until we reach Gethsemane and Calvary and the ultimate expression of abandonment by the greatest of all servants, 'why have you forsaken me?' C. S. Lewis expressed it like this: 'Meanwhile, where is God? This is one of the most disquieting symptoms.... But go to Him when your need is desperate, when all other help is vain and what do you find? A door slammed in your face, and a sound of bolting and double bolting on the inside. After that, silence. You may as well turn away.'[12] The issues for the believer are primarily theological: where is God when the world around you is falling to pieces? Will a man serve God only for gain? Just what kind of God are we serving? Eliphaz, Bildad, Zophar, and Elihu tried to rework the standard spiritual platitudes of the day for Job, but none of them touched the soul of the sufferer, nor usually do they. What is needed ultimately is encounter, but that by definition cannot be on tap, and usually the timing, from a human perspective, is way out. 'Our God is in heaven; he does whatever he pleases.'[13]

Thankfully the God who is always with us does eventually manifest himself. What are the kinds of things that happen in such moments? Again, let Ezekiel be our guide.

---

[12] C. S. Lewis, *A Grief Observed*, (London: Fontana Books, 1966) p. 5
[13] Psalm 115: 3 NASB

The Glory of God

In the height of summer 592 BC, Ezekiel is transported in the Spirit to the banks of the river Kebar, one of the main irrigation canals of Babylon. He sees a great storm coming towards him from the north. As it draws near, he observes it as the chariot-throne of Yahweh carried by four cherubim. At the pinnacle is the Lord of glory.[14] 'It was unutterably splendid, mysteriously intricate, superhuman and supernatural, infinitely mobile but never earth-bound, all-seeing and all-knowing.'[15]

It comes from the north – significant as this was the traditional home of the Babylonian gods and the route by which the exiles went into captivity: Israel's God is all conquering and identifies with his people. The immense proportions, reaching to the heavens, dwarfs anything seen in Babylon, either its great wonders of the world or any gold statue erected by Nebuchadnezzar. Its transcendent radiance pales to insignificance any other god being portrayed to them. Its invincible power, riding on all the forces of nature coupled with the majesty of heavenly and earthly creatures, so great that no power on earth could resist. Its unrestrained movement, wheels within wheels, as lightning, back and forth across the plain at unbelievable speed, so dynamic that no barrier could be erected to hamper its movement and arrival.

Most glorious of all was the sheer magnificence of the Lord seated at the top. Ezekiel struggles with the limitation of language and stutters: 'what appeared to be', 'as if like', 'he looked like', 'like the appearance of', 'the appearance of the likeness of'. The impression he gives is of one who is fully human yet unlike any humanity seen on earth. Metaphors of light, precious gems, fire, and radiance are pressed into service and will have to suffice. Words fail with a glimpse of the glorified Lord.

Israel's God had just shown up and shown up amid all the sordid heathenism and idolatry of Babylonian life, amid a dejected people suffering punishment for their sins, amid the might of world empire. In the face of such a visitation, who is Nebuchadnezzar, what is Babylon?

---

[14] The old Rabbis called the vision *the Merkabah* and suggested that if anyone knew all its secrets they would know the secrets of creation; they insisted that no-one under the age of thirty should read the passage as it was holy ground.

[15] John B. Taylor, *Ezekiel,* (London: TyndalePress, 1969) p. 41

Suddenly there is no past, for if God invades the present, only the present moment with God counts. Suddenly there is no other place, for if God invades this place, only this place with God counts. Time and space are to be instantly re-evaluated and fresh meaning and significance sought.

Ezekiel's spontaneous response was to fall on his face, as had Isaiah previously in the temple and as would John on Patmos later. From such a posture, none have articulated the moment better than Job: 'My ears had heard of you but now my eyes have seen you. Therefore I despise myself and repent in dust and ashes.'[16] Previously held theologies now need be revised and upgraded, inadequate worldviews jettisoned, life itself must be redefined and fresh meaning sought. But even before the head gets to work, first the tortured heart must find its cure. As God draws near there can finally begin the birthing of wonder, some solace for the emotions and the release of worship. 'If we can be brought into actual consciousness of His nature we shall sing on the darkest day, because we shall detect the glory of the coming victory. In order to find abiding hope and abounding joy, we must pass beyond the principles and the practice, to the Person.'[17].

One important matter resolved in such moments is the relentless question 'why?' In the margin of my Bible by Job 42 I have written a quote (no longer traceable) from the old Scottish preacher Graham Scroggie, 'The eternal God does not answer our insistent questions, God does not explain, but he does give to the anguished spirit such a sense of Divine greatness that questioning ceases in the place of submission.'

The recovery of peace is the prelude to further emotional healing and release.

Brennan Manning writes, 'I think of a scene from the play *Gideon*, written by a Jew from Brooklyn named Paddy Chayefsky. Gideon is out in the desert in his tent a thousand miles from nowhere, feeling deserted and rejected by God. One night, God breaks into the tent and Gideon is seduced, ravished, overcome, burnt by the wild fire of God's love. He is up all night, pacing back and forth in his tent. Finally dawn comes, and Gideon in his Brooklyn Jewish accent cries out, "God, oh God, all night long I've thought of nuttin' but you,

---

[16] Job 42: 5, 6
[17] G. Campbell Morgan, *The Messages of the Books of the Bible (Job to Malachi)*, (London: Hodder & Stoughton, nd) p. 159

nuttin' but you. I'm caught up in the raptures of love. God, I want to take you into my tent, wrap you up, and keep you all to myself. God, hey God, tell me that you love me."

'God answers: "I love you, Gideon."

'"Yeah, tell me again, God."

'"I love you, Gideon."

'Gideon scratches his head, "I don't understand. Why? Why do you love me?"

'And God scratches *his* head and answers, "I really don't know. Sometimes, my Gideon, passion is unreasonable."'

Manning concludes, 'This is the God of Jesus and the God revealed in Jesus.'[18]

Ours is a jealous God, jealous for his name and jealous for his people, their time, and their attention. Ours is a Trinitarian God, whose essence is relational, being in communion. It becomes a matter of grave concern to him if other things appear to take priority over his place in our lives and that includes the work he has given in the first place. When Jesus called the twelve to him, it was that they might first be with him and only after that be sent out to preach.[19] We see this worked time and again in his earthly ministry as Jesus looks for their companionship and the strength of their fellowship. In John 6 he asks, 'Are you also going to leave?' and in Gethsemane, 'Could you not watch one hour with me?' The very busyness of life can be a cause of exile, the solution to which is fresh encounter and embrace, a drawing back to the bosom of the Father, a renewal of life in the Spirit.

Some years ago I remember hearing a story told by Judson Cornwall. He recounted how the Sunday morning services seemed heavy in spirit. So one day he began the worship by binding and casting out the enemy. A wonderful sense of liberty and release followed. It seemed appropriate, therefore, to begin the service that way the following week, again with the same result. The formula became the norm. Some time later, during a period of waiting on the Lord, Cornwall sensed the quiet whisper of the Lord in his heart, 'When am I going to get top billing in your church?'

---

[18] Brennan Manning, *The Relentless Love Of Jesus*, (London: Hodder & Stoughton, 1966) p. 85
[19] Mark 3: 14

Exile – God means it for good, for when a fresh awareness of the glory of God restores his top billing, life begins to get the right way up!

The Grace of God

Recommissioned

Ezekiel 'the priest, the son of Buzi,'[20] came from a priestly family, an hereditary destiny. From the moment of his birth in Jerusalem, his life would have been mapped out for him and devoted to the priesthood. From the age of twelve, he would have been at special rabbinic training school. At the age of fifteen, he would have moved to the temple as an apprentice, where the next ten years were devoted to his learning the rites, rituals, and ceremonies. At the age of twenty-five, he was about to enter into his life's calling when Nebuchadnezzar showed up. Suddenly everything was stripped away from him: place of work, purpose of training, destiny of life, identity as priest.

As far as we can determine, there followed five years of silence, the heavens as brass. It does not take much to imagine the psychological trauma of such upheaval on Ezekiel: disorientation and depression at the least.

Even with a strong assurance of call to ministry as I had known, exile can induce the most robust of God's servants to doubt and depression, and when that occurs in the context of pastoral ministry, there will be the additional emotion of guilt to deal with: 'Surely I ought not to be feeling like this.'

It is a specialised field, but even a casual glance down the Maslach Burnout Inventory[21] would make revealing reading for many pastors and leaders. Burnout is a loss of enthusiasm, energy, idealism, perspective, and purpose. It is often attended by exhaustion and negative attitudes, feeling a failure in one's vocational call, having a reduced sense of reward and fulfilment. As it progresses, it can produce hopelessness, dejection that there is no way out, a profoundly

---

[20] Ezekiel 1: 3

[21] Invented by Prof. Christina Maslach, professor of Psychology at the University of California at Berkeley; many Web sites available through the usual search engines.

trapped feeling, lethargy of spirit and culminating in apathy and cynicism.[22]

Thankfully today there are godly counsellors and clinicians who are available with specialised disciplines; I have certainly been grateful for their help. Time, rest, and sabbaticals can all play their healing part, but there comes a moment, as with Ezekiel, when a man finds himself on his face before his God. God's first word is deeply significant: 'Stand up on your feet.'[23] There are times and seasons when a child of God will find himself prostrate before the Lord, but when a recommissioning is about to occur, he is to stand up like a man. 'Not paralysis before him is desired by God, but reasonable service.... It is man erect, man in his manhood, with whom God will speak.'[24]

Even as Ezekiel hears the voice, the Spirit energises him and assists him to his feet. Gracious words pour over him from a gracious God, for having lost the priesthood, he is now to be a prophet, not just to Israel but the nations of the world as well. This commission does not now depend on parentage, training, or connections. It is not even dependent on character, gifting, or purity. Grace has reached out to the most unlikely people in the most unlikely places: to this would-be priest in Babylon; to Aaron, nominated High Priest even as he makes the golden calf; to Peter the rock who promptly rebukes the Christ; to Saul, called on his way to kill Christians.

So grace reaches out again and again to defeated and depressed leaders, men and women singed by fire, trodden down by men and become small in their own eyes. The Lord has great delight to recommission those who have been burned in his service.

A short while after I had experienced the discipline mentioned in the previous chapter, Marilyn and I were invited to lead a tour group to Israel. Spiritually, I was struggling, distracted by the recent events, and disoriented by our move to Woking. We sensed it to be a timely invitation, however, and accepted. I had visited Israel on a number of occasions previously, always enjoyed and benefited from such, but I went this time with a glimmer of anticipation born of our particular

---

[22] Rob Parsons through Care for the Family has done an excellent seminar on video called *Beating Burnout.*
[23] Ezekiel 2: 1
[24] A. B. Davidson quoted by Taylor, p. 61

circumstances. One of the days in the Galilee, the party went on the lake in a fishing boat. The day was strangely still, not a ripple on the water, with clear blue sky above. The boat stopped some 50 yards off the north-west shore by Tabgha, and we gazed in silence for a while at the two chapels there: the more modern Church of the Multiplication, commemorating the feeding of the five thousand, and just along the beach the little chapel *Mensa Christi* (the table of Christ), built traditionally at the site where Jesus appeared to the disciples after his resurrection. It was this little Franciscan chapel that strangely held my gaze, and later as we walked the shore, I got away from the party and sat on the rocks between chapel and lake. I had just read John 21 to the party, and my mind was captivated again by the grace and tenderness of Jesus' restoration of Peter. For me there was no vision of a chariot-throne rushing across the lake, just the impress of the gentle Spirit that the Lord's words to Peter were personalised to me also. The entwining of love restated and work recommissioned in that unique place marked a significant watershed for me toward restoration.

The other dimension to recommissioning are the human expressions of restorative grace the Lord uses. The little group in Woking who received me without any sense of condemnation was the physical hands and arms of the unseen embrace. In his book *Rebuilding Your Broken World*, Gordon MacDonald devotes a whole chapter to the value of people's affirmation and reception in grace of his life and ministry. At one point he writes, 'The grace to rebuild came first from God…. Grace also came from people close to me: family, friends, and a host of men and women I'd never met who found ways to say they wanted to be counted among the givers.'[25]

If exile and desert are experiences you presently relate to, can you hear again the Lord's words, 'Do you love me? Feed my sheep.' No failure is so final, no exile so abandoned, no desert so unending, no ministry so lost that this God of all grace cannot restore. In its restoration, however, it is likely to look very different.

The other thing to note concerning this recommissioning is that ministry is not primarily about location but attitude. Jerusalem may be out of the question, but if God is so manifest in the plains of

---

[25] Gordon MacDonald, *Rebuilding Your Broken World*, (Crowborough: Highland Books, 1988) p. 208 and 209

Babylon, who need be in the holy city? For Ezekiel, the place of restriction becomes the place of release; if God in his glory is not restricted then neither are his servants. Once in a new location, it then needs to be devoted to, learned, and served. 'Seek the peace and prosperity of the city to which I have carried you into exile'[26] is God's instruction through Jeremiah. In light of the gracious recommission, looking back could be a dangerous pastime, to which Lot's wife would testify if she could.

Equally, this new sphere, however remote, need not be less fruitful than before; location is no hindrance to fruitfulness. John the Baptist had no problem with his appointed location, a voice in the wilderness, yet the crowds came to him. God is his own publicist. 'As a result, Jesus could no longer enter a town openly but stayed outside in lonely places. Yet the people still came to him from everywhere.'[27]

Re-evaluation

What is happening to Ezekiel also requires a radical re-evaluation of ministry. From now on, its inner values and outward expressions will be nothing like previously imagined: no longer the anticipated career path, no longer the finely woven costume and dress, no longer the respect of the people and a place among the ruling classes. From now on, it is robustly different: ministry shaped in exile always is. Ezekiel becomes a prophetic symbol, a strange man whose lifestyle provokes questions and whose questions challenge lifestyles. One senses his discomfort at times with the calling, not least the effect on and the involvement of his wife.

In this process, of course, the motives for engaging the ministry would have to be severely examined. I have painfully learned that God is supremely interested in motives. Prophets were never high in the popularity stakes, and it is easy to imagine the scornful questionings, 'Just who is this guy lying on one side playing with bricks, cutting off half his beard and refusing to mourn the death of his wife?' Loss of reputation would likely follow; what then would the ministry hold for Ezekiel?

Jesus as ever is the supreme model of motives. As the early church hymn puts it, 'Precisely because he was in very nature God, he

---

[26] Jeremiah 29: 7
[27] Mark 1: 45

emptied Himself, taking the lowliest place, and in humility became obedient to death, because that's just what God is like'.[28] Having embraced self-renunciation and no reputation, he lived out a life to the glory of God, and as the repeated phrase 'They glorified God' rings out time and again from the gospels, we see he did it well.

In 1 Corinthians 4: 1, Paul employs two graphic word pictures to illustrate these attitudes. He suggests that as apostles they were to be viewed as *'huperetai* of Christ'; a term meaning an under-rower, a galley slave. In the great triremes of the day, under-rowers were slaves on the lowest deck, chained to their oar where the detritus from the above decks would fall on them as they pursued their task in abject ignominy. Luke uses the same powerful image as he describes the apostles as 'eyewitnesses and *huperetai* of the word'.[29]

The other word picture follows immediately, 'And *oikonomoi* of the mysteries of God'. The image here is more familiar, that of household manager or steward. In contrast to the position of the under-rower, the role of managing a large household was a significant responsibility. An *oikononmi* however was always a slave and could never aspire to any other station in life. It was a task for a man under orders, where he was only likely to attract attention to himself when things went wrong.

The task of the under-rower and the steward is to make the captain of the ship and the master of the house look good, to serve them without drawing attention to themselves for that would only divert time and attention from the master's purpose. Moses, the meekest man on earth, illustrates this in his conversation with God at Horeb, in face of the golden calf. God seems intent on wiping Israel out and offers Moses a new role as head of a new great nation, one of the greatest offers ever made to a man. And if he were to accept, what higher court could deny it? Moses, however, instinctively refuses, not even saying, 'I'll think about it'. He knows his place and role, and he knows that to accept would reflect poorly on God in the eyes of the surrounding nations. The conversation reveals Moses as a man seeking no reputation before men or indeed before God, nothing that would in any way detract the glory from God.

---

[28] Paul Hawthorn's translation of Philippians 2: 2–8
[29] Luke 1: 2

Going back to the model of Christ, Paul suggests in Philippians 2: 5 that we have a choice in this matter: 'Your attitude should be the same as that of Christ Jesus'. This, urges the apostle, is something we should be intentional about. As with Ezekiel, often events under the sovereign hand of God overtake us to force the issue, for the flesh is dreadfully slow and resistant to it, but insofar as we have a choice, this is surely the one to make. Then having made it, it will continue to influence every decision and opportunity. It will shape the inner motivation for each task. Is what we are about a chance of self-promotion, or is this something in which God alone will get the glory? The outcome of that question makes for a richer or a more impoverished soul. The servants of God seeking only God's glory have about them a wonderful sense of freedom. No longer do they have to consider the implications of a course of action once God's honour is all that is in focus. The call to affirm no reputation may mark us out, may embolden us, or may cause us to lose friends, but it will be a significant factor in making us men and women of God. As the American poet Robert Frost has it:

Two roads diverged in a wood, and I –
I took the road less travelled
And it has made all the difference.

Arising from his encounter with God's glory, Ezekiel experienced the grace of being recommissioned. The recommissioning reshaped his practice of and motives for ministry so that through pain and humiliation he served out his calling in a far-country. But who can doubt the effect of his life, one of Israel's greatest, classic prophets?

The Government of God

Perhaps the major accomplishment of exile for Israel was that it forced a radical rethinking of previously held theologies. It is not my place or purpose to spell out the substance of those reflections; many more able have done so.[30] Suffice it to say the period of exile achieved remarkable ends for Israel:

---

[30] The literature on this subject is immense. As good an introductory summary as I have come across is chapter seven in Philip Greenslade's book *A Passion for God's Story*, subtitled *The Prophetic Hope*, (Carlisle: Paternoster Press, 2002).

- The remnant that went into exile had to research every document to grapple with the enormity of the destruction that had taken place. In the course of their study, they brought together many of these records and so began for the first time to compile what is now known as the Old Testament.

- Despite the occasional flirtations with foreign gods in the post-exilic period, at its core Israel developed a fierce monotheism. The hope of Israel began to be redefined; the prospect of a new covenant of the heart, inspired by God's true Servant, would point the way from external to internal integrities.

- In the absence of the temple, they developed the synagogue system. This allowed Israel to survive dispersion and would later serve both the early church, providing the gathering system ultimately used by them and Israel, herself, following AD 70.

- It cleansed and purified the land, restoring its quota of Sabbath rest. The worst of the evil religious practices were not heard of again: child sacrifice and cult prostitution were eliminated.

Over and beyond these achievements, the exiles came to believe that the God of Israel was the sovereign maker and ruler of the universe such that the government of the nations was in his hands. God was no longer restricted to the temple in Jerusalem; his glory could be seen in Babylon. Israel's place in exile was not due to the vagaries of world politics, a victim of history, but the purposeful act of its loving God. Even the might of Babylon faded when the time for restoration came up in God's calendar. Cyrus, another foreign dictator, was but a pawn in the hand of Israel's God to achieve this end. Exile gave Israel an explanation of history.

Restoration was always the plan, and it always is. Exile is a searing, purging experience, but it leaves the believer utterly captivated by his magnificent Lord and with a new appreciation of his glory, grace, and government. It is in such times and places that we learn how God works, how he governs and effects his purposes, often so different to that which we had previously imagined. We discover he works slow rather than fast, hidden rather than seen, with the weak rather than the strong, and with the few rather than the many. We learn that we are not the centre of the universe, that God is working his purpose out as year succeeds to year, and our glory is to be some small part of it.

When I was eight years old, my father took me to London to see the coronation procession of Elizabeth II. We stood all day from early morning in Regent Street in the rain. In the evening as we were going home on the train, I must have complained, no doubt of aching legs, empty tummy, and wet clothes, but I remember my father saying, 'Yes, but you will always remember this day and know that you were part of something splendid.'

Whatever form our exile takes, we must understand it is not the result of a Nebuchadnezzar's despotism, an *anno horribilis,* or any random malign influence. As we cooperate with our loving Father, we pass through it to a bigger God, in a more secure place, with a healthier perspective on God, self, and work – one small part of something splendid. And confinement under God's hand has so often led to previously unimagined fruitfulness. Where would we be without David's songs from the cave, Paul's prison epistles, John's Patmos missive, Bunyan's *Pilgrims Progress,* Bonheoffer's letters, or Niemöller's Dachau sermons?

As Alexander Solzhenitsyn expressed it in worship, 'I thank thee O Lord for the concentration camp, for there I discovered the cross'.

And to the cross we must next turn: for the circumstances of our workplace, the challenge of our call and discipline under Father God, and the extremities of exile are all designed to bring us again to the cross. God means it all for good.

Underpinning

Exploration – *based on Psalm 137*

- In the psalm, the effect of being in Babylon is variously expressed. How does the psalmist describe and lament the experience in terms:
  o Physical
  o Social
  o Spiritual

  To what degree, past or present, do you identify with such expressions?

- 'We need laments because we need a way of dealing with strong negative emotions. The choices are few. Either we suppress the pain, which is psychologically harmful, or we vent it on others, which is socially destructive. There is another way. We can express them honestly and fiercely to God.'[31]

  Which psalms have you most identified with during a wilderness season? Which might you best use now to channel your pain to God?

- The imprecatory verses 7–9 sound discordant to our Christian ears. Their ferocity, however, challenges our all too often sanitised emotions and our sense of appropriate violence before God. Being in touch with such pain and channelling it to God is the subtext invitation of these verses. More careful confession can come later; in the mean time, God can handle anything thrown at him.

Excavation – *recommended for digging deeper*

- *Hopeful Imagination, Prophetic Voices in Exile* by Walter Brueggemann, published by Fortress Press.

- *Cadences of Home, Preaching among Exiles* by Walter Brueggemann, published by Westminster John Knox Press.

Exchange – *new foundation for old*

- A song, which is a prayer, written by Darlene Zschech

---

[31] Philip Greenslade, *Songs for all Seasons*, (Farnham: CWR, 2003) p. 110

Beautiful Lord, wonderful Saviour,
I know for sure, all of my days
Are held in your hand,
Crafted into your perfect plan.
You gently call me into your presence,
Guiding me by your Holy Spirit.
Teach me, dear Lord, to live all my life
Through your eyes.
I'm captured by your holy calling,
Set me apart, I know you're drawing me to yourself;
Lead me, Lord, I pray.
Take me, mould me, use me, fill me,
I give my life to the Potter's hand.
Call me, guide me, lead me, walk beside me,
I give myself into the Potter's hand.[32]

Chapter 5

The Cross We Hold

For the message of the cross is foolishness to those who are perishing
but to us who are being saved it is the power of God.... For I resolved
to know nothing while I was with you except Jesus Christ and Him
crucified.

1 Corinthians 1: 18 and 2: 2.

Above the sweeping staircase in the large entrance hall of Spurgeon's
College is a stained glass window in the centre of which is the college
crest incorporating the college motto. The crest consists of an
outstretched hand and forearm grasping a cross interwoven with the
motto *et teneo et teneor*. The traditional interpretation of the motto,
focussing on the cross, is 'I both hold and am held'. For some 150
years, successive generations of students preparing for home or
overseas ministry have had, by this means, the cross firmly placed at
the centre of their calling: which is to proclaim it boldly, in the
confidence that by doing so they will know in turn its sustaining
power. It is a fine piece of blazonry in the best heraldic tradition and a
worthy emblem for God's battalions – to be commended to all,
especially those unfortunate enough not to have gone to the college!

The Centrality of the cross

Perhaps I should say that when I use the phrase 'the cross', as one
might use the phrase 'the blood', I use it as it is used in the New
Testament and has been in church history for two thousand years. That
is to say the phrases are shorthand, metaphors, meaning 'Jesus Christ,
his sacrificial and atoning death at Calvary and all that was
accomplished by that vicarious death'. Forgive me if this is obvious,
but we live with a new age generation who place meaning and spiritual

significance in symbols (particularly a cross) divorced from the Jesus story, their historical roots, and traditional theology, so language and definition is important. The college crest, as with everything else in this Christian life, is all about Jesus; references to the cross focus attention specifically on his accomplishments through his death.

The centrality of the cross in the Christian faith is clear. The gospel records reveal Jesus as moving steadfastly toward Jerusalem as the climax of his work, gently preparing the disciples for what he already knew, that death awaited him. Nearly half of John's gospel is devoted to the last week of Jesus' three-year ministry. Paul's determined focus of ministry was 'to know nothing while I was with you except Jesus Christ and him crucified.'[1] The cross was quickly established as an early symbol of Christianity, and the shape has been the primary model for church architecture over the millennia. Crosses are the focal point in churches whether on wall, on altar, on lectern, on drape, or atop the building. Worship songs old and new celebrate the glories of the cross. Many wear the symbol as jewellery, and it is used extensively in logos, badges, and crests. Christians are a people of the cross.

But is our experience of it any deeper than that of our new age travellers? I can think of nothing more blasphemous or abominable than that the most significant event in world history be reduced to a trinket or piece of furniture. What a travesty should the death that offers eternal life be parodied in superstition or sentimentality. Yet I suspect I've used the words, spoken the formulas, and declared the liturgies with professional familiarity and detachment; have sung of its power - and capitulated to sin soon after. Is it possible to be a servant of the cross and the crucified One, yet scarcely get beyond the symbol? I think so. And if so, what will the Father do for us? I suspect in love he will bring us again to fear Him who has called us; he will teach us the ways of sonship through his discipline, and by the trauma of wilderness and exile, lead us to Calvary.

All the synoptic gospels record Jesus' conditional invitation to discipleship, 'If anyone would come after me, he must deny himself and take up his cross and follow me'; Luke adds the emphatic 'daily'. Discipleship is offered universally to anyone, but its terms are not for

---

[1] 1 Corinthians 2: 2

negotiation. Jesus' 'if' stands alongside many other conditional offers in scripture; what John Piper calls 'unmerited, conditional grace.'[2] What does that mean for those of us called, not just to proclaim the invitation to discipleship, but as followers ourselves, live with its condition?

1. Daily receive forgiveness.

The grace of conviction

I wonder at what point in our lives each of us has had a genuine conviction of sin? By that I mean felt the guilt and shame of it, known the offence it was to God, and recognised that we were deserving of some form of judgement and punishment?

In 2004, along with a small team from the United Kingdom, I twice visited the country of Belarus. One evening in the city of Mogilev, after our pastors' conference was finished, we were invited to attend an evangelistic rally being held by the Baptist Union of Belarus. The church was full with people of all ages. The service was formal, led exclusively from the front, and typical of services in that part of the world: a mixture of testimonies, songs, poetry, musical items, and preaching. There was no congregational participation, not even in singing. The atmosphere was warm but solidly and stoically Russian. As best we understood it through our translator, the sermon was a simple presentation of the gospel; no histrionics, no great teaching insight from the scriptures, no hype of any sort. Compared to a similar rally in the West, it lacked colour, vibrancy, energy, and crowd participation. It was good to be there, not least at such an event taking place in a country where believers live in an increasingly antagonistic spiritual environment. But my expectations for response were not high as the preacher drew to the end of his message. As he made his appeal however, I watched in amazement, humility, and great emotion, for all over the congregation there were tears streaming down people's faces. Inviting forward those convicted of their sin, many made their way to the front: Westernised, attractive young ladies along with peasant babushkas, good looking boys in their teens and wizened farmers, dressed as if they had come straight from the fields. As I

---

[2] John Piper, *Future Grace*, (Sisters, Or: Multnoma Books, 1998) p. 229

watched with tears in my own eyes, I realised I was witnessing something I had never seen before in over thirty years of ministry and attending countless conferences, rallies, and crusades: genuine, heartfelt conviction of sin. I had seen many come forward, stand up, fall down, or kneel down, but not this. Now I am prepared to recognise that some of it may have been cultural, but much of it had to be real. It left me with a profound sense that this conviction of sin was a missing element in much of our Western church scene, and perhaps a fatal absence.

Not that it has always been absent. As a young Christian, I read with some sense of awe the accounts of George Whitfield's preaching to the colliers of Kingswood, Bristol: 'The first discovery of their being affected was to see the white gutters made by their tears which plentifully fell down their black cheeks, as they came out of their coal pits. Hundreds of them were soon brought under deep convictions, which, as the event proved, happily ended in a sound and thorough conversion.'[3]

I am not saying that such a manifestation of conviction is essential for salvation. The acceptance, with or without emotion, of the pronouncements of scripture concerning our spiritual state is the ground of faith. Bonhoeffer puts it like this: 'First, the Christian is the man who no longer seeks his salvation, his deliverance, his justification in himself, but in Jesus Christ alone. He knows that God's Word in Jesus Christ pronounces him guilty, even when he does not feel his guilt, and God's Word in Jesus Christ pronounces him not guilty and righteous, even when he does not feel that he is righteous at all.'[4]

However, without those truths affecting the whole man including the emotions, we must inevitably fall short in our wholehearted appreciation of what Christ has done for us in his death. That certainly has been my experience: conviction of sin with tears, has led to the cross in a way previously unexplored. Not only so, but it has left a legacy of daily gratitude to God for the grace of conviction and an awareness daily of the need to pray with vigilance 'deliver us from evil'; a healthier place at least for this servant of God to be in.

---

[3] Quoted by Arnold Dallimore, *George Whitefield, The Life and Times of the great evangelist of the 18th century revival*, (London: Banner of Truth, 1965) Vol 1, p. 259
[4] Dietrich Bonhoeffer, *Life Together*, (London: SCM, 1972), p. 11

The grace of forgiveness

An interesting problem has arisen on my journey: I find it easier to accept that I am forgiven by God than to forgive myself. All my life I have been in and around church. I know the gospel and for many years have preached the gospel. It is the bedrock of the Christian faith that through Jesus, God forgives our sins. I know there are technical bits like conviction, contrition, confession, repentance, faith, and so on, but one glimpse of the brazen serpent, one hope-filled 'look and live', and this God-of-all-grace forgives, 'neither do I condemn you: go and sin no more'. I suspect it takes less to get saved than we might think! – ask the thief hung next to Jesus. The father runs to the prodigal, showers him with kisses, decks him with new clothing and adornment, kills the fatted calf, and shouts to all, 'let's party!' – all before the lad hardly got out a word!

Why then is it so hard to forgive myself? Perhaps it will be different for all of us, but for me at least there was the powerful coupling of two elemental forces: shame and low self-esteem. This combination reinforced the message that I was worthless, and now everyone knew it to be true. Caught in the vice of these two crushing forces, forgiveness simply didn't touch the pain. I may be forgiven by God, I would go to heaven, but I was destroyed in the process. R. T. Kendall suggests that there are a number of such barriers to forgiving ourselves: being angry with ourselves, the inability to distinguish between true and false guilt, fear, pride, self-righteousness, and self-pity.[5]

I suspect that we evangelicals have a tendency to hurry things. There are of course occasions when transactions between God and man result in immediate transformation. The scripture and church history are full of such stories. But I do wonder, even with these dramatic encounters, whether the individual impacted and changed did not require much longer to work out the full implications. The orientation of our lives may change in a moment but not the ingrained thought patterns, worldviews, and well-worn grooves of behaviour. The flesh with its multi-faceted influences and its far-reaching tentacles is not so quickly subdued.

---

[5] R. T. Kendall, *Total Forgiveness*, (London: Hodder & Stoughton, 2001) chapter six, "The Art of Forgiving ourselves and Forgetting"

On one occasion soon after my public admonition, I was speaking with a respected man of God who asked how I was. I answered that I limped – a reference of course to Jacob following his encounter with God at Jabbok. That was exactly how I felt: inwardly, I knew I had met with God and continued in close fellowship with him, but I felt crippled, broken, not yet whole. This allusion was rather pooh-poohed with the suggestion that I was fully forgiven and should act accordingly. All I can say is that while that may be so in theory, it has taken much longer in practice.

Help was at hand, thank God, in its usual manner in my experience: books! The process began with Brennan Manning, who in his book *The Ragamuffin Gospel* penned chapter ten and called it *The Victorious Limp.* Never shone a chapter heading in brighter lights, never had an adjective been more surprising and hope filled. I almost did not need the chapter content; the title was enough.

He writes, 'The limping Peter's betrayal of the Master, like so many of our own moral lapses and refusals of grace, was not a terminal failure but the occasion for painful growth in fidelity. It is not unrealistic to presume that later, Peter praised God for the servant girl in Caiaphas's courtyard who turned him into a snivelling coward. In this context, small wonder that Augustine would paraphrase the words of Paul, "That for those who love God everything works unto the good, even sin"

'The mature Christians I have met along the way are those who have failed and have learned to live gracefully with their failure.

'On the last day, when we arrive at the Great Cabin in the Sky, many of us will be bloodied, battered, bruised, and limping. But, by God and by Christ, there will be a light in the window and a "welcome home" sign on the door.'[6]

The picture of the disciples hiding away in the upper room has been so helpful to me. It would be fascinating to have been a fly on that wall! My guess is that between them they would have spanned all the emotions of guilt. What is significant and divine is that Jesus, on his sudden appearance among them, makes no reference to it in his conversation. Indeed, he simply moves on as if they had not cut and run, denied him, and generally failed him in his moment of need. He comes and

---

[6] Manning, selections from chapter 10

commissions them, bestowing huge dignity on these rascals. He knows what they are like, what they have done, and what they might be capable of in the future, but this, surprise, surprise, is the raw material of his Kingdom.

What I came to see was that trying to receive God's forgiveness but not forgiving oneself is ultimately an exercise in self-pity and an expression of self-centredness. The journey from self-centeredness to Christ-centeredness begins with an honest acceptance of ourselves as sinners and our total inability to do anything about that. If Christ says that he has shed his blood, washed and forgiven us our sins, and satisfied God's justice, how dare we not forgive ourselves? Where else is there to go if we refuse that liberty? The very embracing of ourselves as 'the forgiven' is the first step in turning us to look outward from self and opening up the way for a healthier spirituality and freedom.

If we are to daily pray, 'forgive us our trespasses as we forgive those who trespass against us', then we must surely daily forgive ourselves also: the cross demands that of us.

As the seasons make their turn

There's a lesson here to learn

Broken wings take time to mend

Before they learn to fly again

On the breath of God they'll soar

And be stronger than before

Don't look back into the past

What was fire now is ash

Let it all be dead and gone

The time is now for moving on

(Janny Grein) [7]

The grace of compassion

Jesus was in one of his favoured places, enjoying the hospitality of a meal with a Pharisee, Simon. Much to the dismay of the host, the town harlot gate-crashed the party, and to his further embarrassment,

---

[7] Quoted by Kendall. p. 143

she brazenly anointed Jesus' feet with perfume, filling the house with its alluring fragrance. What annoyed Simon most was the way Jesus seemed to be enjoying the moment, gazing with loving appreciation at the floozy. Jesus looked up eventually from the girl and addressed both sides of a great religious divide. 'Simon,' Jesus said, trying to penetrate the Pharisee's blindness by paralleling the situation with a story he might comprehend, 'two men were in debt to a banker. One owed five hundred silver pieces, the other fifty. Neither of them could pay up, so the banker cancelled both debts. Which of the two would be more grateful?'

Simon just about got that, so Jesus pushed the illustration into the present scenario. 'Do you see this woman? I came to your home, you provided no water for my feet, but she rained down tears on my feet and dried them with her hair. You gave me no greeting, but from the time I arrived, she hasn't quit kissing my feet. You provided nothing for freshening up, but she has soothed my feet with perfume. Impressive isn't it? She was forgiven many, many sins, and so she is very, very grateful. If the forgiveness is minimal, the gratitude is minimal.'[8]

In making our identifications in that story, we almost certainly instinctively side with the woman: she surely represents our responses to grace. Luke in particular in his gospel, however, does not let off quite so easily. He piles on story after story to challenge such an easy supposition. It is the minimal, superficial awareness of forgiveness seen in Simon, and its attendant meanness, that is forced on us. This attitude is fleshed out particularly in Jesus' story a little later in Luke 15 of the two sons and the prodigal father, especially in the role of the elder brother.

Henri Nouwen with penetrating insight has ruthlessly exposed the psyche of this young man and, with great candour, revealed his own identification with him. That very honesty is a challenge to all who find their work, like the elder son and Nouwen himself, in the father's house.

Listen to Nouwen: 'It is hard for me to concede that this bitter, resentful, angry man might be closer to me in a spiritual way than the lustful younger brother.... The lostness of the elder son is much harder

---

[8] From Luke 7: 36–47 the Message

to identify. After all, he did the right things. He was obedient, dutiful, law-abiding, and hardworking. People respected him, admired him, praised him, and likely considered him a model son. Outwardly, the elder son was faultless. But when confronted by his father's joy at the return of his younger brother, a dark power erupts in him and boils to the surface. Suddenly, there becomes glaringly visible a resentful, proud, unkind, selfish person, one that had remained deeply hidden, even though it had been growing stronger and more powerful over the years.... Looking deeply into myself and then around me at the lives of other people, I wonder which does more damage, lust or resentment? There is so much resentment among the "just" and the "righteous". There is so much judgement, condemnation, and prejudice among the "saints". There is so much frozen anger among the people who are so concerned about avoiding "sin". The lostness of the resentful "saint" is so hard to reach precisely because it is so closely wedded to the desire to be good and virtuous.'[9]

There is a frustrating open-endedness to Jesus' story: just what did finally happen to this elder brother? It is of more than passing interest for those of us working in the Father's house. What we do know with certainty is that the father was on the case: 'his father went out and pleaded with him.' His objective was that this boy might learn to share his father's joy, to discover a lost brother, and to jettison the cold, slavish mentality of a servant. If the younger son had passion without obedience, then this older one had obedience without passion, and the father's invitation was to let it all go, discover passion and compassion, and join the party.

The place for us to let it all go is the cross. This work of the cross in our lives bringing conviction and forgiveness then has a surprising and positive outcome: it really does begin to change our attitude to others as Jesus promised – having been forgiven much, we begin to see others with a softer focus lens.

This becomes a matter of great importance in the performing of our ministry, for ours is a calling which deals in the business of mess, sheep's mess, the excrement of lives plagued by the dysentery of sin. Without understanding the commonality of humanity, why get involved? Without the knowledge of our own sinful ways, who would

---

[9] Henri J.M.Nouwen, *The Return of the Prodigal*, (London: DLT, 2004) p. 71

not stand apart and criticise? Without the experience of mercy and grace, who would not leave the lost to their own deserving end? Thank God that before the cross there is a flat plain; we all stand on level ground, sinners being saved by grace – including pastors.

2. Daily Receive Life

The Grace of Death

Bonhoeffer's famous dictum starkly reminds us, 'When Jesus calls a man, he bids him come and die.' In the first instance, the cross does not offer life but death, does not bring hope but confirms defeat, marks the end not the beginning. What the cross offers us is death, the ultimate expression of our humanity and humiliation. The offer is a kindly one, for about us all too often is the stench of death, and in our more honest moments, we know something needs killing off and disposing of, but it is an offer we all too perversely resist. There must come a point, however, in our pastoral calling, if we have not come there before, when we must die. That point also needs to be revisited daily.

In order to explore this, it might be helpful to re-dig an old well.

Amy Carmichael (1867–1951) was the founder of the Dohnavur Fellowship in southern India, devoted to the rescue of children given by their families to Hindu temple prostitution. She was the author of over thirty-five books, a prolific writer on the spiritual life. Miss Carmichael drew deeply from the Keswick tradition (her call to missions had come as she and her family attended the 1892 Keswick). It was an early experience of frustration, however, that brought about an encounter with the Lord that was to shape her life and writings. Arriving in Bangalore in 1895, Amy was warmly welcomed and treated with consideration by the other missionaries – all except one, who saw it as her task to show this spirited Irish young lady a thing or two. Amy was given menial tasks, restricted and criticised until she began to react most strongly. She records, 'One day I felt the "I" in me rising hotly, and quite clearly – so clearly that I could show you the place on the floor of the room where I was standing when I heard it – the word came, "See in it a chance to die." To this day that word is life and release to me, and it has been so to many others. See in this which seems to stir up all you most wish were *not* stirred up – see in it a chance to die to self in every form. Accept it as just that – a chance to die.'[10]

The phrase became a way of life for the Dohnavur Fellowship, and it shaped her selection procedures with prospective missionaries. To possible candidates, twenty-five questions evolved, which included 'Do you truly desire to live a crucified life? (This may mean doing very humble things joyfully for His name's sake.)' She emphasised that 'missionary work, most of the time, offers little that could be called glamour. What it does offer, as Amy wrote to a prospective candidate in later years, is "a chance to die."'[11]

What Amy Carmichael writes of missionaries applies equally to pastors. The appeal to embrace 'the chance to die' is an invitation to recognise that in and of ourselves we are unable to cope with the sacrificial nature of life. We face the hurts to pride that come from working in obscurity, from frequent periods of lack of appreciation, and from the loss of what most men count as fundamental worker-rights to success, respectability, and security. 'A chance to die' then becomes the pointer to an inward exchange that the cross has made available.

I return to Bonhoeffer and an important insight from *Life Together* – a significant passage for pastors whose task it is to minister in community. Under the heading *Not an Ideal but a Divine Reality,* he writes, 'Innumerable times a whole Christian community has broken down because it had sprung from a wish dream. The serious Christian, set down for the first time in a Christian community, is likely to bring with him a very definite idea of what Christian life together should be and try to realise it. But God's grace speedily shatters such dreams. Just as surely God desires to lead us to a knowledge of genuine Christian fellowship, so surely must we be overwhelmed by a great general disillusionment with others, with Christians in general, and, if we are fortunate, with ourselves.... Only that fellowship which faces such disillusionment, with all its unhappy and ugly aspects, begins to see what it should be in God's sight, begins to grasp in faith the

---

[10] Frank L. Houghton, *Amy Carmichael of Dohnavur*, (Fort Washington, PA: CLC, 2000) p. 111

[11] The two quotes in this paragraph are from *A Chance to Die, the Life and Legacy of Amy Carmichael*, by Elizabeth Elliot (Grand Rapids: Revell, 2005) p. 265 and 176 respectively

promise that is given to it. The sooner the shock of disillusionment comes to an individual and to a community the better for both.'[12]

The point in common here with Amy Carmichael is that God will bring his servants to see that 'unless a grain of wheat falls into the earth and dies, it remains by itself alone; but if it dies, it bears much fruit.'[13] The grain of wheat may consist of many things: a dream of community, ambition for church success or a renowned ministry, the confidence of youthful energy, the assurance in great gifting or any other false god our jealous Father needs to expose. The falling to the ground and dying may equally come in many ways.

For Isaiah and Daniel, this happened through a vision of the glory of God. Isaiah, already a preacher, laments, 'Woe is me for I am ruined! For I am a man of unclean lips.'[14] The most consecrated part of him for ministry was exposed as unclean in God's sight. The old Authorised Version and New King James version of 'ruined' is 'undone', which rather more expresses the idea of the man being stripped of outward appearance to reveal a state of corruption previously unrealised but now revealed in the light of God's holiness. This is exactly the sentiment expressed by Daniel. The New English Bible captures the expression perfectly, 'I became a sorry figure of a man.'[15]

For most, however, what brings us again to the cross is simply the end of one's tether!

Soon after leaving Worthing, a special friend in the States invited me to join him at Jack Hayford's Pastor's Conference at the Church on the Way in California. During the conference, Jack spoke on the death of Sarah from Genesis 23. He made the point that the death and burial of Sarah, necessitating as it did the purchase of the field of Machpelah near Mamre, constituted the first fruits of God's promise of land to Abraham. This, he suggested, is a graphic illustration of the spiritual principle spoken of by Jesus in John 12: 24, 'Unless a grain of wheat fall into the earth and die.' Death always precedes possession and the new working of God. Jack then asked what was it that Abraham was burying in Sarah? He answered the question with three suggestions.

[12] Bonhoeffer, *Life Together*, p. 15
[13] John 12: 24 NASB
[14] Isaiah 6: 5
[15] Daniel 10: 8 NEB

Firstly, he buried the previous channel of blessing; Abraham had learned painfully that Sarah was the only acceptable channel for birth, but following her death, a new fruitfulness was released and Abraham was to have six more children. Secondly, he buried the memory of his failures toward his wife. Thirdly, he buried the love of his life, a wife and marriage close to celebrating its double golden! But what, probed Jack, is the love of our lives especially as it may touch on ministry and be anything aside from the glory of God?

At the end of his sermon, Jack invited us to come to the cross, to bring to the place of Jesus' death our awareness and experiences of death. As ever in the Lord's economy, the timing was perfect for me. Never had a word offered more relevant application and hope. The service was a watershed, which, coupled with the recent events at home, led to a far more realistic understanding of my own frailties, vulnerabilities, and inadequacies. The flesh, I have discovered since then, also believes in and practices resurrection, so there is need for the message to be regularly reinforced. The pastoral ministry, I suspect, is the best place on earth for that to occur – leadership is after all a perpetual probing of character. Which is why the question 'Who is sufficient for these things?' leads us sooner or later to the cross and the grace of a place to surrender that which we now understand as death.

> Upon that cross of Jesus
> Mine eyes at times can see
> The very dying form of One
> Who suffered there for me;
> And from my smitten heart with tears
> Two wonders I confess –
> The wonder of His glorious love
> And my own worthlessness.[16]

The Grace of Life

Don't you think that the forty days between the resurrection and the ascension must have held almost unimaginable excitement and suspense for the disciples? Where next might Jesus suddenly appear?

---

[16] Verse 3 of the hymn 'Beneath the Cross of Jesus', by Elizabeth Clephane

What time of day or night might they find him among them? How long would he stay before he disappeared again? Would he eat with them, could they touch him, what might he say? The very nature of his coming and going would have put them on edge, straining with anticipation. The gospels and Acts chapter 1 tease the imagination as we try to put ourselves in the disciples' shoes. What is undeniable is that the recorded exclamations show their exuberant joy whenever they see Him: 'Rabboni! We have seen the Lord! It is the Lord! My Lord and my God! Did not our hearts burn within us? It is true! The Lord has risen.'

Just as Jesus had dominated their horizon during the past three years, so now he dominates their present hopes and shapes their futures around himself. 'The point is that one cannot say "Jesus of Nazareth was bodily raised from the dead" with minimal involvement.... If it happened, it matters. The world is a different place from what it would have been if it did not happen. The person who makes the statement is committed to living in this different world, this newly envisioned universe of discourse, imagination and action.'[17] If the first reaction to resurrection was spontaneous joy, as time moves on, the event taxes their brains to a reworking of every category of being and theology. Yet even as that happens, the emotional compartment expands exponentially in love for this magnificent Jesus until he becomes the focus of worship in a way fitting only for God Almighty.

'We look at this Son and see the God who cannot be seen. We look at this Son and see God's original purpose in everything created. For everything, absolutely everything, above and below, visible and invisible, rank after rank after rank of angels – *everything* got started in him and finds its purpose in him. He was there before any of it came into existence and holds it all together right up to this moment. And when it comes to the church, he organises and holds it together like a head does a body.

'He was supreme in the beginning and – leading the resurrection parade – he is supreme in the end. From beginning to end he's there, towering far above everything, everyone. So spacious is he, so roomy, that everything of God finds its proper place in him without crowding.

---

[17] N. T. Wright, *The Resurrection of the Son of God*, (London: SPCK, 2003) p. 714

Not only that, but all the broken and dislocated pieces of the universe – people and things, animals and atoms – get properly fixed and fitted together in vibrant harmonies, all because of his death, his blood that poured down from the cross.'[18]

So the knowledge of Jesus is passed from generation to generation; no wonder Peter could still say to those who never had his privileges, 'Though you have not seen him, you love him; and even though you do not see him now, you believe in him and are filled with an inexpressible and glorious joy'.[19]

What a phrase: 'inexpressible and glorious joy' – the birthright not just of pastors and leaders but all the children of the King. And this joy of the Lord then becomes our strength, '"Oh, children," said the Lion, "I feel my strength coming back to me. Oh, children, catch me if you can!" He stood for a second, his eyes very bright, his limbs quivering, lashing himself with his tail. Then he made a leap high over their heads and landed on the other side of the Table. Laughing, though she didn't know why, Lucy scrambled over it to reach him. Aslan leaped again. A mad chase began. Round and round the hill-top he led them, now hopelessly out of their reach, now letting them almost catch his tail, now diving between them, now tossing them in the air with his huge and beautifully velveted paws and catching them again, and now stopping unexpectedly so that all three of them rolled over together in happy laughing heap of fur and arms and legs. It was such a romp as no one has ever had except in Narnia; and whether it was like playing with a thunderstorm or playing with a kitten Lucy could never make up her mind. And the funny thing was that when all three finally lay together panting in the sun the girls no longer felt in the least tired or hungry or thirsty.'[20]

Thank God for the cross as a place where we can bring our stench of death, but the greater part by far is that having come, we can fill our vista with the luminous figure of Jesus. As we daily visit the cross and feel its weight, we discover the yoke remarkably easy and light, for the presence of the risen Christ is with us. Daily he is our first love, drawing our hearts, forging our wills, expanding our thinking,

---

[18] Colossians 1: 18–20 The Message

[19] 1 Peter 1: 8

[20] C. S. Lewis, *The Lion, The Witch and The Wardrobe,* (Oxford: Lion, 1988) p. 149

purifying our consciences, and fully captivating our gaze – the altogether lovely one. Jesus is not just employer, God forbid, but lover, friend, teacher, and Lord, and every other part of his glorious being in relationship with us. First of all has to be the joy of our own salvation and the rich blessings of knowing God and being incorporated in to his family. Hallelujah, what a Saviour!

I have stated that this is not a book about the how of pastoring, rather it is the being of a pastor. But there comes a point here where the two merge. Perhaps above all else it is a pastor's very passion for Jesus that marks out the blessing he is to the flock. What people need more than sermons from paper and pulpit are sermons written in flesh and blood. The people who have most influenced and inspired my Christian life are those who somehow breathe the atmosphere of heaven and naturally reflect the purity and passion of their relationship with God, and all so self-effacingly done that you know there is no artifice but childlike sincerity. It is the people who know their God, and who speak easily of Jesus, that draw us on. Those of my generation will remember the Bisto kids: an advert for a gravy mix where the smell of the gravy is seen floating in the air with the roughly dressed kids following it, noses raised to catch its fragrance and follow it to its source – an apt metaphor for pastoring.

David Hansen develops the statement of Eberhard Jungel that 'Jesus is the parable of God', by suggesting that pastors are a parable of Jesus Christ. 'Jesus is the Parable of God and delivers God to us in the process. Isn't it possible that pastors, to the extent that they follow Jesus, are parables of Jesus Christ and so deliver him to those they encounter?... This is why when I walk into a hospital room, the people seem to experience the coming of God. Just to say that sounds egotistical. But sometimes on hospital calls, it is as if I am not even there. God is there. Sometimes God comes to people when I preach, or pray, or even when I'm just visiting with them. Being a parable of Jesus shows me how it is possibly true when he says: "He who receives you receives me, and he who receives me receives the one who sent me" (Mt 10: 40).'[21]

And all for the joy of knowing him!

---

[21] Hansen, *The Art of Pastoring*, p. 24

"Et teneo et teneor"

We began this chapter with a picture of a hand holding a cross and in turn being held by its grace and power – a most helpful image for pastors in their calling. If daily we treasure the cross to cleanse us through the graces of conviction, forgiveness, and compassion and find in it a place to release death to the gaining of a Christ-filled life, then we are set for all that the day may bring. As C. S. Lewis wrote immediately after the aforementioned Narnian romp, "'And now", said Aslan presently, "to business. I feel I am about to roar.'"

And in terms of the business of our inner world, what follows in the next five chapters is a series of graces made available to us as a result of the cross, the first of which has to do with our identity.

Underpinning

Exploration – there is no more searching passage of scripture than Revelation 2 and 3, where the ascended Lord questions his church and, whatever 'the angel of the church' is, pastors must be included. In the light of the cross, perhaps Jesus would probe:

- Ephesus, Revelation 2: 4 – Have we abandoned our first love? Is there passion in our lives, and is it for Jesus?
- Smyrna, Revelation 2: 10 – Have fears of suffering diverted us?
- Pergamum, Revelation 2: 20 – Has our teaching become watered down?
- Thyatira, Revelation 3: 20 – Have we compromised on purity?
- Sardis, Revelation 3: 1 – Are we preoccupied with reputation?
- Philadelphia, Revelation 3: 8 – Do we worry over small numbers and little strength?
- Laodicea, Revelation 3: 15 and 16 – Have we grown lukewarm?

Excavation –recommended for digging deeper

- *Amy Carmichael of Dohnavur* by Frank L. Houghton, published by CLC

Exchange – new foundation for old

- The Prayer of St. Patrick (his breastplate)

I bind unto myself today
The power of God to hold and lead;
His eye to watch, his might to stay,
His ear to hearken to my need;
The wisdom of my God to teach,
His hand to guide, his shield to ward,
The Word of God to give me speech,
His heavenly host to be my guide.

Christ be with me, Christ within me,
Christ behind me, Christ before me,
Christ beside me, Christ to win me,
Christ to comfort and restore me,
Christ beneath me, Christ above me, 1
Christ in quiet, Christ in danger,
Christ in hearts of all that love me,
Christ in mouth of friend and stranger.
I bind unto myself today...
The strong name of the Trinity.

Chapter 6

The Identity We Own

For we are God's workmanship, created in Christ Jesus to do good
works, which God prepared in advance for us to do.

Ephesians 2: 10

In a moment of high theatrical drama, Jean Valjean wrestles with his
conscience, knowing that for him the outcome of this conflict will
have eternal consequences. In a case of mistaken identity, the police
officer Inspector Javert has dragged an innocent man before the court
thinking him to be Valjean – an ex-prisoner who violated his parole, a
man he has been tracking down for years. What should Valjean do? If
he speaks up, he will have to reveal the alibi he has adopted and show
the world that the man who has become a wealthy factory owner and
mayor of Montreuil-sur-Mer is a sham and still at heart prisoner
24601. To speak up for the condemned man will be to condemn
himself. But if he holds his tongue, perpetuates his new persona, then
the innocent man will not see the light of day again. Valjean realises,
'If I stay silent, I am damned.'

The moment has been captured in the lyrics of Herbert Kretzmer
and the music of Claude-Michel Schonberg in their musical adaptation
of Victor Hugo's drama *Les Misérables,* with a song of crisis and
heart-searching called simply: "Who Am I?"

If I speak, I am condemned.

If I sit silent, I am damned!

Who am I?

Can I condemn this man to slavery?

Pretend I do not see his agony?

This innocent who bears my face

Who goes to judgement in my place.

Who am I?

Can I conceal myself for evermore?

Pretend I'm not the man I was before?

And must my name until I die

Be no more than an alibi?

Must I lie?

How can I ever face my fellow-men?

How can I ever face myself again?

It is the prologue that sets up the drama. Valjean is released on parole after nineteen years in prison for the crime of stealing a loaf of bread – a potent image of life in pre-revolutionary, eighteenth century France. He sleeps that night in the bishop's palace but is rearrested by constables, accused of stealing. The bishop intervenes on his behalf, telling the officers that all in Valjeans' possession was a gift, and furthermore, he tells Valjean that he should have also taken the silver candelabra. In dismissing the constables, the bishop then addresses Valjean, telling him that God's blessing should be seen as part of a higher plan for his life, that he must use this gift for an honest life. He concludes by putting Valjean under a solemn charge, 'By the witness of the martyrs, by the passion and the blood, God has raised you out of darkness; I have bought your soul for God.' Valjean recognises the implications and in a prayer sings, 'What have I done, sweet Jesus, what have I done?… Yet why did I allow that man to touch my soul and teach me love? He treated me like any other. He gave me his trust. He called me brother. He claims my life for God above. Can such things be?… He told me that I had a soul. How does he know? What spirit comes to move my life? Is there another way to go?'

Back in the courtroom, the breakthrough comes for Valjean as he presses the 'who am I' question and comes to his conclusion:

My soul belongs to God, I know

I made that bargain long ago

He gave me hope when hope was gone

He gave me strength to journey on.

Who am I? Who am I?

I am Jean Valjean!

Who am I?

24601![1]

What *Les Misérables* dramatically portrays is the link between grace and identity. Having received mercy and grace from God at the hand of the bishop, Valjean is forced to reassess who he is and own that identity, warts and all, before the world, whatever the implications. He cannot deny what God had made him or therefore how he should behave. The future must now take its course, The story will unfold differently, but the man will be more whole and strong by embracing his destiny. So courageously he declares, 'I'm prisoner 24601, a man who violated parole, a man who has received grace. I'm Jean Valjean.'

Identity

As for Valjean in revolutionary France, so for us in the work of ministry: there will be no escaping situations that challenge our authenticity. Indeed these should be understood as a further step in God's ruthless perfecting of us. Identity was arguably the central issue in Jesus' ministry. For him the question was not 'Who am I?' – that was never in doubt. His settled self–knowledge, however, frequently begged the shadow question from others: 'Who are you?'[2] The more assured an individual is in his identity, the more likely he is to be questioned in today's parlance, 'Who do you think you are?' Either way identity is a key issue.

There may be some robust characters for whom the issue of identity is idle speculation; they are comfortable in their skin, assured in themselves, and not given to introspective doubts. Most of us, however, in the face of the call to and the work of ministry are more likely to identify with Moses' ambivalence, 'Who am I that I should?'[3] I have sometimes joked that ministry would be much easier if I could pastor like Richard Baxter, teach like John

---

[1] From Cameron Mackintosh's production *Les Misérables* by Alain Boulil and Claude-Michel Schonberg, based on the novel by Victor Hugo, lyrics by Herbert Kretzmer.
[2] John 8: 25
[3] Exodus 3: 11

Calvin, evangelise like Billy Graham, pray like Rees Howells, organise like John Wesley, have a voice like George Whitfield, and look like Tom Cruise. The demands of ministry are such that we soon feel the desire to be ten talented people rather than the one talent we perceive ourselves to be. Intellectually, we may know we are God's workmanship through creation and redemption, but we can't help wondering if we were not a Friday afternoon job, such that as we came off the conveyor belt we were missing a couple of vital components.

Without a settled sense of identity, though, we will always be vulnerable. God's purpose through the cross is to establish authenticity and integrity in the knowledge of who we are in Christ, such that having done all, we will stand firm. Nehemiah was under intense pressure from both within the restoration community and from the machinations of Sanballat, Tobiah, and Geshem. Their determination was to create fear and stop the progress of the work – the usual strategy of God's enemies. Following a series of escalating intimidatory attacks, the opposition resorted to their ultimate deterrent and issued Nehemiah a death threat. His friend Shemaiah counselled that they claim the sanctuary of the temple and hide. Nehemiah repudiates such cowardice and boldly answers, 'Why would a man like me run for cover? And why would a man like me use the Temple as a hideout? I won't do it.'[4] In other words, men such as he knew himself to be a man of God, a man commissioned, who simply does not do such things: it was inconceivable. His response was based on knowing his identity.

No pastor worth his salt is going to behave like a dictator in God's house, much less a *prima donna*. Leadership will require occasions, however, when tough decisions need to be made. It is in that context that a pastor's character and sense of identity are likely to be challenged. Inevitably, there will be a swirl of opinion. As likely as not from a minority, there will be attempts to undermine that leadership by questioning motive and integrity. 'Who am I?' or 'Who am I that I should?' are then the doubts that can lead to uncertainty and equivocation. There may not be death threats, but the pressure to flee, freeze, or fight can be strong. What is required is a firm grasp of who

---

[4] Nehemiah 6: 11 The Message

we are and how we find ourselves to be in this position. That is to say men and women who have known God's call, are being shaped by his discipline, are daily receiving God's grace at the cross to the end that we are servants of God. The beauty of this is that it can be done without artifice, contrivance, or pretension. It really is God's grace that we are in Christ, made as we are, gifted and called and all so manifestly undeserving that no apology is necessary. Whether or not Luther actually said, 'Here I stand I can do no other', the statement is a healthy affirmation of identity as well as conviction and destiny and to be owned by all God's servants.

Coming to such a place is to find peace. In it, to some extent, we must stand alone, against the temptation to envy others, and be willing to embrace the uniqueness not just of our fingerprints but every complex outworking of our DNA. 'There is a way of being for each of us that is as natural and deeply congruent as the life of the tulip. Beneath the roles and masks lies a possibility of a self that is unique as a snowflake. It is an originality that has existed since God first loved us into existence. Our true self-in-Christ is the only self that will support authenticity. It and it alone provides an identity that is eternal.'[5] The summons, in the words of Shakespeare, is, 'This above all: to thine own self be true'.

If then I am God's workmanship, by creation and cross, who am I? Who and what is it we are being made into? Paul in Ephesians 2: 10 suggests that our identity and vocation are bound up together, that vocation is grounded in identity, 'For we are God's workmanship, created in Christ Jesus to do good works, which God prepared in advance for us to do.' 'Who am I?' thus becomes consonant with our call, a process of discovery as to how we undertake the assigned task in the purposes of God.

We look firstly at a couple of aspects of identity, then at their implications for ministry.

1. Beloved Son

Listening into Jesus' prayer for his disciples, we hear him ask something that takes our breath away: 'May the world know that you Father have loved these even as you have loved me.... I will continue

[5] Benner, *The Gift of Being Yourself,* p. 15

to make you known to them in order that the love you have for me may be in them.'[6] Jesus affirms that the Father loves these rascals in the same way that the Father loves himself; his prayer is that these men might get hold of that and live accordingly.

No one would doubt that the Father loves the Son. At His baptism and at the Transfiguration, Father's voice echoed with pride as he announced, 'This is my beloved Son.' In the manner of adoring parents parading photographs of their child, so the Father's heart swells with joy as he owns his beloved before a watching world: this is my boy! And that he loves him 100 per cent is not in doubt either; anything less is inconceivable. To imagine God loving us like that, however, is a different matter. As humans, we love partially, dependent on many factors, not least the reaction from the object of our affections: love me and I'll love you and so our love will grow. We imagine God loving Jesus 100 per cent, perhaps loving Billy Graham or Mother Theresa 80 per cent, and loving us perhaps 30 per cent on a good day. Inevitably, we project onto God our own deficient experience of love, concluding erroneously that nobody loves 100 per cent, forgetting that God doesn't *do* love so much as *is* love.

Mankind has an orphan spirit, especially missing the rugged benevolent security of Abba Father. Access to all the benefits of this Fatherhood comes as we take hold of the implications of Jesus' prayer and realise the height, breadth, length, and depth of Father's love for us, for me. Writing to Fred in his little classic *Life of the Beloved*, Henri Nouwen puts it like this: 'Our many conversations led me to the inner conviction that the words "You are the Beloved" reveal the most intimate truth about all human beings, whether they belong to any particular tradition or not. Fred, all I want to say to you is "You are the Beloved", and all I hope is that you can hear these words spoken to you with all the tenderness and force that love can hold. My only desire is to make these words reverberate in every corner of your being – "You are the Beloved."'[7]

When Brennan Manning was researching the origins of the Christian faith in the Clearwater area of Florida, he discovered a fascinating piece of information: 'Over a hundred years ago in the

---

[6] From John 17: 23, 26

[7] Henri J. M. Nouwen, *The Life of the Beloved*, (London: Hodder & Stoughton, 1992) p. 26

Deep South, a phrase so common in our Christian culture today, *born again,* was seldom or never used. Rather, the phrase used to describe the breakthrough into a personal relationship with Jesus Christ was, "I was seized by the power of a great affection."[8] I have come to love that phrase. 'Seized by the power of a great affection' roots the regeneration experience into a dynamic transforming experience of love. It equates to Abba Father parading our own photograph around the courts of heaven and booming out for heaven and earth to hear, 'This is my boy, my girl, my beloved, my joy, my delight' and finding ourselves swept up in a transforming embrace.

Some years ago I was meditating in Matthew 1. The genealogies are not famous for presaging profound spiritual experience, and my faith was not high. However, as I pondered the text, I was suddenly aware that this family tree, written primarily to establish Jesus' line back through King David, was also my family tree. I was an adopted son, grafted into not just any family but God's chosen royal family. God's Spirit was forging a vital connection between them and me, living many years later in these far-off islands. These were my people, my folk. I sensed a bond with them; their lives and stories made me proud to be one of them. As I thought of the generations, I realised I loved them profoundly and would one day revel in talking with them. 'Perhaps I should be called Prince Andrew', I thought in a moment of fantasy, but the realisation of my significance, belonging, and identity was profound; I had gained a history, a distinguished family tree. My place in life had been rooted and established; I was part of a loving royal family; I had been seized by the power of a great affection.

Imagine just how many sermons, conferences, books, and articles are devoted to this central truth of God's unconditional love. It has to be the heart of every counselling session, every prayer ministry, and every pulpit exhortation that there is no limit to his love, no failure so final, and no place too dark that God's limitless love in Jesus is not sufficient. And why? Because the wretchedness of man's orphan lostness makes this the most vital and compelling truth, capable of calming the traumatised soul and bringing the prodigal home – including those lost in the far country of pastoral ministry.

---

[8] Manning, *The Ragamuffin Gospel* p. 189

If, like the church in Ephesus, we have lost our first love, then there is no more important matter than to repent and seek again the flame of passion in the heart. Without it, ministry is a chore, a drudgery, and the most miserable place on earth; with it, ministry is tolerable and occasionally glorious! Take time, go up a mountain, find a cave in the desert, listen to Mozart, gaze at a Rembrandt, laugh with Rowan Atkinson, or do whatever it takes to get in touch with your own humanity and God's embrace. He is closer than you think.

Who am I? A child of God's royal family and greatly beloved!

2. Fully Human

The title 'Christian' has a long and distinguished history, but it has become a weak word needing extensive repair work before it can be effective again. As Hans Küng has challengingly questioned, 'In fact is it not the failure to be fully human which makes being a Christian seem inadequate? Is not the lack of genuine, complete humanity particularly with official representatives and exponents of the Churches the reason why being a Christian is disregarded or rejected as an authentic human possibility?'[9] Perhaps it is better, at least initially, to leapfrog the term 'Christian' to emphasise that God's workmanship in Christ is for us to recover Adam's lost humanity. What God is after is to make us fully human, restored to the role that Satan sought to deface forever but which the cross has made gloriously possible. Küng significantly devotes a whole section to this theme under the title *Being Christian as Being Radically Human.*[10]

But what does it mean to be fully human?

'One in the bundle of life'

If you could invite any guests to dinner, I wonder what the criteria might be for your invitations. The people I would love to invite to our table would be those who laugh easily, and you sense know how to cry; people who are unashamedly passionate about God whatever their theological preferences but who do not take themselves too seriously, people who are compassionate toward those gripped by the dark side of our contemporary society and willing to do something

---

[9] Hans Kung, *On Being a Christian*, (Glasgow: Fount, Collins, 1974) p. 530
[10] Kung p. 554ff.

about it, people whose inner warmth draws you in and whose conversation bestows honour and dignity on all, people who relish the food and the wine but know the value of fasting. So who would I like to invite? Those with great humanity.

Any discussion of humanity has to begin with a meal table! Jesus, the supreme human being, was known as a friend of tax collectors and sinners precisely because he spent so much time dining with them. His accusers could only splutter with indignation, 'Why does he eat with tax collectors and sinners?'[11] But food is what friends do together: 'Let's have coffee'; 'Come for lunch'; 'Join us for a barbeque'; 'Let's do breakfast'. Jesus understood that what happens around our meal tables touches the core of our humanity. Eating together breaks down suspicions, eases conversation, transcends social barriers, and facilitates friendship. It helps create community for human beings. Being human, then, has to do in the first instance with this sense of belonging, of identity and commonality with my fellow man.

If I had a dream guest list for supper, one of the first to receive an invitation would be Archbishop Desmond Tutu. Who could resist his infectious laughter, his breadth of compassion, his storytelling, his passionate fight for the soul of a nation – a man who moves with princes but has never lost the common touch? In his book *No Future Without Forgiveness*, his story of the Truth and Reconciliation Commission of South Africa explains the philosophy which undergirded the attempt to bring warring factions together: it has to do with the word *ubuntu,* as the idea is known in the Nguni group of languages.

'*Ubuntu* is very difficult to render into a Western language. It speaks of the very essence of being human. When we want to give high praise to someone we say, '*Yu, u nobuntu*'; 'Hey, he or she has great *ubuntu.*' This means they are generous, hospitable, friendly, caring and compassionate. They share what they have. It also means my humanity is caught up, inextricably bound up, in theirs. We belong in a bundle of life. We say, 'a person is a person through other people'. It is not 'I think therefore I am'. It says rather: 'I am a human being because I belong.' I participate, I share. A person with *ubuntu* is open and available to others, affirming of others, does not feel threatened

---

[11] Mark 2: 16

that others are able and good; for he or she has a proper self-assurance that comes from knowing that he or she belongs in a greater whole and is diminished when others are humiliated or diminished, when others are tortured or oppressed, or treated as if they were less than who they are.'[12]

It seems to me this is a very helpful insight from the culture of our African brothers. Tutu provides examples where *ubuntu* was able to prevail, as it did predominantly in post-apartheid South Africa, or in Kenya under the wise counsel of Jomo Kenyatta, but also acknowledges situations where it did not. One comment on this latter is especially telling. In recounting a 'chilling retort' by the then minister of police that Steve Biko's death in prison by starvation 'leaves me cold', Tutu says, 'You had to ask what had happened to the humanity of anyone who could speak so callously about the death of a fellow human being.'[13]

The fact that *ubuntu* also fails should not surprise us, for it has been infected with the sin virus like everything else on earth. Its fallen nature, however, can still point us to God, the One who is 'a Being in Communion'.[14] Genesis declares that man is made in the image of such a God, and Paul proclaims that in Christ we are being 'renewed in the image of God'.[15] Our being, our very humanity, is therefore an incorporation into and an extension of the love that exists in the heart of our Trinitarian God. As we hear Father's voice intone our belovedness, so we are drawn to communion, which turns out to be not just into God but also with our fellow men: 'We know that we have passed from death to life, because we love our brothers.'[16] To be human is to love, to belong.

Even this, however, will be touched with our sinfulness, which with honesty and humility itself becomes part of our present humanity. We need to be able to say in effect with Valjean not only 'I am Jean Valjean' but also 'I am prisoner 24601'. 'Sin is more basic than what

---

[12] Desmond Tutu, *No Future Without Forgiveness,* (London: Rider, Random House, 2000) p. 34–35

[13] Ibid p. 36

[14] John Zizioulas quoted by David Atkinson in *The Message of Genesis 1–11* BST series (Leicester: IVP, 1990) p. 38

[15] Genesis 1: 26–28 and Colossians 1: 3

[16] 1 John 3: 14

we do. Sin is who we are. In this regard we could say that sin is fundamentally a matter of ontology (being), not simply morality. To be a human is to be a sinner. It is to be broken, damaged goods that carry within our deepest self a fundamental fatal flaw – a flaw that masks our original creation goodness and infects our very being.'[17]

We pastors are under-shepherds of the Good Shepherd. Being shaped in His likeness, we are being made more and more human. As David Atkinson delightfully puts it, 'In a sense, therefore, while it is proper to speak of Jesus Christ as the true Human Being, we should speak of ourselves as Human Becomings.'[18] Through new birth and incarnation, we are dropped into the midst of a needy people and first of all are called not to do but 'to be' with them, to identify with them in their lot, 'meaningless and a great misfortune.'[19] We have a phrase in English that is not always complimentary but which carries the kind of earthy overtones that may be helpful here: one of the boys. Jesus at table with the Pharisees was one of the boys: he ate, drank, laughed, told stories, challenged, and provoked. The common people loved him because he breathed an authenticity that marked him out from the super-spiritual who had somehow lost their ability to mix easily with the common herd. By God's grace, he makes us one of the boys, one in the bundle of life, ready to laugh and cry and be identified as one sharing this common lot.

I am conscious of gender here and recognise that not all women in ministry would be happy with the phrase 'one of the boys.' Perhaps the reason there is no equivalent feminised phrase is because women are intuitively better at this kind of involvement and identification. For them to get alongside others, chat on the phone, have coffee, send notes seems more natural, whereas for men it often has to be worked at. Men have to be drawn into it as we cooperate with the workmanship of God.

Who am I? I am fully human; I belong here with people, one with them in their joys and sorrows, a sinner being saved by grace. I know my place and dignity in Christ. I am a human being, having a make-over in the image of God!

---

[17] Benner p. 64
[18] Atkinson p. 39
[19] Ecclesiastes 2: 21.

But does this mean that I've got to be the clubbable sort, don a 'hail fellow well met' style, be forced into the alien shape of an extrovert? As an introvert, this becomes an important question for me!

Personality Variety

Marilyn and I were attending our first Myers-Briggs introduction course.[20] As our tutor explained the wide variety of ways in which human beings relate to the world around us, gather information, and process decisions, I turned to Marilyn and, with a twinkle in my eye, said,'So you are not mad after all!' The rest of the group joined in the laughter, which was not just at me but was of the kind when even poor humour releases emotion; clearly self-awareness was dawning, lights were being switched on, and mysteries were being made clear. I was not the only one being enlightened! That seminar and subsequent studies in Myers-Briggs have probably been the single most helpful tool in our marriage. Since then we have used it with great profit as part of our team-building in the church; not only is it extremely helpful but great fun as well.

I give testimony at this point only to emphasise that God loves variety. We celebrate that in creation, between the seasons, in different countries and continents. Variety is the stimulus to poetry and music, to art and worship, yet we live in a conformist society intolerant of those who are distinctive and different. We see that in little things like tyranny to fashion and in big things such as xenophobia. This conformist narrowing must surely be resisted at every turn so that the full panoply of Gods colours, harmonies, shades, and brilliances is released. Man, the pinnacle of creation, is made with rich diversity of personality and giftedness.

Imagine the personality and temperamental differences in that team ministry of Haggai and Zechariah. Zechariah ministers out of revelation but deeply congruent with his personality: dreams, visions, imaginative pictures, and symbols. Haggai I define as the 'Yorkshireman of the Old Testament' who, in a strong broad accent, bluntly proclaims, 'Yea and amen, thus saith the Lord, "I am with

---

[20] Entering Myer-Briggs in any internet search engine will show the wide use of this tool in commerce and industry, at university level, and will show lists of facilitators, including applications for Christians and church.

thee'". If asked where were the visions and pictures like those of his contemporary, I'm sure he would have answered, 'I don't know about that, God says he's with us, what more do you need to know?!'

Spending time unpackaging this amazing bundle of life that is each one of us is an important act of stewardship. Learning something of how my personality preferences worked via Myers-Briggs has been one of the most illuminating and releasing discoveries I have made about myself and permitted ownership of God's handiwork. Cooperating with our Creator and spending time to understand how he has wired us is only sensible, yet how easy it is to neglect these matters of our own soul. This is not a call to a self-indulgent exercise in navel gazing; it has rich applications for how we understand and serve others and create community.

Some years ago, we sang a children's chorus, 'If I were a butterfly, I'd thank you Lord for giving me wings'. The chorus was the best bit: 'But I just thank you, Lord, for making me me'. Amen, here I stand; I can do no other: I'm loved as a beloved son, fully human and utterly unique; thank you, Lord, for making me me.

Identity and Vocation

In Ephesians 2: 10, we see that vocation is grounded in identity: 'His workmanship, created in Christ Jesus for the good works ordained for us.' As Benner puts it, 'His call is always absolutely congruent with our destiny, our truest self, our identity and the shape of our being.'[21]

The pattern is set for us in Jesus. The words, 'You are my beloved Son with whom I am well pleased', spoken to Jesus at his baptism, were of course words of affirmation. But the two phrases used join messianic statements in Psalm 2: 7 and Isaiah 42: 1 to also confirm his mission: so both identity and vocation are in mind.

In the second psalm, the psalmist proclaims that God has set his king on Zion, his holy hill. As worshippers set out to honour God in the psalms, they need to know whether their lot is determined by chance or if there is anyone in charge. These psalms were probably compiled and ordered during the Babylonian captivity, so this is no idle question. Where does the authority in this world lie? Are we no

---

[21] Benner p. 102.

more than pawns to be moved at the whim of the next world dictator? The psalmist trumpets out with confidence, 'The Lord reigns, God is King' and details how that reign will be secured. God then, as it were, breaks in and addresses this king of all the earth as 'Son': 'You are my Son, today I have become your Father.' Relationship and mission statement side by side.

Isaiah in the first song of the suffering servant commands attention to this man: 'Behold my servant!' But not just any menial servant – he is one in whom God delights, is well pleased. Like the psalmist, Isaiah has the world in view; Israel is to be parochial no more. The servant's mission is to bring justice to the nations, not just social order but the teaching of Torah, God's word, in its fullest sense. This calling will, however, be exercised with servant-like sensitivity, 'he will not shout or cry out, or raise his voice in the streets. A bruised reed he will not break, and a smouldering wick he will not snuff out.' Once again, the One delighted in has his job description.

As the shout from heaven echoed around the banks of the Jordan, Jesus was declared to be both Messianic son and suffering servant, fully God and fully human. But that voice communicating identity in both 'Belovedness' and 'humanity' was also expressing destiny. It defined a role as servant/ruler, and all in the context of the needs of the nations. Jesus is thereby reminded that his love relationship with the Father was not only personal but extended to redemptive purposes: as he was to say later, 'it was for this reason that I came to this hour.'[22] This moment that revealed the Father-Son relationship to the world was also identifying the one who would fulfil John the Baptist's prophecy concerning 'the Lamb of God, who takes away the sin of the world' and he 'who will baptise with the Holy Spirit'.[23] A magnificent man, uniquely born for a singular purpose.

In Jesus' high priestly prayer for his disciples, he intercedes that they might know that they were loved by the Father as the Father loved him. That prayer is of course set in the context of mission. Shortly, they were to be sent into the world to continue his work. His prayer for them, and those of us in future generations, was that their realisation of sonship would be powerfully

---

[22] John 12: 27
[23] John 1: 29, 33

strengthened as they enter that part of the Father's work for which they had been destined.

A couple of practical observations:

Work shaped by identity

We should expect that our identity and gifting will shape the manner and spirit in which our work is undertaken. Miroslav Volf puts it like this, 'The gifts of the divine Lover move downward to humans. The image that Luther used constantly is that of flowing: "The love of God flows forth and bestows good."'[24] Being caught up in this love flow morphs us and our work. So Nouwen can elaborate on qualities for leadership in these terms: 'Christian leaders cannot simply be persons who have well-informed opinions about the burning issues of our time. Their leadership must be rooted in the permanent, intimate relationship with the incarnate Word, Jesus, and they need to find there the source for their words, advice, and guidance.... Dealing with burning issues easily leads to divisiveness because, before we know it, our sense of self is caught up in our opinion about a given subject. But when we are securely rooted in personal intimacy with the source of life, it will be possible to remain flexible but not relativistic, convinced without being rigid, willing to confront without being offensive, gentle and forgiving without being soft, and true witnesses without being manipulative.'[25]

We have a number of delightful phrases in English that reflect this: 'a chip off the old block', 'like father like son', 'like mother like daughter', 'you can see who they belong to'. Identity has moved beyond simply having the same surname to children reflecting similarities of personality and behaviour to their parents, a genetic progression. So by the Spirit, as we abide in Christ, should we expect to see such transformation in our manner of being and doing. It's 'the love of Christ which constrains us.'[26]

One of the great dangers, therefore, would be to lose the sense of who we are in the bustle of a busy life. Over recent years in Christian counselling there has been a strong emphasis given to the priority of

---

[24] Miroslav Volf, *Free of Charge*, (Grand Rapids: Zondervan, 2005) p. 42

[25] Quoted by Brennan Manning, *Abba's Child*, (Colorado Springs: Navpress, 2002) p. 127 from Nouwen, *In the Name of Jesus*.

[26] 2 Corinthians 5: 14

being over doing. This had been a healthy emphasis both to establish priority and probably to correct a previous imbalance in favour of doing, drawn from a combination of the Protestant work ethic, pharisaic attitudes and rituals, and the heresy of salvation by good works. We have seen, however, that ultimately the New Testament allows no such distinction between being and doing. Trying to define who we are apart from what we do is nigh impossible. 'But who we are is elusive, even to the most sophisticated, therapeutic probing of the human psyche.'[27] What we do and how we do it is the most reliable way of determining who we are. From that moment of his baptism, Jesus did not sit back to bask in his belovedness but secure in his Sonship touched untouchables, mixed mud with spittle and washed dirty feet. His promise is that we would do greater works than he and that in the process would experience persecution. No man gets thrown in jail for simply believing himself a son of God, though he might be thrown elsewhere!

I do not think pastors and leaders are in much danger of overpreoccupation with illusions and abstractions. What we are more liable to is preoccupation with a doing divorced from being, and that to our great loss. Just as being without doing is a fantasy, so doing without being is dead works. Work must be shaped and affected by who we are in Christ.

Work according to gift

Pastoring is not like working on a factory assembly line. The tasks may be very similar from church to church, but God is looking for us to tackle those tasks in a way that expresses our uniqueness. Every church should look and feel different due to its constituent membership but especially due to the shaping influence of its pastor, who is himself/herself this unique creation designed to work in a particular way. Some churches will be highly-structured, well-organised with mission statements, vision statements, where the flock is well-drilled and organised. Others will be highly relational, feely-touchy! There are churches strong in teaching the Word, where members come to services with study bibles and notebooks, while the one down the road will attract musicians, singers, dancers, and artists

---

[27] Manning p. 139.

as they follow their artistic, bohemian-style pastor. This rich kaleidoscope has nothing to do with soundness of doctrine but everything to do with diversity of personality and gift. An occupational temptation is to feel diminished because we are unable to produce what other pastors seem to produce in their churches, but how liberating to know we are not expected to. Thank God for the Rick Warrens and the Bill Hybels of our fraternity, but I could no more produce what they have than swim the Atlantic, nor am I meant to – hallelujah! Let's throw off the tyranny of conformity and do church, expressing it according to our passion for Jesus, our love for his Word, by our cooperation with the Spirit and according to our unique make-up and style. Years ago I heard John Wimber say that he loved his church, adding, 'Why shouldn't I? After all, we sing songs that I wrote, I get to preach, the people love what I do, it's fun!' Classic Wimber! He never thought it was the only church on offer, nor that it had to be all things to all men, he just had to do it according to the way he was made in response to God's grace, and God could look after the rest.

Having pastored for over thirty-five years, I have come to dislike 'adjective church'. We pastors are challenged to do cell church, seeker-friendly church, signs and wonders church, servant church, mission-shaped church, purpose-driven church, messy church, emergent church, and prodigal-sensitive church. None of these are bad, but they should be seen as expressions of individuals' passions and insights, which may have some value, but the danger is that by trying to incorporate all these facets, God loses out on what he is uniquely looking for us to produce. So at times I feel like shouting, 'Give us a break – let's just do church!' If any adjective is required, let it be 'New Testament', which I submit has to do with churches expressing appropriate diversity, mainly according to God's workmanship in each of us, a unique expression of our personality and gifts and all in the power of the Holy Spirit.

Work for His approval

It is in this love relationship that we find the source of our job satisfaction, an ear tuned both to His 'well done good and faithful servant' and the delight of joyful partnering with God as his grace and gifts are passed on to others. 'Since God creates the self to be indwelled by Christ that self will be fulfilled only if it draws the living water from the well-spring of love's infinity and passes it on to its neighbours.'[28] The temptation is to look for job satisfaction in the product achieved, whether individual response to our ministry, church growth, numbers converted, or expansion of ministry influence, rather than God alone. But the end product is subject to so many variables that even if we knew what it was to be (and I am more and more convinced we have little idea of what God is up to!) it would be beyond our capability to produce it. The end product is simply not our responsibility: what we are called to is faithfulness, 'now it is required that those who have been given a trust must prove faithful.' Which is why Paul made it clear that no human court could evaluate his work: he did not even judge himself, concluding, 'It is the Lord who judges me. Therefore judge nothing before the appointed time; wait till the Lord comes'.[29] Time and again in scripture God has to say to his servants, 'Do not be discouraged', as he knows how easily we could be if we look for satisfaction in the wrong place. He usually goes on to add, 'For I the Lord your God am with you wherever you go.'[30] And it's that communion of Father with us, his children, that nourishes and rewards us, even as it did Jesus in his earthly ministry.

I Must Be About My Father's Business

My brother-in-law, Alan, prior to his retirement, worked in the family business of H. R. Rashbrook & Son. The firm was begun by his grandfather, continued by his father, and over the past thirty-five years run by Alan and his brother, Gerry. There was always a sense of appropriate privilege in Alan for the close link that existed between family and business. Not that it was always easy, nor did it guarantee smooth running, but when families can both love and work together it adds a rich dimension to life and certainly has for Alan. Prior to my call to pastoral ministry, my father and I had talked about how good it would have been to be in practice together as surveyors. There was much that he could have taught me from his wide experience; I sensed his pride in me qualifying in his own chosen profession, and I would

---

[28] Volf p. 52
[29] 1 Corinthians 4: 2–5
[30] For example in Joshua 1: 9

have loved to work closely with my dad. It was not to be, but even now the thought of it moves me. This tradition of family businesses, especially seen here in England, is a fine thing, not least as it lends credibility to the standard of work and service offered, for the family name is at stake. If you employed J. Bloggs and Sons to do your plumbing, there was an understanding that you would get quality whether from father or son because their name was on the line. Interestingly, when Alan retired, he and Gerry could have sold the company but chose rather to close it down as they did not want to run the risk that the family name would be abused if it fell into the hands of those who would not work hard to honour it.

Whatever opportunities our earthly families have afforded us, how much greater is the privilege that we can 'be about my Father's business'.

The Next Step

What next? How are we to cooperate in the fuller realisation of who we are and so give better shape to our calling? From identity we move on to personal discipline – another response to his grace. Not one of mine, nor I suspect many, of our preferred themes but one we try to sidestep to our cost.

Underpinning

Exploration – based on phrases in this chapter

- 'You are the Beloved' – how comfortably does this phrase resonate in your spirit?

- 'I was seized by the power of a great affection' – have you known this past, or is it present, or do you look for it future?

- 'We should speak of ourselves as human becomings' – what does this phrase mean for you?

- 'Beneath the roles and the masks lies a self that is as unique as a snowflake' – how comfortable are you in your own skin?

- 'There will be no escaping situations which challenge our authenticity as men' – who or what most challenges your authenticity, makes you want to run or strike back, gets under your skin?

- 'His call is always absolutely congruent with our destiny, our truest self, our identity and the shape of our being' – how free are you in your spirit to do the work of ministry being true to yourself?

Excavation – recommended for digging deeper

- *The Gift of Being Yourself* by David Benner, published by Eagle

Exchange – new foundation for old

- A prayer of John Wesley:

I am no longer my own but Yours.
Put me to what you will.
Put me to doing. Put me to suffering.
Let me be employed for you, or laid aside for you,
Exalted in you, or brought low for you.
Let me be full, let me be empty.
Let me have all things, let me have nothing.
I freely and wholeheartedly yield all things to
Your pleasure and disposal.

And now glorious and blessed God,
Father, Son and Holy Spirit,
You are mine and I am yours. So be it.
And this covenant now made on earth,
Let it be satisfied in Heaven. Amen.

Chapter 7

The Training We Engage

I beat my body and make it my slave so that after I have preached to others, I myself will not be disqualified for the prize.
1 Corinthians 9: 27

The nearest I came to army life prior to our daughter's wedding was at school when Thursday afternoon was devoted to the CCF – the Combined Cadet Force. We dressed in khaki, polished buttons, dubbed webbing, shone boots, and got shouted at on the parade ground. With the exception of being shouted at, I enjoyed it. It was rugged out door Kenyan life where we learned field craft, handling rifles, including live ammunition, and developed a good *esprit de corps*. Once a year we went on army camp under the tutelage of professional soldiers, where our training and discipline were taken further. Not surprisingly, a good number of pupils from our Nairobi school went into military careers, for there is something about that way of life that has great appeal. Not that it suited everyone. I well remember one studious friend with bottle-end glasses, ginger hair, and sensitive freckled skin for whom the whole thing was purgatory.

Army life entered our family again when Vanessa married Jon, who is a professional career officer. It made for a colourful and spectacular wedding as fellow officers in dress uniform provided the ceremonial arch with drawn swords. As a signals specialist, Jon has worked with many regiments, including the Gurkhas, a unique group of men in the British army from Nepal. The Brigade of Gurkhas was originally part of the British Army in India but following Indian independence in 1947 was given the option of remaining with the Indian or British armies; those joining the British were formed into various regiments.

Their renown springs from their unique fighting spirit and exceptional bravery. Drafted from the tough Nepalese terrain, they fit easily into the rigors of army life, which results in soldiers of exceptional calibre. The following tribute written by the late Sir Ralph Turner MC (Professor of Sankrit at the University of London, Fellow of Christ's College Cambridge, and sometime Adjutant of a Gurkha Riffle Battalion) makes worthy reading. 'As I write these words, my thoughts return to you who were my comrades…. Once more I hear the laughter with which you greeted every hardship. Once more I see you in your bivouacs or about your camp fires, on forced marches or in the trenches, now shivering with wet and cold, now scorched by pitiless and burning sun. Uncomplaining you endure hunger and thirst and wounds; and at the last your unwavering lines disappear into the smoke and wrath of battle. Bravest of the brave, most generous of the generous, never had a country more faithful friends than you.' What had begun as raw peasant recruits ended up through the disciplines of army life to the development of human virtues of the highest order. What a tremendous testimonial that would be for God's divisions!

The apostle Paul uses this metaphor of soldiering as he pens his farewell letter to his beloved Timothy: 'Endure hardship with us like a good soldier of Christ Jesus. No one serving as a soldier gets involved in civilian affairs – he wants to please his commanding officer'.[1] The image he has in mind of course is the Roman Legions, every bit the hardened fighting units of today's Gurkhas. This is not the first time he has urged Timothy to draw on this metaphor. In his first letter he has exhorted him to 'wage the good warfare' and 'fight the good fight'.[2] Significantly perhaps, Paul holds up the army model to a man not unlike my school friend in temperament, certainly not one of nature's warriors. Elsewhere his writings are littered with military imagery: we have spiritual weapons for invisible foes, we are to don the armour of righteousness wielding the sword of the Spirit, we are to be inspired by ancient warriors and stand firm in the victory of Christ.

Throughout scripture, the references to warfare abound literally, metaphorically, and allegorically. In the book of Revelation, the rebellious forces of Satan tremble and capitulate before the vision of one

---

[1] 2 Timothy 2: 3, 4
[2] I Timothy 1: 18 & 6: 12

called Faithful and True who rides out to wage war along with the armies of heaven. Kings and generals and mighty men fail as the One with the sword from his mouth treads the winepress of the fury of the wrath of God. Little wonder the appropriate exhortation throughout the book to the followers of such a King is to be overcomers.

David Watson, writing the foreword to Richard Foster's book *Celebration of Discipline,* said, 'It is commonplace today to speak of the battle of the eighties to be between Islam, Marxism, and Third World Christianity. Western Christianity is, on the whole, too flabby to do anything about it.'[3] The only adjustment needed, I suspect, in that statement, reflecting the passage of another generation, would be the significant decline of Marxism and the even more prominent challenge of Islam. Sadly, Western Christianity, despite many promising claims of revival, remains flabby.

Flabby, however, is not what soldiers of Christ are supposed be. Flabby is a distinctly inappropriate adjective for those identifying themselves as servants of God. Flabby describes humans who are out of shape. What is needed is a bit of square-bashing, some army-style discipline, and even a bit of sergeant-major yelling – though if we can do it without the latter I think we should try! Paul's recipe was, 'I beat my body and make it my slave so that after I have preached to others, I myself will not be disqualified for the prize.'

Growing-up – Discipline and Transformation

This is a critical moment in the argument. Most Christian workers will be happy with this chapter to this point, but from this point, we could all spin off in very different directions. The call to discipline can appeal or repel for all the wrong reasons; you might even agree for the right reasons and promise to start tomorrow! The flesh in its myriad manifestations likes nothing better than to put on a show, including aspects of discipline, even if it be for our ego only. In such cases, the benefit is marginal. What I invite you to consider is both the potential when undertaken in the right spirit and the consequences of neglect.

John Ortberg, in his book on spiritual disciplines, helpfully uses another of Paul's metaphors, that of athletics, and so develops the idea

---

[3] Richard Foster, *Celebration of Discipline*, (London: Hodder & Stoughton, 1981).

of training. He imagines a person selected by computer who turns out to be perfectly designed and created to win the marathon at the next Olympic Games. The response to such selection being a sense of destiny, the awareness that it was for this they were born. But he continues, 'Then it dawns on you: Right now you cannot run a marathon. More to the point, you cannot run a marathon *even if you really tried hard.* ... If you are really serious about seizing this chance of a lifetime, you will have to enter into a lifetime of training. You must arrange your life around certain practices that will enable you to do what you cannot do now by willpower alone. When it comes to running a marathon, you must train, not merely try.'[4] Peterson makes the same point when he says, '*Askesis* is to spirituality what a training regimen is to an athlete'.[5]

Even when performers are at the peak of their careers, there is still the need for regular practice. If Andrea Bocelli stopped singing between performances or Wayne Rooney gave up training between games, they would soon be out of favour with their public. The fact is that anything worth doing requires application and wise training, both to bring us to maximum condition and then to sustain that, thus avoiding the onset of the flab.

Discipline, training, and practice develop and change us; it puts on muscles in the right places and infuses stamina, transforming both our physical and psychological profile: as in the physical so in the spiritual. The goal of spiritual discipline is conformity to Christ-likeness, 'My dear children, for whom I am again in the pains of childbirth until Christ is formed in you.'[6] Elsewhere Paul speaks of 'being transformed by the renewing of your minds'[7] and both verbs 'formed' and 'transformed' derive from the Greek verb *metamorphoo* from which we have the English word metamorphosis. The best picture of metamorphosis is that of the butterfly emerging from its chrysalis, a slow evolving process of change that issues in beauty and freedom. John Stott draws attention to the fact that '*metamorphoo* is the verb used by Matthew and Mark of the transfiguration of Jesus....

---

[4] John Ortberg, *The Life You've Always Wanted*, (Grand Rapids: Zondervan, 2002) p. 42
[5] Peterson, *Under the Unpredictable Plant*, p .74
[6] Galatians 4: 19
[7] Romans 12: 2

A complete change came over him. His whole body became translucent.... As for the change which takes place in the people of God... it is fundamental transformation of character and conduct, away from the standards of the world and into the image of Christ himself'.[8]

One of God's delightful acts of grace is to bring people into our lives who embody and model biblical truth for us. Not that they are perfect, but they become an inspiration, usually at a formative phase of life. Billy Graham[9] pays tribute in his biography to the early influence of Billy Sunday; the evangelist Mordecai Ham, under whose ministry he committed his life to Christ; and Dr. Bob Jones, his first college principle. One of Philip Yancey's most fascinating books, I think, is *Soul Survivor,*[10] where he sketches twelve people who have helped him 'recover from church abuse' and discover spiritual authenticity. Irenaeus, the second century theologian, said, 'The glory of God is a person fully alive' and that is the kind of people we instinctively are on the lookout for.

One of God's gifts to me in this respect has been Campbell McAlpine. Called from a background of army and business, Campbell exercised an itinerant prophetic teaching ministry for over fifty years. His influence extended to every continent and ushered the mighty and the lowly into the presence of God. His pattern of life was to rise very early and spend the first hours of every day in Bible meditation and prayer. He had the grace to admit that he never found discipline difficult (which probably marks him out as different from most us for a start), but that pattern shaped and formed the man. Little wonder he became friend and father in God to hundreds around the world. What is significant about Campbell, and others who similarly inspire, is that they are people who would eschew the very thought of themselves as worthy role-models.

The Classic Disciplines

'Superficiality is the curse of our age. The doctrine of instant satisfaction is a primary spiritual problem. The desperate need today is

---

[8] John R.W.Stott, The *Message of Romans,* BST Series (Leicester: IVP, 1994) p. 321
[9] Billy Graham, *Just As I Am,* (New York: Harper, 1998) chapter two.
[10] Philip Yancey, *Soul Survivor*, (London: Hodder & Stoughton, 2001)

not for a greater number of intelligent people, or gifted people, but for deep people…. The classical Disciplines of the spiritual life call us to move beyond the surface living into the depths.'[11] This famous quotation by Richard Foster opens his book *Celebration of Discipline*. He explains in a footnote that he uses the term 'classical' not merely because these disciplines are ancient, though they have been practised over the centuries, but because they are central to experiential Christianity. He adds that in one form or another all of the spiritual masters have affirmed the necessity of the Disciplines.

It is not my purpose to re-teach all those disciplines here, nor is it necessary as there are many fine books devoted to their exposition.[12] Before looking at just three areas of good disciplined practice relating to the work of the ministry, I simply want to recognise here that every discipline is a response to the invitation of Jesus to spend time with him. They must never be seen as exercises isolated from intimate fellowship with Christ. Depth in the sense called for by Foster is discovered as we answer that invitation from Jesus positively and seriously.

Mark, in his gospel, records, 'Jesus went up on a mountainside and called to him those he wanted, and they came to him. He appointed twelve – designating them apostles – that they might be with him and that he might send them out to preach and to have authority to drive out demons.'[13] Jesus here speaks of a twofold purpose born of his invitation: to be with him and to be sent out. I have previously talked about priestly ministry in inner and outer court and 'carrying the aroma of God'. Here we have it again: service among people should flow from time spent in God's presence. Jesus built this rhythm into his training of the disciples, for he would frequently draw them away from the crowds to spend time with himself. This became an ingrained habit, so that when the workload increased in the early church, they made the executive decision to hand over food distribution to others to be able to give attention to prayer and the ministry of the word. Life became

---

[11] Foster p. 1

[12] Foster for example devotes chapters to the Inward Disciplines: meditation, prayer, fasting, and study; the Outward Disciplines: simplicity, solitude, submission, and service; the Corporate Disciplines: confession, worship, guidance, and celebration.

[13] Mark 3: 13, 14

arranged around times and activities spent with Jesus – and that is what spiritual disciplines are all about. As Bonhoeffer put it in the negative, 'Christianity without discipleship is always Christianity without Christ.'

But how on earth can this occur in the throb of pastoral life with the phone ringing, the funeral directors knocking, sermons to prepare, committees to plan and attend, deadlines to meet, one hundred and one things demanding attention, and all with spouses to love and babies who wake in the night? What's to do when life is manic in the manse and there are vigilantes in the vestry, when the deacons are diabolical and the members are moribund, so that even the call to come aside sounds like a satanic seduction to self-indulgence? Answer: come aside and give up running the universe for a while; you will be amazed at how well churches can do without us!

This will involve us looking at three areas of discipline.

The Discipline of Time

For a happy heart

George Müller of Bristol is rightly honoured for his orphanages, his examples of faith, and his support of Hudson Taylor and many of the CIM missionaries. Müller retired at the age of seventy and spent the next seventeen years as an itinerant evangelist. He suffered the loss of daughter and wife yet evidently lived a joyful and fulfilled life. He was once asked his secret to such a long and happy life, to which he replied 'the first great and primary business to which I attend every day is to have my soul happy in the Lord'.

It was Nehemiah who enunciated the truth, 'the joy of the Lord is your strength'.[14] Sadly, for many of us in ministry, the dominant emotions are more likely to be anger or frustration. When those are to the fore, we quickly lose freshness in ministry, and the results are an ineffective and unfruitful season. At such times, we feel the weight of the world on our shoulders and can all too easily explode in the face of the mildest provocation. We become hard to live with at home, where our defences are apt to be lower to the pain of spouse and family. I wonder how our families would rate our 'fruit of the Spirit level' just

---

[14] Nehemiah 8: 10

now? I dread to think what my family might have said at times and can only be grateful, especially for Marilyn's extraordinary patience – I am convinced I am her greatest means of grace!

Joy is a great defence; its buoyancy can sustain through the pressures that rise. Joy, however, can be both elusive and ephemeral, 'for joy and happiness are not at our command, and cannot be turned on and off like a tap'.[15] What we are able to do is obey the call to 'Rejoice in the Lord always. I will say it again: Rejoice'.[16] The traditional evangelical mode most encouraged, and rightly so, is the use of prayer and the word of God. However, there may well be times when we need to get ourselves into a state of mind ready for those practices. Many years ago I was at a pastors' conference where Dr. Martyn Lloyd-Jones was asked what he did on the occasions when he felt dispirited. I suspect his answer surprised some, for he answered, 'I listen to some Beethoven or, if I'm particularly low, Mozart.' Ajith Fernando, a church planter in his native Sri Lanka, speaking at the UK Evangelical Missionary Alliance conference in 1997 said, 'At this time (of great pressure), I developed the discipline of walking, sometimes two or three miles, until I felt the joy of the Lord return'.[17] For others it will be meditating on the wonders of nature. In today's parlance, 'whatever it takes!'

One of my favourite pictures of Jesus is the little snapshot Luke gives us at the return of the seventy-two, 'At that time Jesus full of joy through the Holy Spirit said, "I praise you Father, Lord of heaven and earth, because you have hidden these things from the wise and learned and revealed them to little children."'[18] Frequently known as a man of sorrows and acquainted with grief, this shows perhaps his more general state, full of joy in the Holy Spirit. Picture the wide smile on his face, his laugh, the tilt of his head heavenward, his raised hands, and the skip to his feet: an inexpressible and glorious joy. That same man lives in us by his Spirit, full of joy, and our happy task is to draw from his well.

So 'whatever it takes' and what it will take is time. Perhaps not long but some, for the sustaining of a happy heart is too important a

---

[15] John Stott commenting on 1 Thessalonians 5: 16, *The Message of Thessalonians*, BST series, (Leicester: IVP, 1991) p. 124

[16] Philippians 4: 4

[17] Ajith Fernando p. 20

[18] Luke 10: 21

dynamic to get squeezed out. C. S. Lewis reminded us that joy is the serious business of heaven! And long before Lewis was so quotable, the wisest of preachers wrote, 'A cheerful heart has a continual feast'.[19] No stereotypes at this point please! A grinning jack-ass is not the answer. Authenticity is essential, for each of us joy will be known and experienced uniquely, but be assured, this is the new birthright for all. The alternative is to become the Eyore of the Christian community, and if my pastoral experience is anything to go by, there are one or two claimants to that role already.

For a nourished mind

Another lovely cameo of Jesus is of him sitting among the rabbis at his bar mitzvah in Jerusalem. There he was engaging the traditional Jewish practice of studying Torah, asking questions, debating answers and interpretations. Rabbinic debate over texts and interpretations continued throughout his ministry where he revealed layers and textures of understanding that spoke an authority beyond anything conjured by the scribes and Pharisees. His teaching and debate, however, was contextually congruent and would have fitted in not just with the Torah scholars of his day but every succeeding generation. Jesus had an exceedingly well-nourished mind, not just in scripture but all the schools of thought surrounding their interpretation.

This devotion to study is widely recognised as characteristic of the Jewish people. Chief Rabbi Jonathan Sacks recounts the following incident in proof: 'I was in hospital recovering from a serious operation. An elderly patient – someone I knew from a neighbouring community – heard that I was there. He came rushing into my room. I thought he was going to wish me well, or ask about my illness, or swap notes about doctors or nurses. Nothing of the kind. With a huge smile on his face, he produced a volume of the Talmud and said, "How wonderful to have you here, Rabbi Sacks. Now we can study together!"' [20]

In training his men, Jesus showed the necessity of this discipline. 'He said to them, "Therefore every teacher of the law who has been instructed about the kingdom of heaven is like the owner of a house

---

[19] Proverbs 15: 15
[20] Jonathan Sacks, *Celebrating Life*, (London: Fount, HarperCollins, 2000) p. 40

who brings out of his storeroom new treasures as well as old.'"[21] Treasures of truth both old and new have to be mined out, cut, polished, and set in a store that they may serve to adorn the knowledge of King and Kingdom.

Confession time: I am playing catch-up with my reading for the many wasted years when it was summer time in the church 'and the livin' was easy'; years when we were exceedingly busy in the heydays of renewal but, like Mark Twain's Mississippi, a mile wide and two inches deep. If we are not careful, intellectual rigour can depart at the same speed as numbers arrive or the pressures increase. A little success can be a dangerous thing, for what's good for the ego is bad for the soul and can in the long run cause ministry deprivation. Beware the barrenness of a busy life! Having said that, God's grace is a wonderful thing, and it has been fun catching up on the reading. Meeting up with friends old and new through their pages is invigorating and humbling – it both inspires and reminds you how little you know. But again it takes the discipline of time, of writing it into the diary, of blocking out a day, of meeting up with like-minded friends, of finding a book mentor. But isn't that what Jesus did?

Jonathan Sacks on the pages referred to earlier tells of the habit of the faithful in the towns of the *shtelt* to seize any moment to share thoughts of the Torah. 'They would share some insight one or other had heard from the town scholar, a novel interpretation of a biblical verse perhaps, or a new perspective on a rabbinical text. For a moment they would forget the poverty and insecurity around them and instead be lifted into a brief, exhilarating flight of the mind and the spirit.' Being in touch with the rich treasures in books lifts us out of the demands of the instant and gives the perspective of the ages; it draws on other conversations with God and settles something of an eternal beat into our souls.

We live in a day when fewer and fewer Christians are reading books – time for pastors to show a lead.

For a healthy body

For a number of years we ran church treks to Israel. The idea was not so much to visit the shaky shrines as to walk the land to get the feel of its topography. Although Israel is a relatively small country, the

---

[21] Matthew 13: 52

distances are significant when you have to walk them. It made me realise just how fit Jesus and the disciples would have been as they traversed the land, moving from village to village and the cycle of trips between Galilee and Jerusalem. Just as Jesus is seen as having a happy heart and nourished mind, so he would have had a very healthy body. And it would not just have been the exercise. We live in a day when care for the body beautiful has almost reached idolatrous proportions, but what it has done is to make us aware of what constitutes good health: proper rest, healthy diet, and regular exercise. All these are evident in the lifestyle of Jesus. I'm not suggesting that Jesus would have set about these things intentionally, but the rhythms of Jewish life with Sabbaths, feasts, fasts, and dietary guidelines would have shaped such. Interestingly and significantly, today one of the countries with the lowest incidence of heart disease per capita in the world is Israel.

Paul reminds us that we are to resist the squeezing influence of the world around us, which in our day would be both the extreme of overpreoccupation with diets and gyms on the one hand and the tendency to obesity on the other. The apostle also acknowledges the place of physical training, 'For physical training is of some value',[22] – though in fairness it does seem grudgingly given! Stewardship of the body as the temple of the Holy Spirit, however, is surely not only proper for our own sense of well being but also respects the call and demands of ministry, which can only be undertaken properly when we are fit.

Each of us needs to find our own way here, but perhaps I can commend the virtues of the humble bicycle. Some years ago, the family clubbed together to get me a bike for my birthday, and I've loved it ever since. As well as providing gentle exercise (that's the way I ride), it has the virtue of the spiritual discipline of slowing and the rejection of another of the world's squeezes: that of hurry. Carl Jüng wrote, 'Hurry is not *of* the devil; hurry *is* the devil.'[23] Cycling from house to house, home to church or to the shops changes the pace, eliminates the curse of multi-tasking, gives time to reflect, and makes contact with pedestrians through a smile or wave, so more realistically touching the patch of our incarnation. And if all that does not

---

[22] 1 Timothy 4: 8
[23] Quoted by Ortberg p. 77

commend the humble bike, we can now claim cycle allowance per mile from the Inland Revenue on our tax returns!

Along with exercise comes the question of rest, where again Jesus has much to model for us. When there is so much in the gospels indicating Jesus' pattern of withdrawal from the crowds and providing rest for tired disciples, it may strike as odd to ask what was Jesus doing on his visit to the region of Tyre and Sidon (Mark 7: 24–31)? His ministry was to the lost sheep of the house of Israel, yet here he is way outside the borders of Israel, far to the north of the northern boundaries of the tribe of Dan, parallel with Damascus, and entering a house intent on secrecy. Could it be that this was intended as rest, a holiday even, before the final events of the Galilee ministry? From Peter's Caesarea Philippi confession (shortly following the trip to Tyre), via the mount of Transfiguration, there would be an inescapable momentum that would lead him to Jerusalem and Calvary – was this the last chance to prepare in quiet? It certainly shows Jesus in charge of his own timing and looking for respite from the demands of crowd and Sanhedrin. If the rhythm of rest and withdrawal was necessary for him, how much more should we take it seriously, learn to slow the drives of the Protestant work ethic, resist the temptations to any Messiah complex, and take regular rest?

The discipline of time then is to encourage muscle and fight the flab, to produce a happy heart, a nourished mind, and a healthy body. Peterson suggests that pastors can become overly busy for two reasons: vanity, whereby we seek to impress others with our importance, or laziness, whereby we allow others to determine our time instead of resolutely doing it ourselves.[24] By taking control of our time, we free ourselves for the truly important and not the merely demanding, including taking proper care of ourselves.

Discipline of Boundaries[25]

When I was at Spurgeon's, I wish someone had told me what, as a pastor, I was and was not responsible for. It has taken many weary

---

[24] Eugene H .Peterson, *The Contemplative Pastor*, (Grand Rapids: Eerdmans, 1989) p. 18.

[25] Recommended reading here is Dr. Henry Cloud and Dr. John Townsend, *Boundaries, subtitled: When to Say Yes, When to Say No, To Take Control of Your Life* (Grand Rapids: Zondervan, 1992)

years to work it out and even now do not always find it easy to live with the distinction. In counselling terminology, of course, these are known as boundary issues. Living with healthy boundaries *vis-à-vis* the flock is essential for inner health and peace of mind, but I have come to see that even with understanding, there must also be a discipline to maintain it.

In simple terms, a boundary defines me. It defines who I am, what is of me, and what I am responsible for, and it does so by distinguishing that from you. A boundary tells me where I end and you begin, and recognising that gives us freedom. Knowing this boundary enables us to take ownership of our lives and be in a place to show others how to take ownership of their own lives. As pastors, we may have various levels of responsibility toward members of the flock, but never are we to take responsibility for their lives: only they can do this. Confusion at this point makes life intolerable for the pastor and breeds immaturity in others; co-dependency is always unhealthy.

Jesus is again the role model to whom we look and to whom we are being changed. Mark recounts in some detail the incident in Gadara where Jesus delivers the man possessed by the legion of spirits, then permits them to enter the herd of pigs feeding on the nearby hillside.[26] Not surprisingly, the people of the region (especially other pig farmers) ask Jesus to leave. Not so the man delivered. As Jesus is getting into the boat, he begs Jesus to let him go with him. Jesus refuses. What is going on here? Has Jesus ceased to look for followers? Could it be that the man has been controlled by other forces for so long that he is looking for another to possess him, take control and be responsible for him? Jesus says in effect, 'I will not control you like these demons did; I will not be your guru; you must learn to take control of your own life, for this is the essence of your humanity.' Significantly in other stories around this event, Mark records Jesus controlling natural elements, demonic forces, and the general environment, but never does he seek to dominate human personality or emotions. So for example, he calms the storm but not the disciples fear: they alone can do that. He is with them in the storm and that is the key to overcoming their fear, but they have to apply the implications for themselves.

---

[26] Mark 5: 1–20

Another classic example is Jesus' encounter with the rich young ruler.[27] Faced with the challenge of the call, this personable young man cannot rise to the implications of full surrender and goes away sad. Mark has poignantly told us that Jesus, looking at him, loved him, but notwithstanding this emotional connection and spark between them, he allows the young man to walk away without any attempt to persuade him otherwise. Jesus respected his boundary.

In these stories, Jesus avoids common boundary violations. With the man from Gadara he avoids the problem of compliance, which would have been to go along with the request rather than confront it with a firm 'no', which he did. With both the same man and the rich young ruler, he avoided becoming a controller, violating their boundaries and creating dependency. In effect, Jesus forces these people to grow up, to take themselves seriously. He shows them a respect that they would not always have for themselves. Incidentally, I suspect more clarity on what God expects us to do and what we have a right to expect him to do would help many believers – especially in the realm of prayer!

What then are we pastors responsible for? Negatively, Ezekiel voiced God's dismay at the failure of Israel's shepherds in these terms: they failed to care for the flock, not strengthening the weak, healing the sick, binding the injured, not searching for strays or providing food. [28] Positively, we may say we are to provide a loving, supportive environment for growth, where the means of grace in corporate worship, ministry of word and sacrament and prayer are available. If appropriated, these have the grace and power to transform lives, but, and this is an all important but, beyond making a good job of providing those things, we dare not go. No man can be forced, coerced, or worried into the grace of God by a pastor, and if we allow such things to drive us, they will destroy us. If Jesus did not win them all, it's certain we can't and won't. Holding that perspective requires the discipline of good boundaries, where we find our peace and fulfilment in God himself, not ministry 'success'. Self-control is not just a fruit of the Spirit; it is a specific criterion for leadership: 'a leader must be self-controlled'.[29]

---

[27] Mark 10: 17–31
[28] Ezekiel 36
[29] 1 Timothy 3: 2

Discipline of Faith

Strictly speaking, faith is not a discipline; that is it is not an ordered, regular practice or abstinence. Faith, however, does have to be sustained at the heart of all ministry, hence its inclusion here.

Faith as a living dynamic central to ministry has a number of elements. It recognises that the work is Christ's, that it is his ultimate responsibility, of his initiating, at his direction, and dependent on his fulfilment. Our part is to live out our calling faithfully and look to him to do that which no man can do, not least open blind eyes, soften hard hearts, and bend stubborn wills. At the end, therefore, only he will get the glory: 'For from him and through him and to him are all things. To him be the glory for ever!'[30] As pastors, leaders, and workers, we should be familiar with these basic tenets of faith as far as the work is concerned: woe betide us if not, for 'whatever does not proceed from faith is sin'![31]

I want to move the discipline of faith closer to home. Soon after beginning in our first church, I was talking with the then Baptist Southern Area Superintendent, Vivian Evans, a man much loved by the men he served. He let slip that when pastors came to see him it invariably had to do with one of three subjects: sex, money, or the diaconate. Well, this is about money.

Back in the late 1960s as a chartered surveyor I was earning £1200 per annum, which, along with Marilyn's salary as a teacher, provided a princely income. We were buying our home and living comfortably – for about a year. While at Spurgeons, I qualified for a maintenance grant of £850 per annum – those were the days! We lived well as Marilyn continued to teach. On accepting the call to Durrington, the stipend was £750 per annum and Marilyn was not encouraged to teach, indeed she could not have as there was now another mouth to feed. We went onto family benefit and quickly began to learn the disciplines of faith.

Though many denominations and churches are taking a more realistic view of stipends these days, financial pressures remain for many clergy. These are not just personal and domestic (i.e., the disparity of remuneration against the cost of living). We also face the

---

[30] Romans 11: 36
[31] Romans 14: 23

challenge of sustaining ministry in the midst of a congregation where there are likely to be some, if not many, affluent people. Assuming that the more base temptation of pure envy is avoided, more subtle temptations remain. The rich have every right to expect hospitality from us as the poor, but they do have a way of arriving in BMWs and talking about the Barbados holiday. Their wives casually wear designer labels while ours parade homemade – a disparity which takes extraordinary grace to span. Some people of wealth can expect to be treated with deference and respect and exert an influence unrelated to spiritual maturity; this can be hard to resist. Friends are those who among other things play together, and there will be times when friendship is curtailed as we cannot afford to join in some of their pastimes. Then there is the enemy of our soul who loves to parade such 'injustices' before us, and the tiny bit of us still not entirely sanctified is capable of putting on quite a show when it comes to money: the little green-eyed monster adorned with pound signs.

But this too is of God, ruthless perfecting to raise us to a different level. What we are invited to is the discipline of faith, which we learn at home but then becomes the ground from which we can teach others.

In those early years we learned three simple lessons, not in the classroom of academia but at the raw edge of physical need. The first was to look to God as our source of supply, to know Him as Jehovah Jirah.[32] Let me select just one story from our family album. The stipend paid to us provided what we needed for just over three weeks in any month, the remainder was our learning time. Marilyn's cousin needed a break and at short notice arrived on our doorstep with her two young children – would you guess toward the end of the month. We were not about to turn her away or give her ground to think poorly of the God we were serving, so we simply took them all in – three extra mouths to feed when we were not sure how our own four would be! We had the policy to only talk to God about it, so we did in earnest. The week turned out as an extraordinary demonstration of the way he can provide: food left on the door step, vegetables from someone's allotment, a few vouchers from Sainsbury's, and a couple of small gifts. The *pièce de resistance* came on the Friday morning

---

[32] I am presently reading *Free of Charge* by Miroslav Volf, published by Zondervan, and the temptation is to simply quote him so helpful is his addressing the subject of receiving and giving; a book warmly commended.

when I got out of bed and saw a bag of potatoes at the junction of our drive and the main road. The bag had obviously slipped off the back of a lorry, split, and rolled its contents down the gutter, which I of course had to clear up to get the car out. The children were sure an angel flicked it off as the lorry had turned the corner opposite. Marilyn's cousin observed that we seemed to love potatoes but otherwise noticed nothing during the time of her stay.

As we searched the scriptures, we quickly were brought to see the interrelatedness of giving and receiving, both as aspects of God's nature and being. So out of gratitude and obedience we learned to give. What eventually we observed was the way this pattern of life began to seep into the church. We learned that 'the reciprocal exchange of gifts expresses and nourishes a community of love. Take reciprocity out of gift giving, and community disintegrates into discrete individuals.'[33] There have been some who have encouraged an almost legalistic, mechanistic application of Jesus' word in Luke 6: 38, 'Give and it will be given to you.' This spirit must surely be resisted. The heart of our call is being conformed to the likeness of this wonderfully generous God who spreads his gifts abroad with liberality just because that is what he is like, without thought or calculation of return.

The third lesson was the one Paul speaks of when he testifies, 'I have learned to be content whatever the circumstances. I know what it is to be in need, and I know what it is to have plenty. I have learned the secret of being content in any and every situation, whether well-fed or hungry, whether living in plenty or in want.'[34] One of the things our son-in-law Jon says is that soldiers, when they are on exercises, are told to eat whenever food is available and sleep at every opportunity as you never know when the next chance might come! That may be rather extreme for everyday living, but the principle of one day at a time certainly was the guide Jesus laid down in the Sermon on the Mount. This focuses us again on faith in the goodness and faithfulness of our loving Father and develops in us a discipline fit for such a walk. Contentment rests on the impermanence of any season in life; this is the grace of God, filling us with hope and fitting us for eternity.

---

[33] Volf p. 87
[34] Philippians 4: 11–12

Having to learn faith for things as basic as food and drink roots faith in the physical, practical, and observable world and steers us away from faith as an unprovable metaphysical comfort. I have limited my examples to such basics; others could be given. It's my conviction that Father wants us to learn to trust him, to know his utter dependability, and he will teach us this at a domestic level so we can speak with conviction and authenticity in the public arena.

One fascinating spin-off from this lesson is the way in which it has made a lasting impression on our children, who now bring up their own families on the same principles!

Disciplined Soldiers of Christ

In addition to the 'enemies' of communism and Islam referred to earlier by David Watson, there is of course the ever-present, insidious, malign influences of the present day 'isms': materialism, consumerism, humanism, individualism, hedonism; specialities of the thief who comes 'to steal, kill and destroy.'[35] The battle we face is not just against flesh and blood but is 'your enemy the devil who prowls around like a roaring lion looking for someone to devour.'[36] The easiest prey will always be the weak, out of condition, flabby specimens around the edges of the herd – what a tragedy if they happen to be to be those who should be leading.

Some eighteen months after the fall of the communist regime in Romania, a few of us were having coffee in a hotel lounge in Cluj-Napoca with Big John. John was one of the leaders of *Oastea Domnului,* the Lord's Army, an evangelical movement within the Romanian Orthodox Church. He was telling stories of the communist years: the privations of the people, the arrests, questioning and imprisonment of the movements' leaders, the lack of educational and career prospects for their members, and the multitude of petty discriminations they faced daily all because of their known faith. The dedication of the members of the church was clearly something he was very proud of: ordinary peasant people with an uncompromising faith in Christ suffering a lifestyle of injustice as a consequence. It was moving to hear of the courage of the saints as they smuggled bibles

---

[35] John 10: 10
[36] 1 Peter 5: 8

around the country, gathered surreptitiously for prayer meetings, or smuggled food to families whose heads of households were in prison. We chatted about the new freedoms and especially the joy of fellowship with many from the West. Then he paused and with a deep Eastern European sigh said, 'But you know, for all the blessings of this freedom, I wish for the old days'. He went on to elaborate, 'You see in those days people joined the church for Christ. Already today just eighteen months later we do not know why they join. When there is a price to pay you know it's real.'

Big John said, 'When there is a price to pay you know it's real'. Putting that the other way round is also true: you know it's real when pastors and people are prepared to pay the price of practised discipline and careful living in response to God's grace.

Of Soldiers, Corps, and Regiments

We have drawn on the image of soldiering in this chapter, just one of the biblical models of discipline. But soldiers are not trained in isolation or for individual battle. The effectiveness of soldiers is only found in their corporate setting. So in the next chapter, we turn to the gift of fellowship and the necessity for us to find rich and meaningful friends, for that is a vital grace in ministry.

Underpinning

Exploration

- What in this chapter did you agree with?
- What did you disagree with?
- Did anything in this chapter make you angry?
- Using the classic disciplines as invitations from the Lord Jesus to come aside and spend time with him, can you date when you last gave time to him in:
  - Quiet biblical meditation
  - Fasting
  - Taking a retreat
  - Reflective prayer
  - Reading and study unrelated to the work
  - Solitude

Excavation –*recommended for digging deeper*

- *The Life You've Always Wanted,* sub-titled, *Spiritual Disciplines for Ordinary People,* by John Ortberg, published by Zondervan

Exchange – *new foundation for old*

- A prayer by Sir Francis Drake (c. 1539–96), originally ordained deacon, taking holy orders and appointed 'among seamen in the King's Navy to read prayers to them'; later as Queen Elizabeth's vice-admiral played a part in the defeat of the Spanish Armada:

O Lord God, when you give your servants

To endeavour any great matter,

Grant us also to know that it is not the beginning,

But the continuing of the same,

Until it be thoroughly finished,

Which yields the true glory. [37]

---

[37] Quoted by Louise and R. T. Kendall, *Great Christian Prayers*, (London: Hodder& Stoughton, 2000) for 27 January p. 374

Chapter 8

The Company We Enjoy

How good and pleasant it is when brothers live together in unity!…
For there the Lord bestows His blessing, life for ever more.

Psalm 133: 1 & 3

To love another person is to see the face of God.[1]

Isolation

The Word of God says that it is not good for man to be alone,[2] yet
many in leadership are just that. Isolation can occur in various ways,
three at least spring to mind. It can be *geographically enforced,* as in
the case of a missionary serving in some remote region. It can be
culturally imposed, as in communities where tradition dictates that the
leader does not make friends among the people he leads. It can be
personality induced, where the individual temperament favours
introversion or is otherwise fearful of allowing others too close. And
all this can occur despite the potential of our restored humanity for a
place in community.

Even in good situations, where the buck stops tends to single
out an individual. One of our church missionaries serving in
Belgium has recently taken on the pastoral leadership of a church
where he had been the youth pastor. He is finding the step-up
demanding and challenging, but what he has found most difficult is
the way so many of the church now relate to him differently. It was
not something he had anticipated. Previously he was friends with
them; now he is 'the Pastor' and fills a different role in their lives.
While some of that may be cultural, the fact is that any senior

---

[1] Line from Les Misérables
[2] Genesis 2: 18

leadership position in any culture carries a unique burden that marks them out. Isolation may be the last thing a leader wants, but by definition, being set apart for the work of ministry produces that. The danger of isolation, however created, is that it leads to the experience of aloneness, and aloneness is a state of heart that has little to do with immediate company. It is rightly said the loneliest place is in a crowd, and when the crowd is a church, the sense of isolation is only aggravated, for we all know that's where Christians are supposed to feel connected and feel they belong. The danger then of aloneness is a vulnerability to temptation. So great is the human craving for touch and contact that lonely people are prey to the lure to seek it in inappropriate or illicit ways. Alternatively, it may be expressed in an unhealthy expectation of a spouse to meet all the individual's emotional and physical needs, putting unreasonable pressure on the marriage.

Recent work by Robin Hay, principal at Redcliffe Missionary Training College, concludes, 'Research on missionary attrition has shown that a "low sense of organisational connectedness" is an important factor contributing to the early departure of the missionaries.'[3] What is true in a missionary situation is equally true of ministry in the local church in any location.

It is not good for man to be alone!

Prequel

They were dotted around the crowd, but when the remark was made, the three intuitively sought each other's eyes, nodded in agreement, and edged away from the group surrounding their young leader. 'You up for it, guys?' asked the first. The wry grin on both sunburned faces was all that was needed for confirmation as they made their way to don simple armour and swords.

'You're just trying to get me killed again,' chided the second as they emerged from the cave – his cheeky grin belying his sincerity.

'We always knew that might be God's will when we signed up with the young pretender', replied the first, serious as always.

---

[3] Robin Hay, *Worth Keeping – Global Perspectives on Best Practice in Missionary Retention,* (Pasadena, CA: William Carey Press, 2007) p. 164

'But this is a bit different,' said the third with enthusiasm. 'Just imagine, breaking into your own home town that's no longer your home and stealing your own stuff!'

The harsh desert years had forged the three into a formidable unit. Their characters were as divergent as their physical appearances, but they had developed a bond that marked them out among their fellows. They had shared their fears in the dark and laughed uproariously at them in the light of dawn. They had bound each other's wounds, rallied each other's spirits, defended each other's honour, and teased each other mercilessly. Increasingly, they understood that the God of Israel was doing a new thing, and the trick was to live with both old and new until God's timing gave the breakthrough. They learned both the restraint of their companion and his release of passion as he poured out his pain to his God in song. Many a night they had joined his rich baritone voice as they sang to the stars and the heavens. They had tested each other's strength of arms and between them discovered the mystery of 'one putting to flight a thousand and two ten thousand'. Theirs was the experience, available to all but discovered by few, that life was simply better in every way when shared together.

Early next morning, they crept back into camp carrying the water between them. A mop of curly red hair emerged from a cave, and the three, with exaggerated courtliness, bowed low and presented the pitcher. 'Water, as requested, O king!' they chimed.

Still rubbing the sleep from his eyes, the young leader said with that special blend of reproof and affection, 'Idiots! You could have got yourselves killed!' And with that, he poured the water out on the ground.

'I don't believe it!' groaned the second and made as if his legs would buckle under him. They dissolved into laughter and headed off to where the food was being fried over the fires, with arms round each other's shoulders. And so a new heart was being given to Israel, the old tired heart of lonely, isolated leadership being replaced by a love to die for.

As a chaplain to soldiers was to say many centuries later, 'If human love does not carry a man beyond himself, it is not love. If love is always discreet, always wise, always sensible and calculating, never carried beyond itself, it is not love at all. It may be affection, it may be warmth of feeling, but it has not the true nature of love in it.'[4]

Main Feature

It had been a bad day as far as numbers was concerned. But then our leader didn't usually seem to count heads or notice whether the crowds increased or decreased. Things had started well with the multitude out early, not surprising given the previous day's feast with loaves and fishes. Then things had got a little tetchy with awkward questions thrown at him and his answers clearly proving more and more conceptually difficult for many. Conversation rocked back and forth around the disputes emerging from yesterday's miracle, Moses' manna and his own contribution as the 'bread of life', whatever that meant – no doubt he would explain it later.

Soon it became heated: outright grumbling, challenging accusations, and not a few deeply offended. Outwardly, our leader didn't seem to give ground at all, just drove in with the argument even harder, even accusing them of rank unbelief. Tough talking and no mistake, no ground asked for or given. Not surprisingly, the discontent became palpable, the atmosphere turned sour, and folk started to drift away muttering and gesticulating as they left.

But it was then your heart went out to him. You see. He turned, tears in his eyes, and such a look in his gaze. How to explain that look? Compassion, anger, hurt, longing, and still something more: a look which said 'I need you guys, are you still with me?' For a moment it looked as if his heart was breaking, his lip wobbled and out popped the question: 'You don't want to go too do you?' – the negative revealing his concern, his longing for affirmation, reassurance. What a man, all heart!

Simon banged back the answer we were all feeling. 'Master, to whom would we go? You have the words of real life, eternal life. We've already committed ourselves, confident that you are the Holy One of God.'[5] The look on his face was worth every bit of Peter's speech, such appreciation and love, though even that was suddenly

---

[4] Oswald Chambers, *My Utmost for His Highest* (London: Marshall, Morgan & Scott: 1972) p. 52
[5] John 6: 68, 69 The Message

tempered as his eyes sought out Judas. He made some reference to him as having a devil, and the pain of that realisation convulsed him again, and the whole gamut of conflicting emotions poured through Him. You could have died for him in that moment!

And in a strange way, the moment (and I guess many others like it) bound us to each other as well. For as we empathised with his grieving, we were drawn into a commonalty of existence, a sympathy of purpose, a mutual destiny all drawn from his experiences. We became a band of brothers by sharing his life.

As a college principal would say many centuries later, they became a company of Christ by 'a subduing Presence... an informing Spirit... a reality, power, and right both supernatural and supernational.'[6]

New Release

John just sat there and wept. They were manly tears of pain and loss, for no parent should have to bury their child. Ten days earlier, John and his wife, Jen, had laid to rest their twenty-one year old son, taken by leukaemia and the Lord. Now the Cluster[7] was meeting for the first time after the event. There was little we professional ministers could say to our friend; perhaps what was more important was just being there. John told the story of James' last days and the triumph of the funeral. He knew all about 'not grieving as others who have no hope', but the grief was still profound. As more of the story unfolded, there came a note of pride in John's voice as he reflected to us his son's faith and courage. The humour inherent in even the worst of tragedies came through, and before long, we were chuckling together. Coffee, a comfortable setting, and companionship was again doing its work, and by the time we gently prayed for John, Jen, and the family,

---

[6] P. T. Forsyth, *The Church and The Sacraments,* (London: Longmans, Green and Co, 1917) p. 27

[7] I pay tribute here to the men of our Cluster, a group of Baptist ministers, now friends and colleagues. Our number has inevitably fluctuated over the years, but the men presently involved are John Bridger from Reigate, John Berry now with Elle El Ministries, Paul Gough from Dorking, Graham Holliday from Bexhill, Peter Jackson from Guildford, Ian McFarlane from Great Bookham, Tony Taylor from Walton, Bryan Pickard from Sherringham, and Wally Fahrer in counselling ministry. We meet for half a day approximately every three weeks and annually for a retreat.

the moment had become profoundly cathartic and healing – the presence of Christ was manifestly present; we were on holy ground.

Such depths are not plumbed every time the Cluster meets, but over the many years we have been together, all of us have had occasion to share our angst, unburden our hearts, spill our guts. The needs have been as wide and deep as any group of nine men are likely to produce: wives, children, grandchildren, churches, leadership, and all the emotions of our humanity that are able to be shared due to the level of trust and knowledge built up over time. It's a safe place and a necessary one. In addition to personal support, of course, there is plenty of 'iron sharpening iron', intellectual rigour, worship, and prayer. Occasionally, others have come to teach, preach, or provoke, but the primary activity is always the sharing of hearts in an atmosphere of prayer. There are other groupings both within and without the local church that offer stimulus and support in various ways, but I have come to believe that everyone in ministry needs something like our Cluster for the sake of sanity and perspective!

As a minstrel sang many centuries ago, 'How wonderful, how beautiful, when brothers and sisters get along!... Yes, that's where God commands the blessing, ordains eternal life.'[8]

The *Koinonia* Principle

Koinonia is the Greek New Testament word that is variously translated communion, partnership, fellowship, contribution – all words that have to do with a sharing participation. It covers activities such as being gathered around the Word of God, agreeing together in prayer, or tangibly handling bread and wine. It is a spiritual and intimate dynamic that implies a vulnerable honesty in the sharing of life stories. Historically, many such groups have discovered an energy under the Holy Spirit that has significantly advanced the gospel through both the better resourcing of those believers and the attractiveness of their lifestyle. *Koinonia* is the essence of church life, the core expression of the common life produced by the work of Christ.

In a passage as relevant today as when first penned, P. T. Forsyth urges the recognition that 'the Church's one foundation, and the trust

---

[8] Psalm 133: 1, 3 The Message

of its ministry, is not simply Christ, but Christ crucified. It is not His Person as our spiritual superlative or even as our home and clime, but His Person as our Eternal Redeemer in His blood. It is evangelical.... It is a new creation of God in the Holy Spirit, a spiritual organism, in which we find our soul. Men unite themselves with the Church because they are already united with Christ... the Church is the social and practical response to that Grace.... It is the living organism of the worshippers of Christ, created by His redeeming Gospel in Word and Sacrament.' [9]

This evangelical point of *entrée* into the church, and its high and holy cost, only serves to emphasise that those of us called to pastoral work in the church must enter fully into its *koinonia* potential. If not, we miss the heart of what has been made available in the gospel. It is surely not good enough to encourage others to appropriate the blessing if we are equivocal about embracing it ourselves. Professional detachment here surely cannot be an option. If we attempt to detach ourselves, we can only be some kind of half-Christian which is no Christian. Those who lead others must themselves be living in the good of every aspect of our salvation as best we know how, including *koinonia,* or else we miss the presence of Christ, which comes through it. Bishop Kallistos Ware in his book *The Orthodox Way* quotes T. S. Eliot's *The Waste Land* with a fascinating explanation:

'Who is the third who walks always beside you?

When I count, there are only you and I together

But when I look ahead up the white road

There is always another one walking beside you....

'He (Eliot) explains in the notes that he has in mind the story told of Shackleton's Antarctic expedition: how the party of explorers, when at the extremity of their strength, repeatedly felt that there was *one more member* than could be actually counted.'[10]

This kind of fellowship provides many practical blessings: accountability, friendship, stimulus, challenge, and laughter to name but the obvious. The greatest, however, is the presence of Jesus, which becomes the more manifest *in extremis* when we share the burdens of

---

[9] Forsyth p. 31

[10] Bishop Kallistos Ware, *The Orthodox Way*, (Oxford: Mowbray, 1979) p. 67

call and office with others. As Forsyth put it, we live as part of 'the new creation… a spiritual organism, in which we find our soul.' It may be neither appropriate to share pastoral burdens with many members of the churches we serve, nor for most would it be fair; all the more reason then for searching out those we can enter into this kind of covenant with. For those serious about finding their soul, *koinonia* is an important key.

One of the most impressive paragraphs among many in Billy Graham's autobiography was his honouring of the team. Men such as Cliff Barrows, Walter Smythe, Bev Shea, and Tedd Smith had been with him for at least three decades, and Grady Smith and his brother T. W. shared ties that went back to their youth. The paragraph records, 'In order to do whatever needed to be done, they have subordinated their personal privileges, reordered their priorities, accepted disappointments and endless changes in schedule, stretched their patience, absorbed criticism, and exhausted their energy. They were the Heaven-sent ones who propped me up when I was sagging and often protected me from buffetings that would have scared me or scarred me otherwise. They did not back away from correcting me when I needed it or counselling me with their wisdom when I faced decisions. I'm convinced that without them, burnout would have left me nothing but a charred cinder within five years of the 1949 Los Angles Crusade.'[11]

These men were Billy Graham's cluster, cell, discipleship group, class meeting, house group, or whatever name in any turn of the wheel it may be called. Modelled by Jesus himself, with forerunners like David and his three mighty men, we are invited to experience the power in *koinonia* to the enrichment of life and the experience of exponential strength whereby 'five of you will chase a hundred and a hundred of you will chase ten thousand.'[12]

Honesty – the Place to Start

I have already referred to the two or three people whom God tends to use in shaping our lives. Another of those for me is Rick Howard. Rick was, for over thirty-five years, pastor of the Peninsular Christian Centre in Redwood City, California. His Bible teaching has

[11] Billy Graham p. 781
[12] Leviticus 26: 8

been valued around the world in colleges, universities, and churches. He has become a firm friend, and what has touched and challenged me most over the years is his honesty and vulnerability, which coupled with a passion for biblical truth makes him something of an iconoclast, which is fun! He has written much on the subject of *koinonia* in his book *The Lost Formula of the Early Church*. This is his own story from that book of how his journey into it began.

I was in a desperate way. Some would have credited my feelings to a rather extended midlife crisis or "manopause", as I prefer to call it. I wanted out! *My pastorate was suffocating me, and my marriage and family life were unfulfilling. A young friend called from Los Angeles. He had been a troubled teenager in my youth group years earlier. Now a successful minister, he used to joke, "You helped me grow up so I could help you grow up." So much for logic.*

"Rick," he said, "I want you to fly to New York next week."

I was speechless. He continued, "There's a pastor's conference there, and I think you should go. Elisabeth and I will meet you there."

"Impossible," I said with my usual open-minded approach. "That Sunday is Mother's Day and I'm swamped," but before I could continue my laundry list of excuses, he interrupted.

"This isn't a request. I've already booked the tickets. They're in the mail. See you there."

Now I could begin an almost endless accounting of that conference. I did go! Many of the speakers were on the "Who's Who" of contemporary Christian heroes. They began with an appeal for openness and then told us to turn our chairs in groups of five, excluding anyone we had come with or knew personally.

Boy, was I threatened! I wanted to run, but by default found myself in a tight circle with four strangers. We exchanged names and settled down while the leader gave instructions.

"I know you've come here from all sorts of places geographically and emotionally," he said. "I want you to take time and go around the circle, each giving the reason that brought you to this meeting,"

"Oh, sure," I thought. "Fat chance of that!"

Very simply and sweetly spiritual, the first three fellow preachers from three very different communions shared saccharin sweet reasons for their being at the retreat. I remember phrases like "better minister", "more useful", and "better Christian".

I looked at my shoes and knew I was next. Barely audible, I said, "I'm tired of the ministry, I feel like my marriage is on the rocks, and I'm really mad at God."

What followed would have made an interesting video. Those first three leaned so far back in their chairs, they practically tipped over. They were not only threatened; they were mentally running down the fire escape. So much for honesty.

But the fifth – I think his name was Bruce, and I remember he was a Congregational minister with one of those ordained heads of white hair – leaned in until he was almost in my lap. He placed his hand on my leg, a rather intimate gesture, and said, "That's exactly where I've been for years. But I'm out. I want to be your friend."

Someone had heard me! You can't do handstands, even in Charismatic circles. I at least wanted to yell "Whoopee", however shocking it would be to other Christians.

The sessions ended with handshakes from the first three ministers and a bear-hug from Bruce – a hug that started to change my life. [13]

If you are anything like me, you can know the biblical models, agree the exposition, acknowledge the spiritual truth, and still do nothing about it, which is when God usually has to move in to bridle the wild stallion (or the stubborn mule) in us. We have already alluded to many of the ways he does that in previous chapters. But if he has a scheme designed to maximise our happiness, security, and fruitfulness, do we really think he won't put the bit between our teeth to break us into that place? I'm no horseman, but I understand that the force generated by six horses in harness is tremendous. They have a capacity to create pull significantly greater than the sum of their individual strengths – just another picture of our same truth. As Rick's story shows, however, we do need to begin with honesty, vulnerability, and openness.

Looking back to the events surrounding my failures in the summer of 1985, I have come to the conclusion that a significant, contributing factor was my isolation. I doubt that was obvious to many at the time – though perhaps it was, and I just did not know it! Outwardly, I was at the heart of an exciting renewal in the local

---

[13] Rick C. Howard, *The Lost Formula of the Early Church*, (Woodside CA: Naioth Sound and Publishing, 1996), p. 29 & 30

church. It was a riot of colour and sound, an explosion of life as charismatic renewal transformed a small, dying Baptist church.[14] There was a core team that met together regularly, indeed almost on a daily basis. We prayed, talked, and dreamed. Folk moved homes so that we could be physically close to the church and each other. Our families intermingled, and we shared goods in common. But always there was part of me that held back. I would now understand that to be due in the main to my ongoing battles with lack of self-worth and a general sense of inadequacy. My wrong thinking said, 'If people only knew what I was really like, how little I know, how inadequate I feel, they would leave immediately'. So despite the potential for this level of *koinonia* fellowship that I am talking about now, I was unable to give myself fully to it then. Opportunities existed for it outside the local church as well. In the wake of renewal, a network of church leaders sprang up along the south coast, with many wonderful pastors and leaders participating. It was not as if there were not colleagues who wanted to be there for me, in fact many pressed in only to find themselves rebuffed. My inner world was closed to outsiders, a confusion to myself and a disaster waiting to happen.

Even thinking of my isolation at that time is painful. The loss of all that teeming life, however, faced me with the agony of my true isolation and loneliness. The secret place of the heart had become the reality of life, so everything had to be stripped away, a sever mercy indeed. What the Lord was after was the opening up of that lonely, inadequate, fearful place to allow others in. I cannot tell you how dangerous that felt. I had been playing out the role and doing all I knew how, but now the Lord was pressing me for the last tatters of my protected self. Soon after joining the Cluster, I told the whole story of the previous few years to the guys. The Christian grapevine being what it is, I'm sure they already knew the headlines, but for me to share my regrets and sorrows was a huge unburdening. There were tears aplenty that day, but for me, they were tears of the profoundest therapy. They covered me in their acceptance and graced me with their inclusion. I had found a safe place to be myself, warts and all, and it felt good.

---

[14] The story is told in my book *Let there be Life* (London: Marshalls, 1983), now out of print.

It would be nice to think that one moment of honesty solved the problem. Those knowledgeable of these things recognise that is not the case. The choice to share the fears and inadequacies of our hearts has to be made regularly and determinedly. This kind of covenant relationship does not guarantee openness – ask many a husband or wife! Having a regular point of meeting however helps, for the door is always open. And if the healing presence of Christ is manifest when two or three are gathered together, then the exposing of wounds for his touch, in that safe context, is grace indeed.

Family

Some of the grandchildren had visited over Easter, and after a full day of activity, it was time to quieten them down before supper. I asked Bella if she would like to watch a DVD.

'*My Big Fat Greek Wedding*' she replied, 'it's one of my favourites.'

A teenager already, I thought, at ten years old. So we watched and laughed together. Later, I asked her why she liked the film.

She replied, 'Her family is like ours when we all go camping to Polzeath together.' What she meant was loud, noisy, and all together, three generations, lots of cousins, aunts, and uncles, and totally in your face. I took her comment and movie reference as a huge vote of approval.

My Big Fat Greek Wedding is a film that should be shown to all students preparing for cross-cultural ministry. It depicts the courtship, marriage preparation, and wedding day of Ian Miller, who hails from a conservative, upper middle class American family that is reserved, cool, uptight with the sophistication and superficiality of country club society, and Toula Portokalos, who is Greek American. Her vast family moves as a herd, one huge extended family, in and out of each others' homes, loud, nosey, emotional, warm and generous, taken with food celebrations and old world values of hard work and family loyalty. Mediterranean Greek meets upper crust Anglo. The merging of the two cultures is of course hilarious.

After battling with some aspects of her vibrant family, at the end of the film, Toula says, 'I finally came to realise that my family is big and loud but they are my family. We fight and we laugh and yes, we spit roast on the front yard. But wherever I go and whatever I do, they will always be there.' Every so often Hollywood plugs into God's story and out pops a gem – for what the director was searching after was *koinonia* in a family setting.

Soon after we commenced ministry at our first church, Marilyn and I took the strategic decision that we would operate an open-door policy: that is people from the church would be free to come and go through the front door as they pleased, it would not be locked. Generally speaking, this was not abused and it made for a lively household. In time, this led to a more significant development. We found the Lord brought people across our paths who needed a home for some purpose of recovery. Often, these were young people who stayed a matter of months, though in one case, Debbie stayed over two years and has become part of our extended family. Mags needed to get away from an abusive relationship, stayed six months, and thirty-plus years later she is still an important part of our lives. Adi, having become a Christian in his late twenties, found it difficult to adjust to a new lifestyle, so he asked if he could make his home with us to learn in a safe environment. This he quickly did then later served five years on the Mercy Ship *Anastasis* while retaining his base with us. Now married, Adi and Catherine still pop in regularly. At the other end of the spectrum, Sheila stayed with us the final nine months of her life as she gradually succumbed to the advances of liver cancer. Sheila was a New Zealander in her late sixties with no family in this country. She had joined the church some years earlier and valued its community spirit. Living in bed-sit-land was no place for her to spend her final days, so she came to us. We gave her a room on the ground floor and folk from the church popped in and out to visit her on a daily basis without overly interrupting the running of the household. Tom was two at the time, and on the days Sheila could only lie on her bed, Tom would be toddling around and talking away innocently to her. A lovely bond grew between them, which wonderfully enriched Sheila's last days. After she died, we had to explain to Tom that she had gone to be with Jesus; some few months later, he laid a place at supper for her announcing, 'Jesus has had Sheila long enough; time for her to come home now.' The enrichment had been two ways!

A couple of days before Vanessa got married, we went out together for a drink. One of the questions I asked her was whether the presence of so many people in her home as she was growing up had presented her with any problems. Initially she joked and said, 'No, they acted as a cushion between us and you!' As we talked, it became clear that the style of living we felt called to had enhanced her experience of people and life and that she would not have had it any other way. Significantly, since their marriages, both she and Debbie have had others living with them as well. It is interesting that when the grandchildren come to stay with Marilyn and I they are quite used to others being in the home and understand that's the way it is in Papa and Grandy's house.

Families of course come in all shapes and sizes, all styles and emphases. No one pattern is inherently better than another, and all can be made to work happily and successfully. What is required in all, however, is the determination to make it work and the dedication of time and priority to achieve that. The work of ministry can be all-consuming and pervasive in an unhealthy way, which militates against family. By God's grace, we saw early on that our priorities were first, God; second, family; and third, work. The danger is to link one and three in practice so that family is squeezed to the margins. When this happens, the result can be cheated wives and angry children, which in turn undermines the integrity of the ministry. There were times when I skirted dangerously close to such margins. The inner insecurities I wrestled with bred a passion to succeed and thereby find some measure of self-worth. During those times, all the credit goes to Marilyn, who never confused the agreed priorities and held the family and our family vision together.

I would not want to convey the impression that all was, or is, a bed of roses! We have been taken advantage of, robbed, had household goods and possessions ruined, been cheated, and let down time and again, but it all goes with the territory. There were times when relationships between Marilyn and I and between us and the children felt stretched to breaking point. I can remember a period when all Matthew and I could talk about was sport, every other subject was too difficult – so thank God for sport, for there are times when any communication is better than none. But family, and in our case extended family, has to be worth fighting for. It is God's core unit of society, and when our call to ministry is complete and there are no more committees to attend, no services to lead, no sermons to prepare, there will still be family; as the bumper sticker puts it, 'Be nice to your kids, they get to choose your nursing home!'

I have already acknowledged that there will be a wide range of views on the way those in pastoral leadership handle their families, all perfectly legitimate. What I have felt to do here is submit a pattern of extended family that can significantly serve not just the individuals concerned but model a possibility for others to consider. If our God is One who 'sets the lonely/solitary in families,'[15] then there need to be at least some families willing to rise to such a call. From the earliest days of the church there has been a strand of God's people who have practised a communal dimension. This has been variously worked out, but the extended family is one such practice. The cost and the risk is high, but those called will discover God's grace, and the rewards are tremendous.

Hospitality

If extended family is not mandatory, hospitality certainly is. We are commended to hospitality from the example of Father Abraham who welcomed three holy visitors and killed the fatted calf for them. The Levitical law required that no farmer should glean his fields but leave food for the poor. Isaiah thundered the prophetic call to share food with the hungry and bring into your homes the helpless, poor, and destitute. Jesus reminded his followers that invitations to banquets should not be to those who will repay but to those unable to return the invitation and in this there will be great reward. The early church in the first flush of the Spirit's anointing voluntarily pooled goods that none might be in need. Paul lists hospitality as one of the qualifying criteria for leadership, adding that it be done ungrudgingly. The first picture given to us on entering eternity is of a banquet where the least qualified are ushered in to their utter amazement and joy. A pastor friend of mine in the States got it right when he said, 'I do my finest work around the meal table' – and his girth bears ample testimony to his priorities!

Hospitality is *koinonia* in a home setting. Hospitality has little to do with entertaining. 'Secular entertaining is a terrible bondage. Its source is human pride. Demanding perfection, fostering the urge to impress, it is a rigorous taskmaster which enslaves. In contrast, scriptural hospitality is a freedom which liberates.'[16] Hospitality seeks to minister, not impress;

---

[15] Psalm 68: 6

[16] Karen Burton Mains, *Open Heart – Open Home*, (Elgin Il: Cook, 1976), p. 25

puts people before things; allows guests to see us as we are; urges others not to admire but invites to share. We have found that the most comfortable way is to keep it simple. Hospitality has a dreadful tendency to escalate, to better what others have done and yield its servanthood to the competitive spirit. Food is only one component of true hospitality, which is the opening of our hearts and our homes, to be seen as we are in all our humanity, by allowing others close. If a glass of water does not go without its reward, then think what pasta and a coffee will reap!

Francis Schaeffer, the founder of L'Abri fellowship, challenged the church to consider the call to costly hospitality. He spoke of the toll on goods, home, and emotions of having needy people brought into community; the unpredictability and risk attached to having folk from the margins of society living in close proximity. He then said, 'This is what the love of God means. This is the admonition to the elder – that he must be given to hospitality. Are you an elder? Are you given to hospitality? If not, keep quiet. There is no use talking. But you can begin.... If you have never done any of these things, if you have been married for years and years and had a home (or even a room) and if none of this has ever occurred, if you have been quiet especially as our culture is crumbling about us, if this is so – do you really believe people are going to hell? And if you really believe that how can you stand and say, "I have never even paid the price to open my living place and do the things I can do"?'[17]

Laughter

We have looked at cluster, family, and hospitality as expressions of *koinonia* and God's grace to us in the gospel to combat aloneness, a significant danger for those in pastoral leadership or missions. If the greatest blessing from *koinonia* is the realisation of the promise 'there am I in the midst', can I suggest the second might be laughter. When people get together, gatherings of friends and family, it's not long before laughter fills the air, and laughter is an absolute tonic; 'a cheerful heart is a good medicine'.[18]

I am convinced that humour is a saving grace, especially the ability to laugh at ourselves. It undermines pomposity, highlights the

---

[17] Mains p. 154 quoting Francis Schaeffer *The Church at the End of the 20th Century*
[18] Proverbs 17: 22

quirkiness of our humanity, and delivers us from taking ourselves too seriously. One of Winston Churchill's war time cabinet members was Sir Stafford Cripps, who was president of the Board of Trade. Cripps was a socialist, an earnest high churchman, and a teetotaller and vegetarian. To Churchill's somewhat more expansive tastes, Cripps was a narrow and pinched personality. As a sacrifice to the war effort, Cripps one day announced that he was giving up the habit of smoking cigars. On hearing this, Churchill quipped with a chuckle, 'Too bad, it was his last contact with humanity.'

Humour, and especially the banter of camaraderie, peels away the potential for pomposity and humbug, which lie waiting to pounce on those poised to pontificate. We are such strange creatures, all too prone to see the hypocrisy in others and blinded to the paradoxes in ourselves. Rubbing shoulders with colleagues facing the same challenges, coming home to your turn changing nappies or listening to the pressures of those in industry around a meal table soon brings us back to earth from our lofty towers. When two or three are gathered together, there's usually a joker in the pack, and before long, sanity and humanity is regained. As Malcolm Muggeridge said, 'Next to mystical enlightenment laughter is the most precious gift and blessing that comes to us on earth.'[19]

The rich tradition of Jewish humour is appreciated in the perceptive words of Jonathan Sacks, 'I love Jewish humour because it lets us laugh where otherwise we would cry. Jewish life has had its share of pain, but what we laugh at, we can rise above. It is an assertion of humanity in the face of dehumanising influences. It is our way of breaking the grip of fears that would otherwise hold us captive. If we can keep our sense of humour, we are not yet prisoners of our situation. Laughing, we defeat despair. Humour is first cousin to hope.... The sociologist Peter Berger calls humour "a signal of transcendence", by which I think he means something in the human situation that points to something beyond.... There is something majestic about human nature that can detach itself from the immediate and soar into the ultimate. Laughter is the refutation of tragedy. A joke is an opening of freedom in the encircling wall of fate.'[20]

---

[19] Quoted by Stephen Gaukroger and Nick Mercer, *Frogs in Cream*, (London: SU, 1990)

[20] Sacks, *Celebrating Life*, p. 38 & 39

So Moshe phones from his home in Jerusalem to his daughter in Brooklyn, New York. 'We have some sad news to tell you, Sarah,' he says, 'finally after these forty years of marriage, your mother and I are going to get a divorce.' 'What?' she cries. 'Impossible! How can you? Don't do anything, Papa; I'll phone my brother, Ari. He'll know what to do.' She rings Ari, tells him the shocking news, and begs him to phone home. Ari gets on the phone, and almost immediately it rings; Moshe is on the line. 'Don't do anything in a hurry, Papa; Sarah and I are going to book a flight to come and see you to talk this through. We'll be there by the week-end.' 'OK,' promised Moshe, 'we'll be here.' After the call was finished, the old man turned to his wife and said, 'You see, sweetheart, I told you I could fix it. The kids will be home for Passover, and they are paying their own fare!'

Was it Kierkegaard who recorded a dream he had one night? In his dream, he supposed God posed him an offer similar to the one made to Solomon: 'what one thing would you like to ask of me?' He thought and then replied, 'To always have the last laugh.' There was a dense silence, and for a while he wondered if he had asked amiss. Then there came from heaven a rich chuckling laughter, and he realised how inappropriate it would have been if God had solemnly intoned, 'Your request is granted.' And this kind of request is far from inappropriate, as C. S. Lewis wrote to Sheldon Vanauken, 'It is a Christian duty, as you know, for everyone to be as happy as he can'.[21]

'"Perhaps," said the sage, putting down his volume of the Talmud, "considering all of life's suffering, it would have been better not to have been born. But how many are so lucky? Not one in a thousand!" If we can laugh, we can bear the pain'.[22]

---

[21] Sheldon Vanauken, *A Severe Mercy,* (London: Harpers, 1979) p. 187
[22] Sacks p. 39

Underpinning

Exploration

On a scale of 1–10, where 1 is low and 10 is high, assess your degree of practical involvement in meaningful *koinonia* in the following settings:

- A Cluster-type small group
- Your marriage
- The lives of your children
- The openness of your home
- The ministry of hospitality

Are you happy with these conclusions? If desired, where could you begin to make changes?

How would you evaluate your happiness, laughter quotient?

Excavation *–recommended for digging deeper*

- Desiring God by John Piper, published by Multnomah Publishers

I recommended this book here not because it deals directly with the theme of *koinonia*, but because its focus is the pursuit of happiness and pleasure, as the subtitle indicates: 'meditations of a Christian Hedonist'. As Piper emphasises, all such is found by glorifying God and enjoying him forever, one such aspect of which is discovered in *koinonia.*

Exchange – *new foundation for old*

- The prayer of the apostle Paul in Ephesians chapter three, the epistle that most explores the corporate dimensions of the Christian faith:

For this reason I kneel before the Father, from whom his whole family in heaven and on earth derives its name. I pray that out of his glorious riches he may strengthen you with power through his Spirit in your inner being, so that Christ may dwell in your hearts through faith. And I pray that you, being rooted and established in love, may have power, together with all the saints, to grasp how wide and long and high and deep is the love of Christ, and to know this love that surpasses knowledge – that you may be filled to the measure of the fullness of Christ.

Chapter 9

The Spirit We Receive

Now the Lord is the Spirit, and where the
Spirit of the Lord is, there is freedom.

2 Corinthians 3: 17

A few years ago, I was introduced to a group of delightful people in
the States running a ministry designed to help people discover a fuller
experience of life in Christ. Their material was excellent and
particularly practical. When asked to comment on their courses,
however, I observed that there was nothing specifically on the Holy
Spirit. I asked, 'If we are talking about spiritual formation, the
development of an adequate spirituality to face the pressures of life,
surely some reference to the Holy Spirit is necessary?' The answer
given was that in their ministry, counsellors and teachers came from a
wide denominational background. Their theology and experience of
the Spirit was of such a range, they did not feel able to formulate
teaching acceptable to all, so they felt it best left out. It was not, of
course, that they individually did not recognise the necessity of the
Spirit to accomplish his work, only that they preferred not to formulate
a guide on the subject for their ministry.

I find myself at a similar point but have come to a different
conclusion. My purpose has been to help us recognise that God is at
work in our lives (in the context of pastoral ministry), to form in us a
spirituality adequate to the work of ministry. This he does by force of
circumstances to focus us again on the work of the cross. Then as we
allow that exchange and transformation to occur, we are brought into
the further experiences of grace. This includes our security of identity
as sons, the benefits of the spiritual disciplines, and the enrichments of
fellowship. The agency in all these workings is of course the Holy
Spirit. Sometimes that working is unperceived by us as it occurs. On

other occasions, it is obvious, uncongenial, even unwanted as our comfort zones are challenged. No inward change can occur, however, without the Spirit's operation.

But is that enough? Is it enough to say all that is growing in me is sufficient evidence of the Spirit, nothing more is needed? I submit not. My feeling is that we are invited to a personal walk in and with the Spirit in a knowable way. His activity should not be restricted to his unperceived working (which is not in dispute). If the Lord Jesus so strongly taught his disciples in the upper room discourses of their need of the Spirit, it was because he expected them to cultivate that relationship. And in the cultivation of that relationship would come their resourcing and resilience for the tasks ahead.

It is that which I would like us to explore. Any superficial study quickly reveals that experiences of the Holy Spirit vary widely. That range of experience should be honoured; no attempt should be made to stereotype a relationship. Nonetheless, I want to encourage a definite personal relationship, such that the Spirit's presence in our life is a vital dynamic reality and an essential part of our whole spirituality.

Questions about the Spirit

The twentieth century saw a remarkable outpouring of the Holy Spirit as fresh waves of grace flowed around the world in many colours, forms, and expressions from that first release in Azusa Street in 1906.[1] Despite this prevalence of the work of the Spirit, there remain many who question, not so much the role of the Spirit in principle but the experience of the Spirit in practice. The person and work of the Holy Spirit has always raised questions. This is so even in the New Testament, though there they tend to differ from the kind of questions asked today. Here are two from Paul: 'Did you receive the Spirit when you believed?' and 'Did you receive the Spirit by observing the law or by believing what you heard?'[2] Both questions

---

[1] Peter Hocken (a Roman Catholic theologian), *The Glory and The Shame*, (Guildford: Eagle, 1993), is as discerning a critique as I have come across. Sub-titled *Reflections on the 20th Century Outpouring of the Holy Spirit'*, it is commended in the foreword by Michael Green in the following words: 'I know of no other book which gives such a balanced, warm, and deep perspective on the Christian scene since the remarkable outpouring of the Holy Spirit at the beginning of this century.'

[2] Acts 19: 2 and Galatians 3: 2

indicate that as far as Paul was concerned, reception of the Spirit was a recognisable part of Christian initiation – recognisable by new believers through an exercise of their faith and recognisable in its absence by apostolic discernment. Clearly Paul expected these young believers to have received the Spirit by faith, to be living in the good of that dynamic influence, and for others to see that this had happened. 'Did you receive the Spirit?' can only be asked if the questioner knows that a clear answer is possible. The Spirit comes with that kind of clarity and makes that sort of difference; he was not expected to slip in unnoticed.

What is true of Christian initiation is true again when it comes to ordination. Most denominations and traditions recognise the testing and training process for a call, which culminates in a service of ordination that includes the laying on of hands for the anointing of the Spirit. This is healthy, for Jesus never intended, indeed expressly forbade, ministry to be conducted without the enduement of the Holy Spirit. 'Do not leave Jerusalem, but wait for the gift my Father promises... in a few days you will be baptised with the Holy Spirit... you will receive power when the Holy Spirit comes on you; and (then) you will be my witnesses in Jerusalem, and in Judea and Samaria, and to the ends of the earth.'[3] The challenge, I submit, for all of us now lies in these New Testament questions: did we receive the Spirit when we were prayed for, and did we receive the Spirit by believing what we heard. If so, one more question is essential: are we still living in the good of that dynamic influence?

I, for one, identify with the response given many years ago by D. L. Moody to the question 'have you been filled with the Spirit?' 'Yes,' he replied, 'but I leak!'

Daily being filled then becomes imperative for us as for all God's people. There are a couple of occupational hazards, however, which it seems to me we need to negotiate in the process lest we find ourselves quenching or grieving the Spirit, so rendering that daily infilling less than vital.

The first has to do with the transition from life to structure. In the first flush of being filled with the Spirit, life for the believer is passion and enthusiasm usually untrammelled by form or convention. Jesus

---

[3] Acts 1: 4, 8

becomes wonderfully real, salvation is deeply secured, and the new saint can't imagine why the church has had so many problems over the years. This can also be the experience of a congregation in a period of renewal or revival. Everything is fresh, vibrantly alive, and God is evidently at work in and through the community. Church history reminds us, however, that such periods of gracious visitation do not usually last terribly long. We may fall in love with the lass, think her perfect and flawless, but after the marriage, there comes the season of working it all out – so with Christ. Those passions do not lessen, but they do deepen into meaningful forms and patterns, liturgies, and rhythms. Life has to be this way; Moses cannot live on the mountaintop forever nor the disciples on the mount of Transfiguration. Ecstasy is not self-indulgence; there's a golden calf down there requiring attention and a man whose daughter has a troubling spirit. When the Spirit comes and splashes the new wine all around, the wise quickly realise the need for new wineskins. So, for example, in our worship we discover spontaneity, chorus', Celtic, Taize, dance, and movement and all blossoms at the inspiration of the creative Spirit. The danger comes at that very point when the form expressing the new is no longer a vessel driven by the Spirit but the hoisting of sail to catch the wind of the Spirit. If the Spirit cannot slip in unnoticed at the beginning, sadly he can and does slip away unnoticed at the end.

Church life by its very nature tends to be structured and organised. Pastoral work requires discipline and routine. Overseeing a group of people necessitates attention to administration; a flock needs to be settled. The danger is the potential tension between responsible maintenance and the doing of that in the creative freshness of the Spirit. Pastoral care, administration of Communion, attending to liturgy, the discipleship of new Christians can by its very regularity lure us to the danger of doing it in our own strength, and if not strength then in our own preference for tidiness. The Spirit first appears in scripture brooding over the chaos, and it seems that's where his best work is done, for creativity inevitably involves mess. Handling an orderliness that is dependent on the Spirit for life and at the same time working with the Spirit as he disturbs, challenges, and provokes through mess to redemption is the trick. As Peterson warns, 'The moment tidiness and conduct become the dominant values, creativity is, if not abolished, at least severely inhibited. For then the souls of men and women come to be viewed as energies to manage, objects to control.'[4]

The second is associated with the first but sufficiently distinct from it to warrant separate mention: that is experience. Experience, like money, is itself neutral. Used well it can breed humility, wisdom, and be a reminder of our constant need of the resources of God. Used poorly it can lead to self-confidence, well-practiced routines, and carefully prepared acts of service that will perform well and serve people efficiently, such that it would only be a bonus if God himself showed up. Many years ago, David Watson observed churches where this had become the norm: 'If God removed His Holy Spirit from the church, 90 per cent of the activity would continue unaffected.' Drifting into such a place – and drifting it must be for no man would intentionally do so – works untold damage to the soul. The loss of wonder at vocation turned to 'doing the job' becomes in the end soul destroying; we were intended for better things. Any sense of dry routine sustained by past experience should cause us to humble ourselves again and cry out to God for a fresh infilling of the Holy Spirit so that ministry be fresh and alive in his grace.

Paralleling Jesus' experience of the Spirit with those of His disciples, Dave Hansen puts it like this: 'Jesus sends his disciples out today to do his work anointed with the same Holy Spirit that led and empowered him. Jesus expects us to do the same things that he did, in the same way, with the same Holy Spirit. It is an amazing privilege, a joyous calling, to be filled with the Holy Spirit for ministry.'[5]

What then might this walk in the Spirit look like as far as ministry is concerned? Just how might this gracious person prod us appropriately as we engage the battle? Amid much that could be said, let me submit three aspects of his power for our reflection.

The Spirit of Sensitivity

I find it easy to identify with the little picture of Joshua as he anticipates the forthcoming battle of Jericho. I sense him pacing back and forth, feeling the weight of responsibility now that Moses has left it all in his hands. What a challenge; what a task! A man approaches,

---

[4] Peterson, *Under the Unpredictable Plant,* p. 165
[5] David Hansen p. 44

and Joshua tetchily demands to know whose side he is on; Joshua needs all the men he can get, numbers are everything, another here or there could make all the difference. The man reveals himself as the commander of the army of the Lord and in effect says, 'It's not a question of whose side I'm on Joshua; it's a question of whose side you are on.' He then instructs him to take off his shoes, for the place where he is standing is holy ground.

Taking off his shoes might have been a strange thing to do for a man in battle gear; soldiers are not supposed to be barefoot. Foot covering was protection after all. But foot covering that protects also insulates against feeling and sensitivity – contrast walking down a pebbly beach with shoes on in winter and dressed for a swim in summer. Taking off your shoes, whatever else it meant, was a call to slow down, pause to reflect, and regain sensitivity. A soldier without shoes is not going anywhere very far or very fast.

What Joshua needed from this moment of encounter was to shed the onerous weight of responsibility, the feeling that it was all down to him, and reconnect to the bigger spiritual picture. He had lost the feel for God's presence, forgotten God's title 'the Lord of Hosts', failed to reckon on the heavenly divisions, and had become preoccupied with human resources and tactics. Reconnecting with the divine was going to shake the Sandhurst and West Point manuals to pieces!

Ministry, as we have already seen, affords plenty of hard knocks. The danger is that we cover up, protect ourselves, thicken the hide, and put on hob-nailed boots. We may lose something in the process, but at least we'll keep our tootsies safe. At which point I suspect Jesus reminds us, 'Ministry is holy ground – time to take off your shoes all over again.'

In his book on the Holy Spirit and the Christian mission, Bishop John Taylor significantly calls the Holy Spirit 'the Go-Between God'. He describes the work of the Spirit in terms of creating awareness, insight, and making connections. 'The Holy Spirit is that power which opens eyes that are closed, hearts that are unaware and minds that shrink from too much reality. If one is open toward God, one is open also to the beauty of the world, the truth of ideas, and the pain of disappointment and deformity. If one is closed up against being hurt, or blind towards one's fellow-men, one is inevitably shut off from God also. One cannot choose to be open in one direction and closed in another. Vision and vulnerability go together. Insensitivity also is an all-rounder. If for one reason or another we refuse really to *see* another person, we become incapable of sensing the presence of God.'[6]

The mission of the church was of course birthed on the day of Pentecost. We are familiar with the story: the dramatic advent of the supernatural, the anointed preaching, the thousands being saved. In such an atmosphere it might be easy to ignore the individual, so perhaps an even more telling insight to the work of the Spirit is given in Acts 3. Peter and John going up to the temple encounter a cripple. The man is more than forty years of age and was a familiar sight begging at the gate Beautiful. Jesus would have passed him by many times without healing him. But come the *kairos* moment Peter 'directed his gaze at him, with John, and said "Look at us"'[7] What happened here was that Peter really saw this man, perhaps for the first time. He invites the cripple to really see them, to catch something of the faith in their eyes. This moment of connection created by the Spirit presaging the man's healing turns out to have greater political, social, and evangelistic significance than the day of Pentecost itself, for it led to testimony before the Sanhedrin and the seismic events that followed. Truly seeing, sensing, making connection where the Spirit 'goes-between' is often the key to unlocking a situation for the gospel.

Sensitivity is needed not just strategically but pastorally also. Florence was in her mid-seventies, now bedridden with illness and frail but still mentally sharp as a pin. I was leading a home communion for her along with Doris and Elsie who shared her home. On previous occasions, I had come prepared with songs or hymns to read together, scripture readings, and a brief meditation, but on this occasion, I sensed the prompting of the Spirit to cut back as we worshipped gently together: shorten the reading, leave out verses of a hymn, drop a chorus altogether, the briefest of thoughts leading to bread and wine. Then as we said the benediction, Florence coughed, fell back on the pillow, and died. The events coincided exactly, a unique crafting of the Holy Spirit leaving us all with a profound sense of awe, an unforgettable experience.

---

[6] John V. Taylor, *The Go-Between God*, (London: SCM, 1972) p. 19
[7] Acts 3: 4 RSV

This was a dramatic experience, of course, but I am sure we all have somewhat similar stories when sensitivity to the Spirit proved crucial, occasions when we seemed to move with awareness beyond ourselves. I am frequently challenged by the thought, however, of how many more there might have been with greater attentiveness to his influence. Numbing weariness with the hours, mindless routine, or self-pity over some petty injustice can lead to the neglect of this gentle Dove, who may then soar away from our cloddish self. The journey we have traced thus far to the cross and then coming to terms with our frail humanity should make us all the more aware of our dependence on divine resources. Without him, we really do not have much to bring to the party, especially in this key area of discernment. Without the Spirit to open our eyes and tune our ears, we become all too easily preoccupied with ourselves. The tragedy then, as Taylor points out, is that this insensitivity becomes an all-rounder, blinding us to God and man alike.

I want to close this section by coming back to Jesus. Surely no one was ever as sensitively perceptive and attuned as he. Time and again the gospels record that he looked, he saw, he listened, he heard, he felt: fully alive to God and fully alive to the men, women, and children around him. One particular woman had suffered much over the twelve years of her bleeding and not just the pain and discomfort. The years had wasted her financially as the doctors had taken her money without cure. She had been declared ritually unclean, thus isolated from Temple and synagogue, socially and spiritually excluded, a wasted human spirit to accompany her wasted body. Then came Jesus. He discerns her suffering and frees her from it. And it is not just her physical condition that is healed instantly, but by exposing her and bringing her to the attention of the crowd, he replaces her isolation with community and her shame with dignity: a masterful pastor at work, wonderfully consonant with the Spirit.

Speaking of Jesus, Taylor says, 'If we look into this life in terms of his absolute oneness with the Holy Spirit we see a perfect reflection of all the marks of the Spirit's activity...: the intensity of awareness and communion, the insistent demand for choice, the self oblation and sacrifice, the double vision of creative insight, and the freedom of the incalculable *ruach*. If we had been able to imagine all the characteristics of the Spirit of God fused and focussed in one human personality we should have pictured a figure like Jesus of Nazareth.'[8]

The Spirit of Prayer

Among all the rich and diverse inspirations of the Spirit relative to prayer, I want to focus on the little and often despised gift of speaking with tongues. I do this for a number of reasons. Primarily because I believe the gift to be biblically mandated, and my simple conviction is that God does not give worthless gifts, neither coming from him should they be despised. Secondly because in these days when aspects of the Spirit's renewal have become more respectable, the actual manifestation of the gifts of the Spirit seem to be less prominent, almost as if we were embarrassed to speak of them in polite company. Thirdly, because it is my testimony that I would not be without it for the world, so I am not afraid to speak a little of it for 'a man with an experience is never at the mercy of a man with an argument'! The bottom line I believe is that in our frail humanity, those of us called to pastoral ministry need all the help we can get and we overlook such a gift at our peril. If God has seen fit to make it available, we do well to consider it, for prayer lies at the heart of our calling.

I need to acknowledge that in my section of the Church, the case for tongues has been overstated. In the Corinthian correspondence, Paul asks the question, 'Do all speak in tongues?', clearly expecting the answer no as the context demands – no, no more than all are apostles, all are prophets, all are teachers, all work miracles, all exercise gifts of healing or all interpret tongues.[9] Tongues is not for all; the gift is not even, I submit, 'the initial physical evidence' of being baptised with the Holy Spirit as some Pentecostal denominations state. I suspect it is not for the thought-out but the confused, not the articulate but stammerers, not the assured but the troubled. Tongues is a little gift for those times when life and its burdens are overwhelming and one's soul is heavy and tortured, when the heavens are as brass and even the invitation to pray feels like another defeat; then tongues is a God-send: a little gift for little people *in extremis*. But how like Abba Father is that!

---

[8] Taylor p. 90
[9] 1 Corinthians 12: 29–31

If Charismatics and Pentecostals have overstated the case of tongues, I wonder if opposition to it is less rational than emotional, especially the emotion of fear. We all have some measure of fear of the unfamiliar and fear of fanaticism. In fairness, we need to acknowledge that enthusiasts for supernatural gifts are not always their best advocates. In this area, most of us have had to suffer human idiosyncrasies, sensationalism, and exploitation – a total over-cooking of the egg. In his address to the Lausanne Conference 2 in Manila, Jack Hayford was encouraging the acceptance of the Spirits supernatural gifts in evangelism and in doing so recognised this very problem, 'Peter faced that long ago. But in rebuking Simon the Sorcerer he provides us with a challenging model. Could the Holy Spirit today be calling us to exercise the choice Peter did then – to sort the chaff from the wheat, to expose the serpent and release the dove?'[10]

While acknowledging that not all speak in tongues, Paul does 'thank God that I speak in tongues more than you all'. In the same chapter, he expresses a wish that all of his readers might benefit from the gift: 'I would like every one of you to speak in tongues.'[11] In other words, while he recognises that not all speak in tongues, this does not stop the apostle both testifying to its value personally and commending to all a pursuit of the gift.

What is 'speaking in tongues'? It can be an unlearned earthly language that expresses a prophetic word in a language known to the hearer but not the speaker. Brother Andrew and others who have worked undercover in repressive regimes bear witness to this. Just a couple of months ago, Heather Hartley, one of our members, came forward for personal prayer toward the end of an evening service. Lynne, our pastoral assistant, prayed for her, but as no specific request had been mentioned by Heather, Lynne gently prayed over her in a language of the Spirit. In a few moments, Heather was quite beside herself, quite choked up emotionally. After the service when she had recovered, she explained to me that the prayer offered by Lynne for her was in Zulu, a language she had grown up with in her native South Africa and was a simple reassurance that the great God was with her.

---

[10] Recorded by Jack Hayford, *A Passion for Fullness*, (Dallas: Word Publishing, 1990) p. 25
[11] 1 Corinthians 14: 18, 5

Almost more than the message, however, she was overwhelmed with the personalising of it to her understanding. Lynne was happily bemused! However, that is not the usual usage. More normally it is the expression of an unknown language, sounds, and syllables, a flow of utterance bypassing the cognitive faculties. But what would be the value of that?

I have come to understand its value and benefit as follows: we are told that one aspect of psychological health is the ability to harmonise our inner feeling with our outward expressions. We are psychologically whole if what we are feeling can be articulated and expressed appropriately. An inability to do so can cause inner tensions and frustrations leading even to physical illness. Dustin Hoffman's performance in the film *Rain Man* was a compelling introduction to the world of autism, which is an extreme form of the condition where mind and emotions are discordant.

In any week, most of us are likely to explain technicalities rationally at work, resist the temptation to swear at dangerous driving, shout at the dog, whisper sweet nothings in our beloved's ear, and roar with the crowd at the match. Such a range of expression is appropriate and natural to a healthy person. When we were at college, our elocution instructor told us the following story, which illustrates the point perfectly: there was a Spanish married couple both of whom were linguists. In everyday conversation, they spoke Spanish, but when they argued, they spoke Italian; when they made love, they spoke French, and when they did the accounts, they spoke English! In other words, the language, feel, style, and volume was appropriate to the occasion – though we English may feel that the joke was on us.

In English, we perfectly accept the role of sounds in this process. We understand that careful articulation of words found in the Oxford Dictionary is not necessary in every situation. People hold new babies in their arms and say 'coochicoo' – often over and over again. It is perfectly normal for someone hitting their thumb with a hammer not to break into Shakespeare but simply shout, 'Ouch'. When sinking into a hot bath after a day's work in the garden, one tends to savour the moment with a grateful expression of, 'aaaaahhhh'. All these noises work not because they are carefully formed sentences with appropriate grammar and syntax but because they release the emotion of the moment – and we all do it, and we all accept it is normal to do so.

Speaking in tongues simply takes the process one step forward in the same direction. It is cooperating with the Holy Spirit within us, releasing sounds that connect with the burden or joy of the soul, who then carries them to God in prayer. 'And he who searches our hearts knows the mind of the Spirit, because the Spirit intercedes for the saints in accordance with God's will.'[12] It is said that Churchill had a vocabulary of some fifteen thousand words; the average today is five thousand words, so all help is welcome.

My sister Barbara, before her death, was head of the speech therapy department in one of the area health authorities in Yorkshire. Before she became a Christian herself, and long before she spoke in tongues, she was fascinated by the subject from a professional point of view. Her department dealt primarily with children experiencing speech difficulties and impediments, and she recognised that an inability to speak fluently added significantly to a child's frustrations, hampering his or her development. Her task as a speech therapist was to ease that by increasing fluency, which is why she found her job so rewarding. She later thought that, with respect to this little gift, the Spirit was also a speech therapist doing the same job as hers by producing a greater harmony between the inner and outer self via the mechanism of speech!

Paul urged the church in Ephesus as part of their vigilant warfare to 'pray in the Spirit on all occasions with all kinds of prayers and requests.'[13] Let your prayers, says Paul, be inspired by the Spirit – you being in the Spirit – where each event and occasion is prayed for appropriately drawing on the wide armoury of prayer weapons at our disposal. Among these there will be those times when words fail and our souls are overwhelmed, but despite being at the end of our tether, there is still something we can do; we never have to feel completely helpless. It is then that the gift of speaking in tongues helps release the burden, provides fellowship in the Spirit, and keeps us sane and healthy, for by God's grace, and the use of this little gift, we can always pray.

As Paul encourages, 'Follow the way of love and eagerly desire the spiritual gifts'[14]

---

[12] Romans 8: 27
[13] Ephesians 6: 18
[14] 1 Corinthians 14: 1

The Creative Spirit

Calvin has some colourful phrases to describe the 'empty chaos of heaven and earth' upon which God began the work of creation: 'empty and waste', 'confused emptiness', 'indigested mass', and 'disorderly heap.'[15] Scripture reveals that to such comes the creative love of the Father, the Word and the Spirit of God. It is the picture of the Spirit in particular that I want to focus on: 'and the Spirit of God was hovering over the waters.'[16] The image is of a mother bird incubating, hatching, then stirring the nest to stimulate a full participation in life. Von Rad steers away from the brooding idea associated with 'hovering' and adds synonyms such as 'vibrate', 'tremble', 'move', 'stir'.[17] These ideas come together in the picture of God's work over Israel in Deuteronomy 32: 11: 'Like an eagle that stirs up its nest and hovers over its young, that spreads out its wings to catch them and carries them on its pinions.' The result is something wildly beautiful: light from darkness, order from chaos, energy from sterility, potential from despair, elegance from ugliness, maturity from babyhood. The 'confused emptiness' and the 'disorderly heap' are transformed into something good, something very good. Little wonder 'the morning stars sang together and all the angels shouted for joy'[18] or as C. S. Lewis expressed the link between music, worship, and creation, 'Thus, with an unspeakable thrill, Lucy felt quite certain that all the things were coming (as she said) "out of the Lion's head". When you listened to his song you heard the things he was making up: when you looked around you, you saw them.'[19]

Von Rad reminds us that the text of Genesis 1 is 'Priestly doctrine – indeed it contains the essence of Priestly knowledge in a most concentrated form,' which he then explains thus: 'This second verse speaks not only of a reality that once existed in a primeval period but also of a possibility that always exists. Man has always suspected that creation is always ready to sink into the abyss of formlessness;

---

[15] John Calvin, *A Commentary on Genesis*, (London: Banner of Truth Trust, 1965) p. 70ff

[16] Genesis 1: 3

[17] Gerhard von Rad, *Genesis*, (London: SCM Press, 1966) p. 47

[18] Job 38: 7

[19] C. S. Lewis, *The Chronicles of Narnia (The Magician's Nephew)*, (London: Collins, 1988) p. 65

that the chaos, therefore, signifies a simple threat to everything created.... For the cosmos stands permanently in need of this supporting Creator's will.'[20] Or as Eugene Peterson has put it, '"Create" is not confined to what the Spirit did; it is what the Spirit *does*. Creation is not an impersonal environment, it is a personal home – *this* is where we live. The work of the Spirit in creation no longer is confined to asking the questions, "When did this take place? How did this happen?" We are now asking, "How can I get in on this? Where is my place in this?"'[21]

Twice more in scripture the Spirit is pictured as an activating executor of God's will, bringing the same immanent presence and creative energy to the work of recreation. When the dove descended on Jesus at his baptism and the wind and fire anointed the disciples in the Upper Room, new dimensions of redemption were inaugurated but still at the gracing of this creative Spirit. Genesis, Gospels, and Acts combine to declare that this is still God's world and he is in the business of bringing order out of chaos. 'That is yet another word of comfort and hope to people whose experience is marked by chaos, by ugliness, by disorder, by "confused emptiness": God is the sort of God who comes into confusion and makes things new. He hovers over your darkness and says, "Let there be light." People of God: take heart!'[22]

H. R. Rookmaaker was professor of history of art at the Free University of Amsterdam, and following his death, a series of his essays was published under the title *The Creative Gift*. Francis Schaeffer said of these, 'These essays represent the finest thinking in the area of art and creativity. Until his death, Dr. Rookmaaker was known as a scholar of the highest calibre, and as a man of deep Christian commitment.' Rookmaaker recognised a general Christian involvement with the Spirit, much as outlined above, but then says, 'There is a more limited kind of creativity which leads to a particular creation like an invention or a work of art. Between (the general kind of creativity) and this latter, for which the term is usually reserved, is

---

[20] Von Rad p. 49

[21] Eugene H. Peterson, *Christ Plays in Ten thousand Places*, (London: Hodder & Stoughton, 2005) p. 22 & 23.

[22] David Atkinson, *The Message of Genesis 1–11,* BST series (Leicester: IVP, 1990) p. 25

no material difference.'[23] Using the gifting of Bezalel and Oholiab in Exodus 31 as an example of this creativity in the narrower sense, Rookmaaker says, 'Since Bezalel makes the designs, he is a shaper of culture *par excellence*. He is a man who discovers new possibilities; he opens up creation and cultivates it, and he does so with wisdom and understanding.'[24] Later in the same chapter on creativity in love and freedom, he adds under the heading "Creativity is Nothing Special", 'When we speak about creativity, we do not mean only art. Creativity is part of everyone's work, wherever the best solution to a task is sought in love and freedom'.[25]

What it comes down to, says Rookmaaker, is this: 'Creativity is part of everyone's work', it is individual, and as creative individuals, we shape our world around us. And this is our calling as servants of God, partnering with him in the Spirit and therefore in the creative process and all the while proclaiming, 'Good news! Good news!' A significant dimension to this is the Spirit's creation of community, one aspect of which is our work *milieu* in the church, for as Moltmann writes, the Spirit 'creates the community of all created things with God and with each other, making it that fellowship of creation in which all created things communicate with each other and with God, each in its own way.'[26] I have earlier recognised that we have to learn to be flexible and adaptable in this work, for when the Spirit comes, he firstly comes to 'uproot, and tear down, to destroy and overthrow' before he 'builds and plants'.[27] This prophetic disturbance creates a mess; as I heard one pastor at a conference in the States say, 'Pastoring is prancing in the poop!' But having exposed what is amiss in individual or community, what a joy to see the infinite variety of ways in which the Spirit applies the finished work of Christ to the making of all things new.

The encouragement here is to see that as well as approaching our work creatively, we also need, at a personal level, to engage with creative activity that will be truly recreational for us in body, mind,

---

[23] H. R. Rookmaaker, *The Creative Gift,* (Westchester Il: Cornerstone Books, 1981) p. 69
[24] Rookmaaker p. 69
[25] Rookmaaker p. 74
[26] Quoted by Atkinson p. 26
[27] C. F. Jeremiah 1: 10

and soul. An antidote to the weariness and attrition previously referred to is to embrace something creative instead of blobbing in front of the box. This will vary widely according to our interests: music composing or playing, gardening, photography, water or oil painting, cooking, needlework, or any of one hundred and one activities. For in the doing of them we find the recreative energy of the Spirit, renewing the inner man, slowing us down, forcing us to reconnect with the sights, sounds, and smells of the world around us. We draw from the creative Spirit himself as we splash colour, mix herbs, or plant a new border. The process disconnects us from what we thought was immediate and urgent and reconnects us with the healthier rhythms of nature. Life begins to take on fresh textures, richer hues, and a gentler pace.

The creative arts link us with the contributions of common men and women over the ages who have reached out, risked creating, and whose legacy is there for us to applaud and enjoy. They draw us on into a brighter future as we discover and express hope, aided by the Creator who makes all things new. They border on the sacramental. And all the while the Spirit of God hovers and broods over us, wooing us on.

I dabble with watercolours, enjoy portrait photography, but it is writing that is recreational for me. On holiday, I jot down observations of buildings, trees, and scenes around and weave them into word pictures. Journaling also helps me think, forces me to observe and note, sift and prioritise. I prefer prose to poetry but occasionally feel the urge to shape the moment in verse. Often for me the doing of such reveals, discovers, and clarifies what one thinks but did not realise until the creative process is embarked on. The adventure for me begins as the pen embraces the virgin page. Some years ago I wrote an (unpublished) novel. A friend of mine read it and on returning the manuscript to me said, 'I never knew you knew so much!' We roared with laughter as we both realised what he was insinuating, but I could join in easily, for he actually spoke more of the truth than he realised with his bumbling comment. Writing works like that for me; it draws out and connects and is, as I say, high adventure. Much of what we produce will be for private use, perhaps hardly referred to again after the moment of creation, but the birthing is what is important, the moment of release. Indeed if anything beyond the expression is in mind, it probably prostitutes the act anyway. That others may enjoy and benefit later only adds wonder to the act.

Rookmaaker has some strong words to say to those who would only see these things in utilitarian terms: 'We must beware the danger of Christian utilitarianism. This is the most appalling trap into which one can easily fall'.[28] His concern is that art, creativity, and expressions of the gifts of God are not harnessed only to the pursuit of evangelism, for that would be to lose their intrinsic beauty and be a form of prostitution. 'The music of Bach, the art of Rembrandt, are in themselves a witness because they show what it means to adopt Christian standards, to use one's talents in order to make the very best work one is capable of; this in itself honours God.'[29] And, I would add, most fulfils and develops us his servants, reviving, refreshing and sending us back into the fray recreated, fully alive again to the creative Spirit.

What a lot we got!

I am so conscious that this brief foray into the work of the Holy Spirit barely scratches the surface of his gracious working. But even the little leads us to worship: Thanks be to God for this inexpressible gift!

As we have journeyed through these chapters, we have seen that everything needed for our inner resourcing has been provided. God's grace is rich toward us. Many of Jesus' parables tell us, however, that with the receipt of such bounty comes accountability. Accountability is ordered to breed responsibility, and it is to this subject we turn next.

---

[28] Rookmaaker p. 154
[29] Rookmaaker p. 155

Underpinning

Exploration

Life is best told in stories. How would you tell the stories of the Holy Spirit in your life?

- How did you first come to know Him?

- How do you find He inspires you?

- What stories can you tell of His increasing your awareness and perception?

- How do you find He most inspires your prayers?

- What are your favourite ways of creatively being recreated by His inspiration?

Excavation –*recommended for digging deeper*

I turn here not to a book about the Holy Spirit as such; each will have their libraries and opportunities to dig deeper. Rather, I return to the Jewish writer Chaim Potok and his two novels about a painter Asher Lev. A rare talent, Asher Lev paints the world as he sees it but in doing so shocks and alienates the Hassidic community of which he is a practising member. The books explore the tensions of the creative gift and the cost to the most talented. At the end of the first book, the Rebbe has asked Asher Lev to leave Brooklyn and go, in effect, into exile in Paris. Potok captures the moment in a soliloquy by Asher:

'Asher Lev paints good pictures and hurts people he loves. Then be a great painter, Asher Lev; that will be the only justification for all the pain you will cause. But as a great painter I will cause pain again if I must. Then become a greater painter. But I will cause pain again. Then become a still greater painter. Master of the Universe, will I live this way all the rest of my life? Yes, came the whisper from the branches of the trees. Now journey with me, my Asher. Paint the anguish of all the world. Let the people see the pain. But create your own moulds and your own play forms for the pain. We must give a balance to the universe.'

- *My Name is Asher Lev* by Chaim Potok, published by Fawcett press.

- *The Gift of Asher Lev* by Chaim Potok, as above

Exchange – *new foundation for old*

• A prayer for inviting the Lord to fill you with the Holy Spirit, written by Pastor Jack Hayford, founding pastor of the Church On The Way, chancellor of the King's Seminary in Los Angeles and president of the International Church of the Foursquare Gospel.

Dear Lord Jesus,

I thank you and praise you for your great love and faithfulness to me.

My heart is filled with joy whenever I think of the great gift of salvation you have given to me so freely.

And I humbly glorify you, Lord Jesus, for you have forgiven me all my sins and brought me to the Father.

Now I come in obedience to your call.

I want to receive the fullness of the Holy Spirit.

I do not come because I am worthy myself, but because you have invited me to come.

Because you have washed me from my sins, I thank you that you have made the vessel of my life a worthy one to be filled with the Holy Spirit of God.

I want to be overflowed with your life, your love, and your power, Lord Jesus.

I want to show forth your grace, your words, your goodness, and your gifts to everyone I can.

And so, with simple, childlike faith, I ask you, Lord, to fill me with the Holy Spirit. I open all of myself to you to receive all of yourself in me.

I love you, Lord, and I lift my voice in praise to you.

I welcome your might and your miracles to be manifest in me, for your glory and unto your praise.[30]

---

[30] Hayford p. 273

Chapter 10

The Accountability We Owe

*I have fought the fight, I have finished the race, I have kept the faith.
Now there is in store for me the crown of righteousness, which the
Lord, the righteous judge, will award to me on that day – and not only
to me, but also to all who have longed for his appearing.*

2 Timothy 4: 7 & 8

Church history rightly applauds the heroic work of General William
Booth, founder of the Salvation Army. His courageous decision to
break with the traditional norms of his day and take the gospel onto the
streets to the poor was much derided. Yet with faith and zeal, he and
his band of followers launched a movement combining the evangelical
faith with practical acts of compassion for the most needy and lost
members of society, which has spanned the world.

It is well known that Booth was motivated by the plight of the
poor and homeless, firstly in the Midlands, then particularly in the East
End of London. What is less known is that he also had a vivid
awareness of heaven and how actions on earth might be viewed by
celestial beings and the Lord of Glory himself. On one occasion, he
was preaching at Birmingham Town Hall, where with mounting
intensity he portrayed the dilemma of a seducer on Judgement Day.
'Here she comes – the woman seduced! Her golden hair is falling over
her shoulders – she is screaming "That is the man! That is the man!"
Suddenly, to the horror of all, a voice from the gallery cried in
torment, "My God – he means *me*!" Then, with an appalling crash, he
leaped clean over the balcony to the floor of the hall, stumbling
miraculously up the aisle to collapse at the Penitent-form.'[1]

---

[1] Richard Collier, *The General Next to God*, (London: Fontana Books, 1983) p. 219

Such a perspective on judgement galvanized his own labours, and it was a perspective he urged on all in the movement. In the allegorical manner of Pilgrim's Progress, he wrote a widely published article (or vision as he called it) in the first person singular of a young man's death and visit to heaven entitled *In Heaven, but not of Heaven.*[2]

The vision begins by recounting that as a young man he would have been considered quite a shining light with regard to religious activity: attending church, teaching Sunday School, visiting the sick, and giving money to support Christian work. He then sees himself become dangerously ill, and despite the work of various physicians and proper medication, he draws near to death. Friends come and pray with him but to no avail; he slips into a strange faintness, and his next sensation is of a new and celestial existence; he was in heaven.

A rich description is given of what he saw and the people he encountered, a magnificence which strains language to the limit. However, the impact of such a 'land of pure delight' was to increase his own sense of unworthiness of being there and the futility of the life he had led on earth. The thought of heaven as his dwelling forever began to fill his soul with 'unspeakable regret'. As he meets more and more people whose glory reflects the sacrificial lives they have lived, the more he begins to yearn that he be given a second chance on earth. Eventually he becomes aware that the King's procession is approaching. Earthly pageants he had seen on earth looked but 'the light of a feeble candle to a tropical sun in comparison'. He describes rank after rank of patriarchs and apostles, then the holy martyrs followed by an army of warriors who had fought for Christ in all parts of the world, those who, 'with self-denying zeal and untiring toil, had laboured to extend God's Kingdom and save the souls of men.' Finally, he meets the Lord, where we need to hear Booth's own words:

'That face, that Divine face, seemed to say to me, for language was not needed to convey to the depths of my soul what His feelings were to me: "Thou wilt feel thyself little in harmony with these, once the companions of my tribulations and now of my glory, who counted not their lives dear unto themselves in order that they might bring honour to Me and salvation to men." And He gave a look of

---

[2] The article first appeared in the Salvationist magazine *All the World* in 1892 and was reprinted in a book by Booth in 1905 entitled *Visions,* now out of print.

admiration at the hosts of apostles and martyrs and warriors gathered around Him.

'Oh, that look of Jesus! I felt that to have one such loving recognition – it would be worth dying a hundred deaths at the stake. It would be worth being torn asunder by wild beasts. The angelic escort felt it too, for their responsive burst of praise and song shook the very skies and the ground on which I lay.

'Then the King turned His eyes on me again. How I wished that some mountain would fall upon me and hide me forever from His presence! But I wished in vain. Some invisible and irresistible force compelled me to look up, and my eyes met His once more. I felt, rather than heard, Him saying to me in words that engraved themselves as fire upon my brain:

'"Go back to earth. I will give thee another opportunity. Prove thyself worthy of My name. Show to the world that thou possessest My spirit by doing My works, and becoming, on My behalf, a saviour of men. Thou shalt return hither when thou hast finished the battle, and I will give thee a place in My conquering train, and a share in My glory."'

William Booth died on 20 August 1912, aged eighty-three years. His funeral attracted over forty thousand people and brought London to a standstill. It was attended by Queen Mary with the Lord Chamberlain, and the acting Lord Mayor of London, with wreaths from the King and Queen, Kaiser Wilhelm of Germany, and American Ambassador Whitelaw Reid. *The Daily Telegraph* avowed: 'He belonged to the company of saints', and the New York Times claimed, 'No man did more for the benefit of his people.'[3] Despite such lofty adulation, it was the reformed drunkards, addicts, and prostitutes of the East End of London who made the greatest contribution, and they honoured the man who 'cared for the likes of us'.

Having preached and written much on the subject of heaven, the General who laboured so tirelessly for the lowest of the low on earth was surely now among heaven's aristocracy. But even here he judged the aristocracy of that place with his own unique measure, as he wrote in the *Vision:* 'What a sight it was!... And around and about, above and below, I beheld myriads and myriads of spirits who were never heard

---

[3] Collier, p. 223 & 224.

of on earth outside of their own neighbourhoods, or beyond their own times, who, with self-denying zeal and untiring toil, had laboured to extend God's Kingdom and to save the souls of men. And encircling the gorgeous scene, above, beneath, around, hovered glittering angelic beings who had kept their first estate – proud, it seemed to me, to minister to the happiness and exaltation of these redeemed out of the poor world from which I came.'

Accountability

This awareness of heaven's perspective and his own accountability was also a motivating dynamic in Paul's life, for he makes frequent reference to it. Let one suffice for now: 'For we must all appear before the judgement seat of Christ, that each one of us may receive what is due to him for the things done while in the body, whether good or bad.'[4] Years ago as a student in London, I heard Dr. Martyn Lloyd-Jones say in preaching, 'Nothing is more important than knowing who we are, why we are here, and where we are going.' It was one of those seminal moments for me when God impressed a truth in my soul which then finds confirmation at nearly every subsequent reading of scripture! I wanted to go to heaven, but I understood instinctively that while that was all of grace there was also a stewardship to give an account of.

The phrase 'the judgement seat of Christ' can appear intimidating. We do however live in a world with an innate sense of justice. A frequent cry from children is, 'It's not fair!' That desire for fairness expressed instinctively by children is echoed in most people throughout life, over issues large and small. Hate them as we may, we accept the necessity of exams for establishing standards. We want things to be right, and one of the great hopes of God's judgement at the end of the age is that ultimate justice will be established on the earth and, in particular, the vindication of his name. The Psalms are full of rejoicing at the prospect of God's judgement. The call goes out for the heavens, seas, fields, and trees of the forest to rejoice and sing before the Lord, 'for he comes, he comes to judge the earth. He will judge the world in righteousness and the peoples in his truth'.[5] C. S.

---

[4] 2 Corinthians 5: 10
[5] Psalm 96: 11–13

Lewis wrote in *Reflections on the Psalms,* 'We need not therefore be surprised if the psalms and Prophets are full of longing for judgement, and regard the announcement that judgement is coming as good news.' So to learn that God evaluates his children's lives should not seem strange to us, rather a fitting and appropriate point of judicial summary as we move from time into eternity.

The nature of that however needs framing. Consider the difference between the exercise of judgement at the Old Bailey and the Chelsea Flower Show. Both are processes of judgement, but the atmosphere and outcome is very different. If one was before the judge at the Old Bailey, the whole direction of one's future life stands in jeopardy. When appearing before the judges at Chelsea, however, everyone goes home for tea even if one's presentation was deemed under par. The judgement seat of Christ has nothing to do with sin. We will all stand before the Lord in robes of righteousness, part of the Bride of heaven and without condemnation. There is no possibility of losing one's salvation at that point, providing we have fully trusted in him as Saviour and Lord in this life. As someone has said, 'Our difficulty at the judgement seat of Christ will not be with passports, but with baggage. That is the way it usually is when one travels.' Whatever else may come up, the bottom line is that we are and will be home in the fullest and richest sense of that word.

There is a further distinction however, which needs to be made between the judgement seat of Christ and the analogy of the Chelsea flower show. Chelsea is essentially a competition, but in this Christian life, we are not in competition with anyone else, neither will there be any sense of comparison with others on that day. It is not as if the Lord will line us up with Martin Luther, John Wesley, Gladys Aylward, and William Booth and say, 'Now let's see who did best'. For each of us it will be a personal interview with the Lord.

It was Jesus, himself, who spoke much of this event. Evaluation, accountability, and judgement was built into many of his parables and shot through much of his teaching. He told stories of talents and tasks that would one day have to be accounted for, and where some made better use of their gifts than others, all of which would be revealed at the day of the King's return. The apostles built on this foundation. So Paul urges, 'For we must all stand before God's judgement seat.... So then, each of us will give an account of himself to God.'[6] The final word in the New Testament on the subject remains again with Jesus: 'Behold, I am coming soon! My reward is with me, and I will give to everyone according to what he has done.'[7]

The Test of Fruitfulness

What the Lord will be looking for is fruit – fruit in terms of character and good works.

A fascination and concern for all of us in pastoral ministry is the disparity we often observe between those who rapidly move to maturity in the things of God, have a hunger to learn and grow and who produce solid Christ-like character, and those who never seem to get beyond the basics: some thirty fold, some a hundred fold. The writer to the Hebrews chides his readers that by this stage they should have matured to meat but still had to be fed milk. Those still at the milk stage when they should be at the meat stage are left unskilled, undiscerning, and unfruitful.[8] Continuing immaturity should always be a concern as these scriptures highlight.

How much more should those of us called to his service attend to these inner issues of being transformed to his image and likeness. This is a lifelong commitment where much patience is required and focus retained. Wise words from Peterson are helpful here: 'Formation of spirit, cultivation of soul, realizing a lived congruence between the way and the truth – all this is slow work requiring endless patience.'[9] He goes on to say that in the American society, which prizes fast cars, fast food, and how fast we can get things done, slowness and patience is often jettisoned and we become diminished by our speed. The warning is valid to all in Western societies. Holding the end in view will help us retain focus with patience and resist the pressures and priorities of a passing influence. Was it Eleanor Roosevelt who, toward the end of her life, went blind and when asked by a friend how God could permit this answered, 'Well, my dear, he must be putting the finishing touches to my character'? Ruthless perfecting to the very end!

---

[6] Romans 14: 10, 12
[7] Revelation 22: 12
[8] Cf. Hebrews 5: 11–14
[9] Peterson, *Christ Plays in Ten Thousand Places* p. 337.

One of the great adventures in life is to discover 'the good works which God prepared in advance for us to do'.[10] These works will be unique to each of us, again, no comparisons, and it is this gifted work against which we will be measured. If we have a geography exam coming up, it will do us no good to swot up on history; 'Many will say to Me on that day, "Lord, Lord, did we not prophesy in your name, and in your name drive out demons and perform many miracles?" Then I will tell them plainly, I never knew you."'[11] The kindness and justice of God is revealed in that he simply does not expect us all to produce the same thing, even when called to the same job. If some are ten talent people and others five, it stands to reason the outcome will be different. Even nature teaches us that plants and shrubs and trees all grow to differing size and beauty. As a pastor, what I am called to be is the best my gifting and talents can realise, and I long ago came to terms with the fact that for me those were not capable of producing a mega-church. Once we get the 'Yonggi Cho, largest church in the world' syndrome out of our systems, we can get on with our personal assignment and do that 100 per cent, knowing that it is only that for which we will be called to account.

Tested by Fire

Paul indicates the twofold nature of the evaluation process in 1 Corinthians 3: 10–5. Using the building metaphor, he refers to the foundation and the fabric.

'For no-one can lay any foundation other than the one already laid, which is Jesus Christ.' Whether the shaping of the inner world of our soul or the outer activity of work, all has to be Jesus. Jesus, his Word and his Spirit, is the only solid, immoveable and unshakeable foundation of truth upon which we can build anything which will last beyond time and carry over into eternity. When we come before him, what will be searched for are reflections of himself.

The materials Paul alludes to contrasts wood, hay, and stubble with gold, silver, and precious stones. The former represent materials ready to hand, life made easy for the lazy, the use of things requiring

---

[10] Ephesians 2: 10
[11] Matthew 7: 22, 23

little effort: the drawing on our own wisdom, understanding, traditions and culture. The latter are qualities requiring digging and panning that do not quickly appear but are the result of diligent search and work: the application of enquiring spirits and stretched minds to the discovery and use of quality materials for life and work. The good news is that the wood, hay, and stubble are burned up – thank God that such will not be allowed into glory as reminders of our sloth.

I suspect that when we stand before the Lord we may be utterly surprised by the evaluation meted out. Without wanting to let any of us off the hook, I do not think we are very good at this stage of the journey at such self critique. In the middle of his vigorous correspondence with the Corinthians, Paul refuses to allow them to make judgements of him and even declares he has no intention of stopping to judge himself. 'I care very little if I am judged by you or by any human court; indeed I do not even judge myself. My conscience is clear, but that does not make me innocent. It is the Lord who judges me. Therefore judge nothing before the appointed time; wait till the Lord comes.'[12] I suspect that all too often we bring a more carnal and worldly evaluation to our lives than we realise, often discounting what is pleasing to God and celebrating things that have more to do with our egos – look at how many times the disciples were rebuked by the Lord for their lack of discernment. Brennan Manning hints at this in his forward to *Abba's Child*, 'The road I've travelled… is pockmarked by disastrous victories and magnificent defeats, soul-diminishing successes and life-enhancing failures. Seasons of fidelity and betrayal, periods of consolation and desolation, zeal and apathy are not unknown to me.'[13] So we do well not to engage in too much premature navel gazing but leave it all to One who is wiser and more generous and forgiving than we are likely to be with ourselves. 'If our hearts condemn us, God is greater than our hearts, and he knows everything.'[14]

Just as it takes the winter frost, the spring rains, and the summer sun to produce good apples, so it takes all the seasons of life to shape a character and effect a fruitful life. We do well to remember that in all

---

[12] 1 Corinthians 4: 3–5
[13] Manning, *Abba's Child* p.15
[14] 1 John 3: 20

this work the primary agent is God himself, as Paul emphasises in the above verse, 'We are God's workmanship... created in Christ Jesus, which God prepared.' God, God, God who works this grace in and through us. Ours is the relatively simple job of keeping in step with him, which is helped by keeping our eyes on the prize, for nothing will sound better on that day than, 'Well done, good and faithful servant!... Come and share your master's happiness!'[15]

Rewards

Like all good pastors, I have tried faithfully to teach the scriptures and set before the folk biblical truth on the after-life. Topics such as heaven and hell, judgement, the nature of the resurrection body, the new heaven and the new earth, and the crowns of reward have been expounded. I have taught series on the book of Revelation, the second coming, and the role and place of Israel in prophecy. I believe all those glorious truths and roundly celebrate them, but most of the time, I feel like the wobbly legged marathon runner whose only concern is just to get over the line! Amazingly, for those us deeply aware of our need of mercy and grace, there is more than just making it, but most days, just making it seems enough.

There is a cosmetics advert on television that always ends up with the punch line, 'because you're worth it.' Well, my conviction is that whatever happens in glory everything will focus on Jesus not us – because he's worth it! I love the Authorised Version rendering of Isaiah 53: 11: 'He shall see the travail of his soul and be satisfied.' To contemplate the Lord Jesus, the suffering servant, having fulfilled the Father's purpose by completing his course, then faithfully exercising his heavenly high priestly ministry of always interceding for us, finally to see the fruit of his labours with deep satisfaction, will be enough. He will be satisfied, feeling it was all worth it. He will find joy and delight in those around him, and to sense his happiness will be our joy. The rapturous applause of heaven will declare his story, and he alone will be the focus of rapt attention. If he then says, 'Come and share your master's happiness', how great will that happiness be!

---

[15] Matthew 25: 21

Finishing Well

One of our young grandsons was running in his first school's sports day. After much frustrated waiting, the five year old boys finally lined up, and Finbar took off with enthusiasm. He was holding a good second position as he ran past that part of the crowd where his family were cheering. 'Come on, Fin! You can win it!' they yelled. Hearing his name and ever the showman, he stopped, flung out his arms, took a bow, then carried on, and predictably came last.

In the bigger scheme of things, this did not matter too much, but no one ever wins races by taking a bow before the end. In his second epistle, Peter was concerned that his readers finished the Christian race well. His exhortation in chapter one, verses three through eleven, is pertinent for us at this point.

Firstly in verses 3 and 4, Peter begins by reminding us of the resources and privileges which are ours through God's grace.

His divine power has given us everything we need for life and godliness through our knowledge of him who called us by his own glory and goodness. Through these he has given us very great and glorious promises, so that through them you may participate in the divine nature and escape the corruption in the world caused by evil desires.

Peter's purpose is the same one that has occupied us: how we might live effective and godly lives. He tells us that God has given everything necessary for this, in particular through the resources of his power, the appropriation of his promises, and the knowledge of his Son. Once engaged with, these will issue in a spiritual regeneration, a new spiritual birth, a sense of family relationship with God himself. Effective living and godly lives must and can only begin in such a manner.

Secondly, in verses five through seven, Peter builds on this beginning by setting out a ladder of inner spiritual development.

For this very reason, make every effort to add to your faith goodness; and to goodness, knowledge; and to knowledge, self-control; and to self-control, perseverance; and to perseverance, godliness; and to godliness, brotherly kindness; and to brotherly-kindness, love.

Effective living, says Peter, begins with our inner world and the pursuit of godly virtues. The appropriate response to 'participation in the divine nature' is to muster all the effort we can to partner with God in its development. Addition and growth is expected, and we have our part to play. The aim is to complement our basic faith with qualities that reflect Jesus' character. Pastors, missionaries, and others in leadership are not exempt from this priority of the inner world of godly virtues; we too have to climb the ladder of spiritual development and formation.

Thirdly, in verses eight and nine, Peter links the growth of these inner qualities with increasingly fruitful living.

For if you possess these qualities in increasing measure, they will keep you from being ineffective and unproductive in your knowledge of our Lord Jesus Christ. But if anyone does not have them, he is short-sighted and blind, and has forgotten that he has been cleansed from his past sins.

Peter expects that being united with Jesus Christ will make people effective and productive members of society. Clearly, there is a creative force and energy that emanates from the character of God within us. Nothing could be worse, he suggests, than remaining unfruitful in this life; it would only show that the potential of the glorious start had somehow been reneged on. Fruitfulness in ministry should be our expectation also as the overflow of God's gracious life and Spirit courses through us his servants.

Finally, in verses ten and eleven, Peter urges believers to get to grips with these truths so that there will be no spiritual declension, rather an assured anticipation of the eternal kingdom.

Therefore, my brothers, be all the more eager to make your calling and election sure. For as you do these things, you will never fall, and you will receive a rich welcome into the eternal kingdom of our Lord and Saviour Jesus Christ.

Peter alludes to two welcomes that we receive from God: the first into his family by new birth, the second which awaits us beyond the grave. In the light of this, he urges that we make sure for ourselves that we have got hold of the real thing. If we do so two things will happen. Firstly, we will stand firm as Christians in this life, nothing will shake us, and secondly, we can be assured of an entry into eternity unashamed. Both these blessings are foundational for faith-filled and adventurous leadership by God's servants. But again note, the final motivation is heaven.

Brennan Manning tells a story that seems to perfectly sum up the disposition and posture of a man of God who is putting this teaching of

Peter into practice. He had been given a copy of a note found in the office of a young pastor in Zimbabwe, following his martyrdom for his faith in Christ. The letter reads as follows:

'I'm part of the fellowship of the unashamed. I have the Holy Spirit power. The die has been cast. I have stepped over the line. The decision has been made – I'm a disciple of his. I won't look back, let up, slow down, back away, or be still. My past is redeemed, my present makes sense, my future is secure. I'm finished and done with low living, sight walking, smooth knees, colourless dreams, tamed visions, worldly talking, cheap giving, and dwarfed goals.

'I no longer need pre-eminence, prosperity, position, promotions, plaudits, or popularity. I don't have to be right, first, tops, recognised, praised, regarded, or rewarded. I now live by faith, lean in his presence, walk by patience, am lifted by prayer, and I labour with power.

'My face is set, my gait is fast, my goal is heaven, my road is narrow, my way rough, my companions few, my Guide reliable, my mission clear. I cannot be bought, compromised, detoured, lured away, turned back, deluded, or delayed. I will not flinch in the face of sacrifice, hesitate in the presence of the enemy, pander at the pool of popularity, or meander in the maze of mediocrity.

'I won't give up, shut up, let up, until I have stayed up, stored up, prayed up, paid up, preached up for the cause of Christ. I am a disciple of Jesus. I must go till he comes, give till I drop, preach till all know, and work till he stops me. And, when he comes for his own, he will have no problem recognising me… my banner will be clear!'[16]

Now that's a young man determined to finish well and receive a rich welcome into the eternal kingdom of our Lord and Saviour Jesus Christ!

Further Up and Further In

In the final book of the Narnia series, the adventure is nearly over and a door is shut on the old, frozen world. The children take a little while to adjust to the sudden warm daylight, the blue sky above them, and the flowers at their feet. But there is laughter in Aslan's eyes, and C. S. Lewis pictures the great lion bounding with energy and fun.

---

[16] Brennan Manning, *The Signature of Jesus,* (Aylesbury: SP Trust Ltd, 1992), p. 29 & 30

'He turned swiftly round, crouched lower, lashed himself with his tail and shot away like a golden arrow.

'"Come further in! Come further up!" he shouted over his shoulder. But who could keep up with him at that pace? They set out walking westward to follow him.'[17]

Later the call is taken up by the mighty unicorn, Jewel; Farsight the eagle; and even Reepicheep, the talking mouse, hero of the Battle of Beruna and explorer with King Caspian to the World's End, who all add their voices, 'Further up and further in!' In the end, the call is irresistible, and the children find themselves carried with powers beyond their imagining until they arrive at the end of Shadowlands, for now they 'were beginning Chapter One of the Great Story which no one on earth has read: which goes on for ever: in which every chapter is better than the one before.'[18]

Lewis' magical phrase 'come further up, come further in' has of course enduringly entered Christian vocabulary, a wooing and enticing call to each new generation. It provides us with definition of our homing instinct as we yield to the soaring of the divine dove within us. It articulates the divine love, courting, and commanding us to follow the desires of passion for a glorious consummation of the love begun below. Further up and further in powerfully reminds us that this world in its present form is not our final home; we are here for a season and short at best. We can therefore attend to business here on earth, face whatever trials and hardships come our way, endure the worst that life can throw our way, for we are destined for better things: higher things and richer things. Today again the Lion of the tribe of Judah would say to us: 'Come further in! Come further up!'

Let the final encouragement be the words of scripture: 'Not that I have already obtained all this, or have already been made perfect, but I press on to take hold of that for which Christ Jesus took hold of me. Brothers, I do not consider myself yet to have taken hold of it. But one thing I do: Forgetting what is behind and straining towards what is ahead, I press on towards the goal to win the prize for which God has called me heavenwards in Christ Jesus.'[19]

---

[17] C. S. Lewis, *The Chronicles of Narnia, The Last Battle*, (London: Collins, 2001), compendium version p. 753.

[18] Lewis p. 767

[19] Philippians 3: 12–14

Underpinning

Exploration

- The conducting of funerals is for most of us pastors a regular and privileged service. Through this we are faced with the realities of death, burial, and the declarations of resurrection and eternal life far more frequently than the average believer. The consideration of ultimate issues is therefore part of the fabric of our lives. Rather than explore this in detail, perhaps one question will suffice: In your experience, what is it that makes some funerals so much easier to conduct than others, and in the light of that, how easy would someone find it to take your funeral should you die today?

Excavation – *recommended for digging deeper*

- *This Was Your Life* by Rick Howard & Jamie Lash, subtitled: *Preparing to Meet God Face to Face,* published by Chosen Books of Baker Book House, which includes in an appendix the full text of William Booth's vision of heaven.

Exchange – *new foundation for old*

Father, thank you for the grace which saved me, the grace which goes on saving me, and the grace which will lead me home.

Thank you that you purpose and work all things for my good: hard work, Fatherly discipline, seasons of exile for they lead me to the Cross.

Thank you for the Cross – for daily granting the graces of conviction, forgiveness and compassion; and the exchange of death for loving life.

Thank you for establishing in me a new identity, enabling me to embrace your disciplines, for the enriching of human fellowship and for the gift of the Holy Spirit.

Thank you for the gifts of life and work and the health giving recognition of my accountability.

Thank you for glory begun below and the hope of glory beyond the grave.

'To him who is able to keep you from falling, and to present you before his glorious presence without fault and with great joy – to the only God our Saviour be glory, majesty, power and authority, through Jesus Christ our Lord, before all ages, now and forever more! Amen.'[20]

---

[20] Jude 24–25

Chapter 11

The Dependency We Confess

Have confidence in your leaders and submit to their authority,
because they keep watch over you as those who must give an
account. Do this so that their work will be a joy, not a burden,
for that would be of no benefit to you.

Hebrews 13: 17 TNIV

If it were said, 'Good pastors make good churches', few would
disagree. Some uncharitably might even reply, 'I should hope so
indeed; that is their job'.

But if it were said, 'Good churches make good pastors', it might
give pause for thought. However, that is exactly what the title verse of
this chapter in Hebrews says: church members are called to certain
responsibilities toward its pastors and leaders so they will be happy in
their work. Bluntly, it concludes if they are not happy in their work,
members will derive little benefit from them. This earthy Hebraic
thought can be summarised like this: it's in your own self interest to
make their work a joy!

Paul's understood this principle well. His apostolic pattern was
to be quite candid about his circumstances so that he might appeal to
his readers for their prayers. Understanding breeds compassion,
which leads in turn to intercession. There is not one true servant of
God who is not dependent on the faithful support of God's people for
the effective working of their ministry; God deliberately makes us
interdependent in this way. This is a dependency pastors should
gladly confess.

The stance of this book to this point has had pastors primarily in
view with church members, as it were, looking over their shoulders.
We have explored the various pressures, temptations, and seasons
God brings to his servants and his purpose in doing so. As we close,

church members must come more fully into focus. To complete the circle we must ask, 'What does scripture say about our attitude toward pastors; how are we to treat our leaders; how might we make their work a joy and so expand the influence of their service?' Bluntly: how can we help maximise the effectiveness of their ministry?

Two Extremes to Avoid

King Saul was as mad as a hatter. He threw spears, plotted to kill young men, prophesied naked, and consulted mediums. His inner life was a hideous mess of insecurity, fear, and anger. Outwardly, he pursued the young troubadour with venomous purpose. For over seven years, David was hunted down like an animal. Born of Saul's hatred, the erstwhile shepherd lived in caves with other refugees, forced to scavenge desert places simply to stay alive. Moved from pillar to post, his life was shaped by Israel's king, a monarch who declared David to be public enemy number one.

Suddenly it was all over. Saul and Jonathan lay dead on Mount Gilboa. Knowing something of David's persecution at Saul's hand, a young Amalekite ran to tell David the news. Thinking to curry favour with him, he elaborated the story of their death, claiming to have ended Saul's miserable life with his sword, thus being the one to liberate David from his troubles. Never, however, had a man got it so wrong – an error in judgement of such proportions it would cost him his life.

Did he begin to sense that error as David and his men erupted in mourning and weeping, as he saw them tear their clothes? As the day drew on and David fasted and cried out in unabated anguish, did it begin to dawn on him something was radically wrong with his evaluation of the situation?

Finally, David addresses him and pinpoints the failure: 'Why were you not afraid to lift your hand to destroy the Lord's anointed?'[1]

The difference between David and the Amalekite was not in their understanding of what Saul was like. Everyone knew Saul was the epitome of man in freefall, a leader who would be a byword for spiritual declension to generations to come. No, the difference was that

---

[1] 2 Samuel 1: 14

David never lost sight of the fact that even in that condition Saul was still God's anointed (set apart by God for God's service by his Spirit) and that only God could remove him. Ironically, of course, it was God who had removed Saul – but in his own time and way. The lesson from the narrative is clear: even mad kings and leaders need to be respected for the sake of their anointing and call. For David, the passing years under Saul's antagonism shaped his character, developed his leadership skills and forged godly attitudes. God alone knows when that process is done, so God alone knows when the season is ready to change. To hasten the end at our own hand is to interfere with matters we too often understand little better than the Amalekite.

David then exemplified the correct attitudes of honour and respect due to leaders and clarified in the process that such is not based on competence or even behaviour but on identity and call. Even under a poor regime, God is able to make all things work together for our good. One extreme to avoid then is a failure to respect our leaders.

The other extreme to avoid is a failure to remember leaders' humanity.

The radical honesty of the Early Church's narrative finds humorous expression in Acts 10. Peter enters the home of a Gentile oppressor, Cornelius, a Roman Centurion. It's the Gentile oppressor who falls in reverence at the feet of the 'despised Jew'. Far from milking it, the bluff northerner in his broad brogue corrects the situation, 'Don't be so daft man, up on your feet, we are but men ourselves.' Common sense quickly dispenses the antidote to hero worship along with its accompanying pedestal.

There is something in human nature that loves heroes. They are in fact important, which makes the issue more subtle, for we need role models and mentors. The extreme of putting them on pedestals, deeming they can do no wrong and standing in awe of them, however, is to be avoided at all costs as Peter firmly establishes. For all men and women have feet of clay, all pastors and leaders are works in progress, and none are other than fallible human beings. It is a moment of critical danger when someone falls at our feet.

And there is a unique danger here regarding those who lead services, teach, and preach. At the most basic level, these people talk to us. It may be a one-sided conversation set among many, but for lonely people, the one who talks to me is highly valued. At a more profound level, these people speak to us the oracles of God; they channel rich truths and transforming graces into our lives. These people are the servants of God, and out of appreciation, it is easy to confuse the messenger with the Master. The moment the pendulum begins to swing into unhealthy attitudes, however, other dynamics insinuate themselves into the picture: dependency and hero worship become the ground for pride and the dark underbelly of exploitation and abuse.

So, then, two extremes of attitude to be avoided: failure to respect the anointing and failure to forget their humanity. They are *extremes,* and the challenge is always to nuance attitude and behaviour appropriately, but setting the outer boundaries is a good place to start.

Three Facts to Remember

We are less likely to run to extremes and error if we have a glimpse at the responsibilities pastors and leaders carry. Of course the whole book has been designed to show this, but it might be helpful to summarise at this point.

They Bear the Burden of Vision

Books on leadership recognise that many elements are needed to make an effective leader, but all agree that any leader worth their salt will be a person with vision. Lord Montgomery of Alamein said, 'Leadership is the capacity to will and rally men and women to a common purpose and the character which inspires confidence'. Dr. John R. Mott, one of the early leaders of the Ecumenical Movement, said, 'A leader is a man who knows the road, can keep ahead and who pulls others after him'.

The vision, then, may be the common purpose or the way ahead; it may be some revelation of God himself that burns to be shared, an ideal for the Christian community presently in ruins, a desire for godly influence to penetrate society, a sense of urgency for the lost, for justice, for the environment. That vision, however, will be both a passion and a burden: 'the burden which Habakkuk the prophet saw'.[2] The passion is easy to understand, but the burden comes when the leader wrestles with the huge disparity between what has been seen

---

[2] Habakkuk 1: 1

and what currently exists: the gulf is too great, the task so daunting, the resources so few. Living with vision, therefore, is to live with tension, frustration, and sense of driving passion.

And living with someone who carries the burden of vision should come with a government health warning. Biographies are replete with stories of long-suffering husbands and wives whose spouses were caught up in the drivenness that achieved great things. The London Underground announcer frequently booms out 'Mind the gap!' as train and platform don't align; equally minding the gap between vision and present reality should be boomed around our churches as a reminder to be gentle with those who carry the vision for our community – those who have a dream need to be handled with care and respect.

They Bear the Anxiety of Caring

Earlier in the book, we traced some of Paul's inner world as he grappled with the range of pastoral issues thrown up by the earliest churches. 'Apart from other things there is the daily pressure upon me of my anxiety for all the churches'.[3] No super-spiritual leader this, no glib quoting of 'take no anxious thought' rather a man who cared deeply, feeling every troubled breath of his extensive flock. He was anxious, fretful, hovering like a mother over a sick child waiting for the fever to break.

And there is much to be anxious about. Ted Roberts, an American pastor I heard at a conference some years ago, told how every Monday he required his full time church staff to wear a badge that said, 'Shepherding is prancing in the poop'. Plain, honest Anglo-Saxon has to translate that as 'prancing in the shit', even if the alliteration does not work so well. New believers and even those who should know better find it hard to disentangle themselves from the world, the flesh, and the Devil. Mess happens to the best of us, especially in the realm of relationship where pastoral ministry finds its task compounded. Paul surveyed his Corinthian congregation with a discerning eye and deemed them not many wise, not many powerful, not many of noble birth, rather foolish, weak, lowly, and despised. Most of us smiled as a colleague, echoing Paul, prayed in a fraternal, 'Dear, Lord, please give me a few whole people!' Tom Wright writes

---

[3] 2 Corinthians 11: 28

of a conversation he had with a new vicar. He says the man was a scholar, wise, outgoing, full of ideas, devotion, love, and goodness. You might have thought, said Wright, any church would be glad to have him as their leader. Asking how he was finding it then, the man replied 'trying to be the leader in this church is like trying to take a cat for a walk'.[4] The miracle is that in the midst of such constituted congregations pastors love them just the same!

It would not be so bad if pastors and leaders could sometimes switch off and walk away, but just as a leader worth their salt has to have vision, so they need to have the caring heart. We respect those in other professions who are the carers. Doctors, nurses, social workers, care workers are prized for their compassion and their availability to those in need. We honour their professionalism devoted to looking after the vulnerable in society. Just as we would not lightly criticise such workers out of respect for that devotion, so we should honour our pastors and leaders. Those who carry our needs on their hearts and in their lives of service should be viewed with appreciation and understanding.

They Bear the Weight of Accountability

The last chapter spelled this out pretty thoroughly. The point of mentioning it here is to look at it from the point of view of the flock. The verse from Hebrews at the beginning of the chapter speaks to this context of pastoral accountability: treat them appropriately and well for they must give an account for their watch over you. The writer goes on to elaborate 'that their work (even in the here and now) might be a joy, and not a burden' NIV. The word 'burden' is the Greek *stenazontes,* which is better translated 'grief' NAS, or 'groaning' ESV. 'It is a grief often known only to the pastor, his family, and to God. Because lack of submission is an expression of selfishness and self-will, unruly congregations are not likely to be aware of, or to care about, the sorrow they cause their pastor and other leaders.'[5]

Sadly, the scriptures have more than enough examples of congregations causing this kind of grief. Jeremiah is a prime example

---

[4] Tom Wright, *Hebrews for Everyone,* (London, SPCK,2004) p. 176

[5] John MacArthur, *New Testament Commentaries Hebrews,*(Chicago, Moody Press 1983), p. 446

from the Old Testament. He is known as 'the weeping prophet' so antagonistic was Israel's reaction to his ministry. God had warned of this, promised to protect him, and it did not thwart his ministry. But the inner pain was great: 'I am ridiculed all day long; everyone mocks me'.[6] Many of David's psalms of lament and complaint are because of his enemies, enemies who were not external to Israel but the covenant people of God: 'If an enemy were insulting me, I could endure it; if a foe were raising himself against me, I could hide from him. But it is you, a man like myself, my companion, my close friend, with whom I once enjoyed sweet fellowship as we walked with the throng at the house of God'.[7] These wintery psalms where grief-stricken leaders sing out their blues before the Lord are profoundly cathartic and have provided generations of leaders the release and purging required. They plumb the depth of agony for the faithful servant and help articulate the negative emotions which would otherwise cripple the soul. Perhaps their greatest value, however, is Messianic. They reveal something of God's suffering servant who came to his own and his own received him not, who was despised and rejected by men, a man of sorrows and acquainted with grief.

But what a tragedy.

Thankfully there are examples of congregations being a joyful blessing to their leaders, and how fulsome are those leaders in their appreciation. The letter to the Philippians stands out in New Testament literature as to just how good it is when church and pastor are in harmony. 'I thank my God every time I remember you. In my prayers for all of you, I always pray with joy because of your partnership in the gospel.... I long for you all with the affection of Christ.'[8] Similar notes are struck in the letters to the Thessalonians, 'Timothy... has told us that you always have pleasant memories of us and that you long to see us, just as also we long to see you.'[9]

The fact is we all work better in an environment where we are appreciated and valued. Pastors are no different. And when the eternal implications of judgement are taken into consideration, should not

---

[6] Jeremiah 20: 7
[7] Psalm 55: 12
[8] Philippians 1: 3–5, 8
[9] 1 Thessalonians 3: 6

those who name themselves Christians make it as easy as possible for their pastors to receive the 'well done good and faithful servant'? I'm not sure how it would go for me when I took my place before the Judge if my behaviour had caused one of the Lord's servants to suffer loss; the thought hardly bears thinking about.

Four Things to Do

How then should congregations treat their pastors and leaders? What guidelines do the scriptures provide? In fact many, but we will pick four to comment on.

1.   Honour Them as Gifts

Both Old and New Testaments describe leaders as gifts of God to his people. 'I have given the Levites as gifts to Aaron and his sons.'[10] 'When he ascended on high... he gave gifts to men... some to be apostles, some to be prophets, some to be evangelists, and some to be pastors and teachers.'[11] Perhaps none put it more delightfully than the Queen of Sheba. Having seen Solomon's well-ordered kingdom and heard his wisdom, she said, 'Because of the Lord's eternal love for Israel, he has made you king, to maintain justice and righteousness'.[12]

Knowing that leaders are gifts from God raises the stakes. Pastors and leaders by this reckoning can never be fodder for hire and fire. These are men and women handpicked by God himself and given as gifts. It is this sense of grace that dictates due honour. And this honour should be notwithstanding any quirk or handicap. Paul refers to his first meeting with the Galatians as potentially fraught with difficulties due to his illness and disfigurement, quite possible an extreme eye infection. He acknowledges that this was a trial to the people as much as it was to himself, but they did not treat him with contempt or scorn. 'Instead, you welcomed me as if I were an angel of God, as if I were Christ Jesus himself.'[13]

Here in the UK honour is a virtue in decline. The very term 'authority figure' seems strangely alien in today's world. Ours is a day

---

[10] Numbers 8: 19
[11] Ephesians 4: 8–11
[12] 1 Kings 10: 9
[13] Galatians 4: 14

when teachers have to fight for order in the classroom, policemen are referred to as filth, and notices are placed in doctor's surgeries reminding the public that those working there do not have to tolerate abuse. We need, therefore, to take great care that the prevailing disrespect in the world is not carried unthinkingly into church. Contempt is a particularly unchristian attitude, for it is the very opposite of 'honour one another'.

I frequently visit the States where my observation is that interpersonal honour and respect is more highly prized and practiced than here in the UK. Sons and younger men not infrequently call their fathers and older men 'Sir', shop keepers and waitresses usually give polite, respectful service, pastors are often called 'Pastor' or 'Pastor Andrew'. At first this seems a little quaint to an English ear, but that only emphasises how far our own culture has devalued honour. The simple use of the title Pastor is pleasing for it gives recognition to the gift and is a reminder to give honour where it is due. To be on the receiving end of such respect is a delightful experience and leads in turn to a higher regard for those making the remarks. Conversation in turn becomes easier and elevating. Battling cynicism, disrespect, and impoliteness by contrast and conversation becomes hard work and depressing.

If anyone is worried that pastors and leaders are being promoted more than deserved, it should be remembered that when Paul calls them gifts from the ascended Christ, it is in the context of everyone living with humility, gentleness and patience, bearing with one another in love, making every effort to maintain the unity of the Spirit in the bond of peace[14]. Pastors and leaders simply have other gifts and callings among the many, and fall within the same quiet directives. 'Which means that treating others in a depersonalised way (*not* bearing with one another in love) violates the very nature of those who share the calling.[15]

Honour recognises a world made by God, people as made in his image, believers as children of the most-high King, pastors and leaders as gifts from his hand. Honouring men, women, and children aright is,

---

[14] Ephesians 4: 2—4
[15] Eugene Peterson, *Practise Resurrection,* (London: Hodder & Stoughton, 2010) p.175

in the end, a reflection of an attitude that honours God himself. And when those are right, life and work is sweeter all round.

2.   Love Them as Family

Enough has been said to establish that at one level there is no difference between leaders and people, shepherds and flock; the clergy, laity distinction becomes pejorative if it hints at anything other than different grace callings. To press the point we need to introduce another metaphor, that of family.

As with so much, it is Israel who gives us perspective. Aaron and his sons were brothers to Moses and Miriam. The priests were from the tribe of Levi, one tribe among twelve and all sons of Jacob. Whether kings, priests, or prophets, all Israel's leaders were first and foremost family. Their distinctive role was due to their gift and their call, not their consanguinity. So they participated fully and equally in both their own nuclear/extended family and the family of national life. Their place in society was settled, land was granted, family life encouraged, and all the emotional support that these gave would sustain their ministry function.

Nothing works without love! Even the great theologian missionary apostle Paul could cry out, 'Open wide your hearts to us!'[16] No super-apostle here, no leader six feet above contradiction, no regular third heaven visitor untouched by earthly considerations. Simply doing his duty by them was not enough. He could teach, exhort, and inspire, but without love, he knew his words would not get to the hearts of his congregation. Without love, the greatest ministry of the most gifted minister will only produce sterility. They needed to know Paul loved them, but equally importantly, he needed to know they loved him. For too long he had been the disciplinarian, now he yearns for the tender side of their relationship. Function and faithfulness were not enough; love is the indispensable ingredient that binds the family of God together, that unites pastor and people and produces fruitfulness. It is love that leads to life.

Peterson puts it like this, 'God is love. Love is the core of God's being. Man and woman, made in the image of God, are also, at that core, love. This is who we were created to be, persons who love,

---

[16] 2 Corinthians 6: 13

persons who receive love. When we love we are most ourselves, living at our very best, mature.'[17] Wow! That is how I for one want to live, and that is surely how we would want all pastors and leaders to live, love and be loved. Loving like this reinforces our own sense of identity: in loving I am expressing the heart of my new self in Christ. Rather like the Hebrews verse with which we began this chapter, this love for pastors and church family does me good in turn as it confirms and reinforces who I am – not for pride but worship.

If loving is ontological, that is it has to do with the nature of my being, the 'how to' then becomes the tricky bit. Years ago there was a poster of a mother with her arms outstretched. The caption simply said, 'Mothers work on cuddles'. The poster reminds us that love is more than an emotion. For love to be real, it needs to be expressed, to be tangible. Pastors are no different, though 'cuddles' may not be the best way forward! Pastors come with their uncertainties and fears, they have 'bad days at the office' like anyone else, they battle with tiredness and colds, and they are simply part of the human lot. What is needed time and again is the encouragement that comes from loving gestures: a word of thanks, a small gift, a pat on the back.

Birthdays are a good time to put this into practice. One of my dearest and wisest friends is Allen Randolph, who has pastored the same congregation in San Antonio in Texas for over thirty-five years. Each year they really go to town in wishing Allen happy birthday. They put on events, arrange dinners, meet downtown, and much of it is creatively woven by Gayle, Allen's wife. I mentioned once that their exuberance in celebrating his birthday might seem a bit over the top back in frosty Britain. He explained that it was not the birthday so much that mattered to him; it simply happened to be an occasion for a party that both bound pastor and people closer together and provided an environment for the church family to have fun together. Our job, he said, is to role model celebration and be creative in drawing people together in wholesome, natural settings. Parties do that of course, which is why food is such an essential ingredient in fostering fellowship, and using the pastor as a focus just makes sense all round. We do it for member of our nuclear family, so why not for members of our spiritual family? There is so much to learn from our brothers and

---

[17] Peterson, p 213

sisters in other cultures; I fear that in our determination to avoid 'pastor worship' and remain 'ever-so-'umble' we can unhealthily suppress the natural desire to thank and bless that which comes from within the congregation. Providing we understand the dynamics and don't get carried away, receiving love with grace and thankfulness can only be to the good.

3.   Support Them as Worthy

I wrote earlier about our experiences in Worthing when the philosophy of the church treasurer was of the ilk, 'I'll keep him poor, Lord, and you keep him humble'. It doesn't work of course and, more to the point, is both dishonouring and unbiblical. I have acknowledged that no one worth their salt enters Christian ministry with a view to material gain, and there are many churches who with the best will in the world would struggle to remunerate their pastor much above subsistence level. However, the key is a willingness to be as honouring and generous as possible when that becomes possible. Many of us have gladly undertaken work at the call of God and the congregation knowing the stipend would be minimal but in the faith and expectation that as the work grew so would the financial resources and with that a more adequate support. As with so much in the Kingdom, it's the underlying attitude that is everything.

Finances arouse strange reactions. Not infrequently, pastors are surrounded by leaders who specialise in business and money matters. Should those people bring their expertise directly from the world's practices without shaping them to biblical or Kingdom principles, conflict can arise. This is never more critical than when dealing with church staff salary packages. I know of too many pastors who have suffered what can only be described as petty tyrannies and put-downs from those whose business acumen is esteemed more than warranted by their level of spiritual maturity. Of course when expertise and maturity combine to handle finances with Kingdom principles and generosity, it is a blessing to all. It needs be remembered always that there are simply no 'purely financial decisions' in God's Kingdom, for everything has to do ultimately with people. 'Purely financial decisions' will either bless or pain the Lord's children including pastors. Whether we like it or not, a person will feel valued and appreciated by how they are treated, and finances is often a reflection of other motives. Treat someone like a hireling, and the danger is they become a hireling and lose the dignity of a shepherd.

In writing to Timothy, Paul actually raises the bar rather than lower it. 'The elders who direct the affairs of the church are worthy of double honour, especially those whose work is preaching and teaching. For scripture says, "Do not muzzle the ox while it is treading out the grain," and "the worker deserves his wages."'[18] This text is a delight for exegetes, for Pauls two quotations come firstly from the Old Testament (Deut 25: 4) and secondly from the lips of Jesus (Luke 10: 7) and are coupled together under the title 'scripture'. Forgive the digression; another reason of course a preacher may appreciate the text is that it in turn shows appreciation for the workman. Paul here deplores a niggardly attitude just as he has deplored money-grabbing earlier in the letter (3: 3). In the Sermon on the Mount Jesus showed God's attentiveness to provide for the birds of the air and the lilies of the field, and again here the animal kingdom is pressed into comparison with Paul saying, in effect, 'If God is so concerned for ample provision for oxen treading out corn, how much more will he be concerned to see that those who devote time and energy to their ministry are well rewarded.' And with God looking out for his servants, it would be a wise move for those deciding remuneration packages to tend toward the generous than the miserly: no parsimony for the parson, it is a false economy!

But what is 'double honour', how much might an adequate reward amount to in real terms? Some years ago, I conducted a little survey to discover what percentage of church income was spent on staff salaries (i.e., pastors but also administrative and other support staff). The figure varied greatly from church to church, but a clear pattern emerged. In general, the larger the church, the lower the staffing percentage and vice-versa. In churches around five hundred members, staffing costs tended to be in the 33 to 40 per cent region. Churches with less than fifty members could have 60 per cent or more of their income needed for pastoral support. More work needs to be done here, but it would be interesting to know if churches were intentional in this or simply reactive. Other factors come in, of course, not least the

---

[18] 1 Timothy 5: 17–18

percentages devoted to missions and what might be called 'nonproductive designated giving' as far as a local church is concerned. My only point here is to urge that amid all the other considerations of a church's budget, the welfare of the pastors maintains a high priority. As our verse at the head of the chapter states, the happier they are, the better you will be served!

4.   Pray for Them as Labourers

In 1851 at the age of seventeen, Charles Haddon Spurgeon became the pastor of a handful of believers at Waterbeach in Cambridgeshire. Within five years, he had become the best known minister in the Metropolis, ministering to thousands on a Sunday and tens of thousands around the world through his printed sermons. His arrival in London came at the invitation to the pastorate of the New Park Street Chapel in Southwark; he was twenty years old. In his acceptance letter dated 28 April 1854, Spurgeon wrote, 'I feel it to be a high honour to be the Pastor of a people who can mention glorious names as my predecessors, and I entreat of you to remember me in prayer, that I may realise the solemn responsibility of my trust. Remember my youth and inexperience, and pray that these will not hinder my usefulness.'[19]

Spurgeons life and ministry was characterised by a blazing passion for Christ, which he recognised needed to be stoked with prayer. In his *Lectures to My Students*, he urges the necessity for the pastor to be a man of prayer,[20] but as we see in his acceptance letter, he appealed to others also for their prayers. This is no more or less than the apostolic pattern: 'On him we have set our hope that he will continue to deliver us as you help us with your prayers. Then many will give thanks on our behalf for the gracious favour granted us in answer to the prayers of many.'[21]

---

[19] C. H. Spurgeon, *C. H. Spurgeon Autobiography 1* (London, Banner of Truth Trust, 1973) p. 259

[20] 'If your zeal grows dull, you will not pray well in the pulpit; you will pray worse in the family, and worst in the study alone. When your soul becomes lean, your hearers, without knowing how or why, will find that your prayers in public have little savour for them.' C. H. Spurgeon, *Lectures to My Students* (London, Marshall, Morgan & Scott, 1965) p. 14

[21] 2 Corinthians 1: 10, 11

Charles Swindoll, the world-renowned pastor, teacher, and author tells the following story. One day his secretary passed on a message from an elderly lady in hospital requesting that he visit her. At the time he was the senior pastor of a church in Fullerton, California, which had grown so large under his leadership that he had other pastors to undertake hospital visits; however, knowing the lady, he agreed to visit her himself. When he got to the hospital bed, she said, 'Pastor, I will not be with you much longer; you must get someone to take my place.' Being not sure what she meant, he asked what that place was. She replied, 'At your service of Institution, when you first came to be our pastor, we were a small church, and you said that you needed folk to pray for you so that the ministry might prosper. I heard God speak to me in that service, and since then I have prayed every single day for you. Soon I am going to die, so you need to get someone to take my place.' Swindoll recounts that he was overwhelmed at the faithfulness of this elderly saint and was more than certain that when the full story of that church was revealed in heaven, it would be her name that topped the list of honours.

Prayer brings so many things together. If we honour our pastors and leaders as gifts from God, love them as we would regular members of the family, support them as worthy servants of the Most High God, then it will be natural and easy to pray for them. And as the writer to the Hebrews reminds us, it is this partnership that helps make their work a joy and at a practical level be of most benefit to us.

Strengthening the Shepherds

We have traced something of the ways of God as he lovingly shapes the inner world of his servants. We have noted the seasons of the soul, the resources available and the context of congregation. It is appropriate to conclude with this appeal to the wider people of God, to join with God himself in this mighty project by playing your part. Jesus said, 'The Son... can only do what he sees the Father doing.'[22] That watchword for his life is a good one for his followers. This support and encouragement of pastors and leaders is a chance to partner with God himself to the enrichment of his servants, and to better advance the Kingdom.

---

[22] John 5: 19

Mighty oaks are not made in a day. This growing up into Christ which is the calling for us all, will be ongoing for your pastors and leaders as well as yourself. They also are works in progress! If they are accountable then so are we, for my emphasis throughout has been that we are inter-dependent. Our attitudes and our role relative to them are important. I trust you will find joy in serving them appropriately, to enable them all the more to serve you and others well within God's glorious church. Make their work a joy, for this will be of great benefit to you!

Underpinning

Exploration – *How well do you know and support your pastor?*

- What are the names of his/her children?
- Do you know his/her birthday?
- What is his/her day off?
- Do you pray for him/her before he/she conduct Sunday service?
- Do you pray for him/her at any other regularity?
- Have you ever communicated thanks or appreciation to him/her?
- Where did he/she go for their last holiday?
- Have you invited his/her family round for a drink or meal?
- Would you know which parts of his/her job he/she enjoys most?
- If there was a need, would you be willing to give more to see your pastor paid better?

Seven out of ten and you are doing OK; four out of ten and you could do better; three or below, are you sure you are in the right church?

Excavation – *recommended for digging deeper*

- My spiritual father, mentor, and friend, Campbell McAlpine, wrote a book with penetrating insight into leadership called *The Leadership of Jesus–The Ultimate Example of Exceptional Leadership* (Tonbridge, Sovereign World). Reading this book with your pastor in mind will move you into their world with richer understanding.

Exchange – *new foundation for old*

A prayer of response:

Father, thank you for the gift of my pastor_____

Forgive my shortcomings in support of him/her.

According to your Word, I pray that he/she

- May know the Spirit of the Lord rest on him/her, the Spirit of wisdom and understanding, the Spirit of counsel and of power, the Spirit of knowledge and of the fear of the Lord, and he/she will delight in the fear of the Lord.[23]

- May the Lord anoint him/her to preach good news to the poor, bind up the broken-hearted, proclaim freedom for the captives and release from darkness for the prisoners, proclaim the year of the Lord's favour and the day of vengeance of our God, to comfort all who mourn and provide for those who grieve.[24]

- May they keep the pattern of sound teaching, with faith and love in Christ Jesus and guard the good deposit that was entrusted to them – guard it with the help of the Holy Spirit who lives in them.[25]

May they endure hardship like a good soldier of Christ Jesus[26] and know that God will meet all their needs according to his glorious riches in Christ Jesus.[27]

- Whatever they do, may they work with all their heart, working for the Lord, not for men, since they know that they will receive an inheritance from the Lord as a reward.[28]

So Lord I lift _____ to you for your blessing, in Jesus name.

Amen

---

[23] Isaiah 11: 2
[24] Isaiah 61: 1–3
[25] 2 Timothy 1: 13–14
[26] 2 Timothy 2: 3
[27] Philippians 4: 19
[28] Colossians 3: 23–24